PUBLIC SECRETS

This book is an attempt to explain why three democracies have such different attitudes to and legislation on the control of government information. It does so by examining the historical development of government control of information in Britain, the United States and Sweden. This means that the book challenges the usual view that government secrecy is best understood as a symptom of a lack of commitment to democratic values or as evidence of an undemocratic conspiracy. Rather, no country is seen as having freedom of information and no country as having all of the flaws and none of the virtues of democracy. There are indeed differences in the degree to which legislation prohibits the unauthorised release of government information but this is merely the starting point of the analysis of government information policy. The important point is that each political system provides governments with different interests in controlling, and authority to control, information. Each system has a particular structure of authority and the relationship between elected representatives and non-elected officials creates a boundary between politics and administration which in turn explains the balance between secrecy and disclosure.

Dr K. G. Robertson has been involved in the discussions of the reform of the 'British tradition of secrecy' for several years. He was a member of the Justice (the British branch of the International Commission of Jurists) Committee on Freedom of Information.

PUBLIC SECRETS

A Study in the Development of
Government Secrecy

K. G. Robertson

St. Martin's Press   New York

ISBN 0–312–65566–5

Library of Congress Cataloging in Publication Data

Robertson, Ken.
  Public secrets.

  Bibliography: p.
    1. Official secrets.   2. Secrecy (Law)   I. Title.
JF1525.S4R62   1982   351.81′9   81–5666
ISBN 0–312–65566–5   AACR2

Contents

Acknowledgements

I wish to acknowledge the tremendous impact which Professor Stanislav Andreski of the University of Reading has had upon my intellectual development. I owe him a great debt for showing me how stimulating and challenging sociology can be. I also wish to thank the following people who graciously read the manuscript: Professor Peter Campbell, University of Reading; Professor Edward Shils of Chicago and King's College, Cambridge; Professor Maurice Vile, University of Kent; Neil Elder, University of Hull; Dr Harold Relyea, Library of Congress; Goran Regner, Ministry of Justice, Stockholm. Many people also unstintingly offered their advice and assistance but I would particularly like to mention: Professor Francis Rourke, Johns Hopkins University; Thomas Sussman, Senate Committee on the Judiciary; Congressman Jack Brooks; Mark Lynch, Freedom of Information Clearing House; Dr Janet Morgan, Cabinet Office, London; Victor Moore, University of Reading; Sigvard Holstad, Ministry of Justice, Stockholm; Ingvar Gullnäs, Attorney General of Sweden; Professor Stig Hadenius, University of Gothenburg; Ulf Lunkvik, Chief Ombudsman, Sweden; Bertil Wennergren, Supreme Administrative Court, Stockholm; the Swedish Institute; and the members of the Justice Committee on Freedom of Information. I am also grateful for the financial assistance which I received from the Social Science Research Council, the British Council and the University of Reading Research Board. Ms Joan Morris typed the manuscript and Mrs Helen Chevis typed the book with consummate skill.

The above, of course, are in no way responsible for my errors.

K.G.R.

The author and publishers wish to thank the following who have kindly given permission for the use of copyright

material: the Controller of Her Majesty's Stationery Office
for the extracts from documents in the Public Record Office
and from official government publications; Faber and Faber
Ltd and Alfred A. Knopf Inc. for the table from Samuel H.
Beer, *Modern British Politics*; and Routledge & Kegan Paul
Ltd for the extract from M. Shaw, *Anglo-American Democracy*.

1. Introduction

INTRODUCTION

Countries which are generally acknowledged to be democratic
vary in the amount and kind of government information which
is available to the public. Given this one can do one of
two things: question whether any particular country deserves
the label 'democratic'; or accept that a democracy may have
either a high or low level of secrecy. The latter position
is more useful since it avoids judging political systems
like beauty queens, awarding points for the possession of
desirable characteristics. The sociologist tries to understand secrecy by placing it in its context.

The analysis of each country is divided into two parts.
The first is concerned with how the structure of politics
and government, the distribution of power and interests,
produces a particular balance between secrecy and disclosure. The second part is concerned with how this structure has changed over time and how this is reflected in the
changing laws related to secrecy and disclosure.

This approach then differs from the traditional view
which looks at secrecy in terms of the definition of democracy or in terms of rights, such as the right to know.
This is not to say that nothing will be said about these
issues but there is a very great danger that democracy will
simply come to be a term of approval. However, there will
never be a democracy which has all of the virtues and none
of the flaws. The interrelationship between the various
elements of a political system is a matter for empirical
investigation and not definition. The conclusion of this
investigation is that the boundary between 'reason' and
'politics' determines the point at which disclosure ends
and secrecy begins.

THE MAIN ARGUMENT

The argument is that the main factor which determines the degree to which government information is available to the public is the type of authority elected representatives have over officials and, in particular, by whether officials are directly subordinate to a unified political authority. The analysis of the three countries will show that the existence of a high or low level of government secrecy is dependent upon the structure of political authority in each country.

Responsibility, its extent and clarity, is the most important aspect of the structure of political authority for an explanation of the level of government secrecy. A political system which requires that a clearly identifiable group of elected representatives take responsibility for all the actions of the State provides a strong incentive to that group to control the dissemination of information, since no information about their actions will be neutral politically. All government information will be seen by the 'responsible group' as having consequences for both their ability to exercise the degree of control which the structure of responsibility (as defined above) implies that they have, and for their political survival since any information may affect their reputation and popularity.

A structure of political authority in which a particular group of elected representatives has limited responsibility for State actions will lead to a situation in which the disclosure of government information will not be seen as undermining their degree of control, since the structure of responsibility does not imply that they have complete control in the first place. Where responsibility is unclear or divided, the link between the availability of government information and the threat to political reputation is more tenuous and the incentive to control information correspondingly less.

A high level of protection of government information will be found in a society where administration is a matter which is formally the responsibility of a particular elected body, such that administration is seen as affecting the political survival of a particular body of elected representatives. Where this is the case there will be an effort to protect the information which government has at its disposal since the realm of politically sensitive information will be widely defined and will include all or most information which bears upon the relationship between the government and the citizen, namely government administration. Where no body of elected representatives sees the activities of the administration having repercussions on political survival, then the range and type of information which will be seen as having relevance to the rise and fall of governments will be more narrowly defined. It is the extent to which information is seen as part of the political struggle for office which determines the level of control of information. There are then two variables, the motive to exercise control of information and the ability to implement the degree of control desired. Britain provides a classic case of a political system which provides clear motives for controlling all government information, since all information about the government is seen as having relevance to its political survival and also provides the government, through the cabinet system, with the authority to implement the level of control which it desires. In Sweden the motive to control access to information is much less since the administrative agencies are independent. In the USA the executive may have a motive for secrecy, but it does not have the control over the legislative body necessary to carry out its desire. In the USA the legislative body can only exercise its function by limiting the executive's motive for secrecy, and the legislature does not have the responsibility for administration which would provide the legislative body with a motive for tightly controlling the flow of information.

The analysis of each country is divided into two parts. The first part describes those aspects of the political system which provide the conditions within which public administration and the law of government information operate. The second part describes the system of government administration and the legislation which affects the flow of government information to the public. The first part is concerned with certain institutions in their role as information producers, the elected assemblies, the courts and other agents of administrative supervision, and with the tensions and accommodations characteristic of each political system. The second part describes the development of a politically neutral civil service, a loyal civil service, the structure of control of the service and the rules governing the release of government information. The central theme, however, remains the same, that of showing that it is the structure of responsibility which elected representatives have for state administration which determines the degree of citizen access to government information.

Although the political process will produce certain kinds of government information, it is often a different type than

that which is available under freedom of information legislation. It is often of a more political nature concerned
with extracting the ideological basis of a decision, the
connection or contradiction between one policy or another
and with debating how popular such a decision will be.

   There are three main types of information which governments possess and which are sought after: information
concerning the legality of a decision; the knowledge which
lies behind a particular decision; and the political basis
of a decision. Freedom of information legislation tends to
provide access only to the first two categories, and
elected assemblies and the press to the second. There are in
all countries other institutions, however, which provide
access to the first two types, in particular the courts and
other agents of administrative supervision. The argument
will be that freedom of information legislation can only be
understood in relation to the institutions which provide
access to similar types of information, the courts and other
agents of administrative supervision. The first part of the
analysis of each country examines how effective elected
assemblies and the other institutions are at extracting
government information. It will be argued that the structure
of responsibility also provides the explanation of the
constraints which exist upon the effectiveness of the above
institutions.

THE THREE COUNTRIES COMPARED

Elected Assemblies

The British Parliament is based upon the principle that the
government is composed of those who command the support of
the majority of the House of Commons, the popularly elected
assembly. This means the largest or majority party with the
largest minority party forming the official opposition. If
the majority party has a majority over all other political
parties, then the government has few obstacles to the
implementation of whatever policies it considers to be in
the interest of the nation and will be such as to strengthen
the position of the party in any future election. This
situation does not mean that a British government can do
what it likes. It has to reach accommodation with many
groups, as does any government, but it means that there are
no parliamentary, legal or constitutional obstacles to what
some would see as an 'elective dictatorship'. The composition of the committees of the House, which examine

legislation or the operations of government, is also based
upon the majority principle such that the majority of the
members of the committee will belong to the majority party.
This creates an obstacle if these committees are to be
independent or objective critics of government actions. The
government has every incentive to ensure that these committees do not become part of the 'opposition', although
there are certain areas in which there has always been
agreement that objective investigation is to the advantage
of both Parliament and the government; for example, public
expenditure and delegated legislation. Members of Parliament
seek information from Ministers by asking parliamentary
questions. However, the parliamentary question does not
provide access to the documents upon which the Minister's
answer is based and although many questions are requests for
information and are treated as such, many are of a political
nature in which the major objective is to embarrass the
Minister and thereby to gain prominence in the media for the
failure of the government. Parliamentary questions have
vitality, at least as far as the media and most members of
the public are concerned, because they involve the clash of
personalities and policies and not because they are part of
a systematic or effective attempt to scrutinise the operations of government. The information and investigating
techniques of Parliament are affected by the structure of
political authority in that no attempt is made to pretend
that information is neutral and not part of the struggle for
political office.

In the USA the President has no direct power to affect the
political survival of any Congressman or Senator. Indeed,
Congress does not necessarily pass a larger proportion of
legislation desired by a President, when Congress and the
President are both of the same political party. Congress and
the President have separate constituencies, and although the
system of government requires that they reach an accommodation if effective action is to be taken, it also creates a
situation in which neither party is able to require the sub-
mission of the other. Each of the branches of government has
its particular resources upon which it can call to safeguard
its prerogatives and the interests of its electors. One of
the most potent of the resources of Congress is its power of
investigation. Congress considers it to be part of its duty
to oversee the implementation of the legislation which it
has passed and the use that is being made of the expenditure
which it has allocated, and although membership of the
committee reflects the distribution of the parties, the
absence of direct presidential control over the political
fate of Congressmen means that Congressmen can establish a

political reputation as effective critics and protectors of
the interests of their constituents by acting independently.
The majority party in Congress, even though it may be of the
same party as the President, does not see extracting information from the President as acting as part of the opposition to the President, but as carrying out their legislative function in an effective and independent manner. The
President will not see Congress as independent, but as
acting as an opposition.

The Swedish Riksdag is a Parliament, but it is one in
which much of its conventions and organisation reflect the
attributes of Congress rather than the House of Commons. For
example, the committees of the Riksdag are powerful, both in
their effect upon legislation and in their right to call for
papers; their power is particularly important when the
government lacks a majority in the Riksdag, but when it is
strong their role tends to be restricted to matters of
detail of little or no political significance. One of the
committees of the Riksdag also has the constitutional right
to supervise the actions of the cabinet by inspecting the
advice which the cabinet has offered to the King in Council.
Although the King no longer acts as a political force, this
practice is a residue of the separation of powers between
King and Parliament characteristic of the pre-democratic
constitutional period. However, the powers of the Riksdag to
investigate the activities of government are limited. This
is because most of government administration is carried out
by independent boards and the Swedish constitution prohibits
Parliament from asking questions of a government Minister
about anything for which he is not responsible. As the
Minister is not responsible for the boards, no question concerning their activities can be asked. This is demonstrated
by the fact that not until recent years did the Swedish
Parliament have a question time or consider the questioning
of Ministers to be of importance. In the eyes of most Swedes,
the Swedish Riksdag is not the most important information-
producing institution. The courts, the Ombudsman and the
legal access to documents through the principles of remiss
and the Freedom of the Press Act are more important.

The Courts

The position of the courts in the three countries is also
significantly different. The courts in Sweden and the USA,
for different reasons, are far more closely involved in the
daily workings of government administration than are the
British ones. Both Sweden and the USA consider the legal
control of government administration to be a crucial part of

the constitutional, democratic State.

In Britain the courts play a part in producing information, but they have been constrained by the constitutional convention of ministerial responsibility. The major legal principle which the British courts have used to control administration is that of *ultra vires*, that no action can be lawful which is outside the authority legally granted to an administrative body. The government, then, cannot make the law to suit itself; it must act within its lawful authority. The British system of administrative appeals is not based upon ensuring strict adherence to legal procedure, either by the courts playing a direct part in the process, or by the setting up of administrative courts or similar bodies. There has been no attempt to judicialise administration in Britain either by the courts insisting upon this as a criteria of 'due process' or by the government seeing this as an aid to the control of administration. The courts in Britain have not acted either directly or indirectly as important information producers. They have not sought to act, to create or impose high standards of disclosure.

In the USA the courts have had the Constitution to rely on as a source of authority to question the operations of government. The American courts have sought to impose certain standards of conduct upon government administration, one important element of which has been that decisions be based upon the record and that the record be available to a citizen in dispute with his government. The American courts have felt that where government action concerns life, liberty and property, a decision arrived at in secret or using secret information is contrary to the principle of 'due process' required under the Constitution. The courts have sought to ensure not only that the government has the legal authority to make the particular decisions, but also that it has followed legal procedures in arriving at its decisions. This demand began some forty years before the passing of freedom of information legislation.

In Sweden there exists a system of administrative courts in which the independent boards have been held to account. The administrative courts have not only the right to examine the legality of the boards' decisions, but also to examine the facts upon which the decision was based and to replace the boards' decision with their own. The right of appeal and the right to go to an independent legal authority to have the appeal judged have been seen by the Swedes as an essential part of a constitutional legal state. Sweden parallels the American emphasis upon the importance of the legal control of administration and the judicialisation of administration. Sweden is a society in which government

administration is independent and in which a number of
independent controls have been created to supervise the
actions of the administration: the Ombudsman, the administrative courts, and the right of access to information.
These are all part of a package of controls, the effective
operation of each is seen as requiring the presence of the
others.

This summary indicates some of the ways in which the
system of government differs between each of the three
countries but, as already stated, this is not very illumi-
nating unless one points to those differences which are
significant or most important. It is the relationship
between officials and elected representatives which will be
found to be the area within which the balance between
secrecy and disclosure is determined.

The Civil Service

Part two of the analysis of each country is concerned with
showing that the role allocated to the civil service is the
main factor in determining the degree of citizen access to
government information. The reason for including in this
account the topics of neutrality, loyalty and the hierarchy
of government authority is that these topics show what the
position of the civil service is in each country. Under the
heading of 'Neutrality' is included a description of the
rules governing the political activities of civil servants
and the criteria by which civil servants are appointed and
dismissed.

There is an obvious connection between excluding civil
servants from public political activity and controlling the
amount of information about their views available to the
public. The reason for this is the danger that the views of
civil servants will become part of the struggle for office
characteristic of a democratic political system and that
this may undermine the neutrality which restrictions upon
the activities of civil servants are attempting to create.
The problem then becomes one of identifying what determines
what is defined as being illegitimate political influence
of the civil service upon the decisions taken by elected
representatives. The two positions which may be adopted are
that it is either the 'hidden' or secret influence, or the
overt public participation which is illegitimate. The factor
which determines which of those positions will be selected
is the structure of authority to which civil servants are
subject.

If the civil service is directly subordinate to a single
elected body, then participation will be conceived in very

broad terms such that any open political activity, or information concerning the views of the civil service, will be
seen as a challenge to the authority of the elected body.
Where this is the case it will be overt participation which
is feared, as in Britain. Where this is not the case, such
that the hierarchy of authority is either limited or unclear,
political activities by civil servants will be less narrowly constrained since the threat of public participation
will be more limited and less specific in whose authority it
challenges. In this instance, it will be the secret influence which is most feared, as in the USA and Sweden.

Administration and Politics

In Britain there is a hierarchy of authority which extends
through the bureaucratic hierarchy to an elected representative who is a member of the government. This means that
whatever arguments may be offered as to whether the elected
representative, the Minister, is actually in charge of
administration, the Minister will be on the defensive when
the actions of his department are matters of public comment.
The Minister is, therefore, going to see controlling information about the actions of his department as part of his
defensive strategy. The British system of government highlights a problem of all democratic polities, that information about the government is not simply relevant to the
individual citizen as part of the process of administering,
but also of interest to the opposition political parties as
part of the competition for office. The structure of political authority in Britain makes it difficult, if not impossible, to separate the information which is neutral, of
concern only to the individual citizen in his contest with
government, and that which may affect the survival of the
government.
   In the USA there is a divided responsibility for supervision of the federal bureaucracy. The laws which govern
the actions of administrators are made by those who have no
direct responsibility for administering those laws; those
who are responsible for administration have limited positive
control over the actions of the legislature. This means that
the structure of rewards and costs is such as to allow the
executive and the legislature to blame each other for any
inadequacies of government which may be revealed. For
example, if a nuclear power station is found to have had
inadequate safety, this can be seen either as the failure
of the legislature to enact clear and detailed regulations
for the nuclear industry, or as the failure of the executive to interpret the existing laws in a sufficiently

rigorous and stringent manner. The situation is even more
diffuse in that the legislature can claim that it failed to
enact detailed regulations because it was wrongly advised by
the executive; the executive can claim that its failure was
due to lack of funds provided by the legislature; the nuclear regulatory agency itself can claim that the legislature had interfered with its attempts to be stringent by
holding hearings on its activities, or that the executive
hierarchy interfered with its interpretations of the law; in
fact, the list of excuses provided by the structure of
responsibility is almost endless. It may be a fiction to
state that any one body can actually be responsible for the
multitude of actions which government undertakes, but it may
be a useful fiction. The difficulty with the American system
of government is that there is no place where 'the buck'
actually stops. The lack of such a clear resting point for
responsibility means that no branch of the government has a
strong incentive to protect the bureaucracy against continuous public scrutiny, since errors by the bureaucracy are not
immediately or directly laid at the door of any elected
representative. However, where responsibility can be more
clearly allocated, such as to the President in the area of
foreign affairs, then a far greater effort to keep secrets
can be expected. This, however, is not because national
security actually requires a high level of secrecy. It is
true that it requires some, but the actual level of secrecy
cannot be explained on 'rational' grounds. It is, as always,
a matter of power and interest.

The Swedish Constitution makes it illegal for either
Parliament or a Minister to instruct a civil servant as to
how to interpret the law. Public administration is carried
out by independent boards, which are not answerable to any
political authority as to how they interpret the law. This
means that a Minister is not responsible for the actions of
the boards and that therefore what the civil service does
has little or no political effect upon the survival of
governments. Politicians then have little interest in controlling public access to the documents and information held
by these boards, since such information does not have any
immediate consequences for the reputation of the government.
The information which these boards hold is seen as neutral
and expert knowledge, which has the same status and political implications as the information or knowledge held by any
other institution or interest group. The information held
by the boards may have political implications, but it has no
special status, it poses no more of a threat to the survival
of governments than any other information held by any other
body. The government then has little incentive to control
the flow of such information.

2. Democracy and Secrecy

In this chapter I will be examining the argument that democracy and government secrecy are incompatible, that there is a conflict between government secrecy and the fundamental requirements of a democratic polity. This claim will be assessed in relation to the three ways in which disclosure of government information is justified - as a right, as a value, and as a means. These justifications will be assessed in terms of three fundamental characteristics of democracy: representation, participation and accountability. Although the three justifications which have been given for disclosure of government information are not incompatible, they do have different objectives and implications. The chapter will end with a discussion of the arguments of Max Weber.

THE PUBLIC RIGHT TO KNOW

The view that access to information is a right is predicated upon the requirement of accountability which, it is argued, will be meaningless unless there exists a legal right of access to government information.[1] The argument is that without such a right a government will be able to manipulate information for its own ends, mainly to preserve itself in office. This danger is considered to be so great as to require legal access to government information, even if this involves certain costs. The ability of governments to manipulate information is seen as opposed to the rule of law: it is arbitrary. Arbitrariness is associated with despotism and not democracy. Without legal access to government information, it is feared that governments will use information selectively, releasing only that information which is to their credit or undermines the credibility of their opponents, and that this reduces the requirement of accountability to a meaningless incantation.

The objective of a public right to know is the prevention
of the manipulation of information, or arbitrariness, and
to give substance to the democratic requirement of accountability. Its implication is that democracy requires the
creation of a legal right of access to government information.

DISCLOSURE AS A GOOD

A high degree of disclosure of government information is
also justified because it is seen as expressing and fulfil-
ling certain values; it is a good. It is a value associated
with other values such as participation, knowledge and freedom of ideas.[2] It is argued that government secrecy produces
apathy and ignorance. It is also argued that these are
dangerous to democracy since they produce a citizenry who
will be unwilling and unable to participate in political
life, participation being seen as a fundamental requirement
of a democratic polity.

Absence of participation will produce a separation of
government from the people leading to a 'credibility gap'
and a breakdown of communication between government and
people. Governments will cease to be responsive to the
electorate, and will treat the people with disdain because
they see the people as ignorant and uninterested. This is
seen as the end of popular government, an essential requirement of democracy. It is also seen as a situation in which
the citizen does not develop, become more mature, responsible and aware, and that democracy ought to be a political
system in which individuals learn and become 'better
citizens'. This they will fail to do without participating.

Disclosure is valued because of the kind of person and
citizenry which it will create - one which is active, lively
and knowledgeable - and to give substance to the democratic
requirement of participation. Its implication is that the
good society requires the maximisation of the free movement
of ideas and knowledge.

DISCLOSURE AS A MEANS

The third justification of the claim that democracy requires
the disclosure of government information is that it is a
means of ensuring that the actions of government will be
representative of the interests of the citizenry.[3] It is a
means of ensuring that the government is acting in accordance with the plural interests in the society and is not

suppressing or ignoring any of these diverse interests. It is also a means of checking on the 'rationality' of government actions, that government actions are being taken on the best available information. Government secrecy raises the question of what the government has to hide, whether corruption or other malfeasance of office. Disclosure is also seen as a means of checking that only those who are responsible for taking decisions are actually doing so and not civil servants, interest groups or sinister conspirators. It is this view which lies behind most of the campaigns for a reduction in the amount of information which governments keep secret. It is based upon fear and suspicion of governments and sees disclosure as a means of 'watching the watchers'.

The objective of disclosure is as a means to prevent governments from abusing office or otherwise acting against the interests of individual citizens or of the many and diverse groups of a pluralistic society. It is also a means of giving substance to the democratic requirement of representation. The implication is that government secrecy is evidence of the fact that the government is doing something which it could not justify to the public and that disclosure acts as a 'disinfectant'.

CRITICISMS OF DISCLOSURE AS A RIGHT

The main problem with the argument that the citizen has a right to know is that it fails to solve the problem of what is the appropriate balance between secrecy and openness. To state that such a right exists fails to specify what one has a right to know about and also how this right is to be weighed as against other competing rights. However at first sight it seems appealing to argue that one should have a legal right to know certain information. This has the advantage, it can be argued, of eliminating discretion and thus preventing manipulation of information by the authorities. The problem with this approach is that one cannot eliminate all discretion since politicians will always be capable of keeping certain aspects of their thinking secret and discussing certain of their plans with others of a like mind, in secret. There can never be, then, a right to know all that a citizen might like to know. There can only be a right to know certain specified and carefully defined types of information and making a statement of general principle in this way does not help to solve the problem of what type of information the citizen ought to have the right to know about.

The principle of the right to know, then, even when expressed as the rule of law, still does not tell one what
this minimum is or what the consequences of introducing it
would be. However, one can argue that certain participants
in the political process should have no discretion at all as
to what to reveal - civil servants. One can argue that the
civil servant is not responsible to the electorate for the
decisions which he makes and that, therefore, he should not
be able to take authority without being answerable for its
use. Releasing information is a form of authority which
should not be left to the individual discretion of the civil
servant, since it would be power without responsibility.
However, even here there are problems of morality, defining
the circumstances when it would be immoral for the civil
servant not to reveal certain information about government
actions even if this was to become involved in politics. One
can argue that in certain circumstances the civil servant
has a higher duty than the preservation of the structure of
authority characteristic of democracy, a duty to humanity.
This is an extremely difficult issue, one which is linked to
the complex problem of the duty to obey the State, but the
main problem associated with allowing civil servants a moral
basis to 'whistle blow' is that it will rarely be clear that
the civil servant has made an obviously moral, as opposed to
political, choice. Governments feel suspicious of civil
service leaks because they naturally see them as being
attempts to discredit the government, support the 'opposition', or express a personal ideological commitment.

CRITICISMS OF DISCLOSURE AS A VALUE

The argument that 'openness' is a good suffers from many of
the same problems as the right-to-know principle. It is only
one of many values and must be weighed against others, and
this cannot be done by examining any one in isolation but
only by examining the interdependence between the various
elements which are part of a democratic political system.
This entails the analysis of how the elements do in fact fit
together, based upon empirical research.

CRITICISMS OF DISCLOSURE AS A MEANS

As stated earlier, the argument that a high level of disclosure is a means towards the achievement of certain goals
is the most common one among those who have commented upon
the problem of government secrecy. The view that disclosure

is a means relieves the argument of the pressure to justify
disclosure on any grounds, other than its practical consequences for the operation of a democratic polity. Disclosure becomes a solution to particular problems and this
requires that disclosure be judged as to how effective a
solution it may be, whether it is the best solution to those
particular problems, and how it would affect the other
arrangements characteristic of each political system. This
then is a pragmatic approach to the problems of secrecy.
Disclosure becomes a means of preventing the government from
abusing its power or acting in ways which are detrimental to
the interests of the many groups of a plural society. Disclosure is not only justified on positive grounds, but also
because it acts as a preventive; to prevent certain negative
situations from occurring.

IDEOLOGY AND SECRECY

The ways in which disclosure has been seen as a means will
be discussed in relation to four ideological positions.
Criticisms of government secrecy can be found at all points
of the ideological spectrum. They all tend to have a fear of
conspiracy as their common denominator, although the nature
of the conspiracy which is suspected obviously varies. This
fear of conspiracy, however, creates a new problem, namely
the difficulty of distinguishing between the desire to make
governments open in order to make them more democratic, and
the desire for openness which is based upon an 'irrational'
or groundless fear that governments are conspiring to betray
'the people'. This raises the question of whether those who
see conspiracies would be satisfied by *any* institutional or
legal structure by which the 'will of the people' was to be
decided. One can always argue that however many safeguards
there may be to prevent governments 'subverting' democracy,
they are not enough and that there still remains the 'real
truth' which is yet to be discovered. This raises the
question of what conditions tend to produce a fear of conspiracies and although this is outside the scope of the
present study, the suggestion is offered that it is the
absence of clear and definite lines of responsibility which
tends to produce such fears. The four positions which will
be considered are the left-wing, the anti-statist, the
rationalist and the liberal.

Disclosure and Betrayal

The left-wing argument that a high level of disclosure of

government information is necessary, is justified in terms
of the claim that left-wing parties are incapable of resist-
ing pressures to make compromises and that only by continuous scrutiny can this be avoided. The left often claim to
have knowledge of what is in the interest of the working
class and this provides them with grounds for arguing that
only by constant vigilance and access to government documents can these interests be protected. Given that one knows
in advance what is in the interest of the working class,
socialist government discretion is limited and failure to
implement the 'obvious' programme becomes a matter of betrayal. The fear of betrayal is particularly acute for the
left wing because they consider that all the major centres
of power are determined to prevent the implementation of a
socialist programme and that only by exposing these pressures can socialist governments be assisted to withstand
them.

Disclosure and Power

The anti-statist fear of government secrecy is based upon a
fear that governments are continuously engaged in accruing
power and that only by constant vigilance can this process
be prevented. There is also the fear that because governments are powerful, other groups in the society may secretly
attempt to capture that power. This often takes the form of
racism, fear of hidden communists, or fear of bureaucrats.
Disclosure becomes a means of limiting and checking the
power which the State has at its disposal.

Disclosure and Reason

The rationalist fear of government secrecy is based upon a
fear of politics. Politics is seen as contaminating and as
an activity which should be restricted to as small an area
of government activity as possible.[4] Rationalists fear that
many decisions which are taken are not the result of the
best knowledge, and the product of careful objective analysis, but the result of party or political interest.
Examples of such accusations would be that a cut in spending was made merely because it would be popular and win
votes, or that a decision to nationalise a particular company was the product of dogma and not 'sound' economics.
The reason for labelling this position 'rationalist' is
because it is based upon the claim that all problems are
capable of rational analysis and that only the conclusions
of such an analysis should influence government decision-
making. The struggle for office and the consequent need to

be popular are seen as contaminating the purity of objectivity. Disclosure is seen as a means of making it more
difficult for governments to be ideological and to make
decisions which are not solely based upon rational analysis.

Disclosure and Liberty

The liberal position has been the dominant ideology demanding a high level of disclosure of government information.
The ideology of liberalism is well expressed by Plamenatz in
the following quotation:

> The modern or liberal idea of freedom emerges with the
> attribution of rights of the mere individual against those
> in authority over him. By the mere individual we mean the
> individual considered apart from any specific role ... the
> rights whose exercise constitutes freedom, as the liberal
> conceives of it, are held to be universal and important.
> To have them it is enough to be a man - or to have
> specifically human capacities. (All political philos-
> ophers accept) ... the liberal idea of freedom if they
> claim for man, by reason of his humanity, the right,
> within limits strictly or loosely defined, to order his
> life as seems good to him.[5]

The essence of democracy is then not seen as consisting of
a method of organising political power in order that those
with power should carry out certain social objectives, but
rather it is considered to be the system under which certain
inalienable rights are best preserved. Democracy is seen as
desirable because it guarantees the freedom of the individual to pursue what he considers to be his objectives, with
the least restriction upon these, compatible with the
safety and freedom of others. This view does not allow the
right of the majority to deprive the individual of these
rights, or indeed to take action which would infringe the
right of the individual to 'order his life as seems good to
him'. In fact the concept of 'majority rule' is held in
suspicion by the liberal because it verges on the brink of
totalitarianism or, in de Tocqueville's famous phrase, 'the
tyranny of the majority'.
    There are two main reasons why those who advocate the
liberal view tend to favour the release of information. One
is that it is necessary if individual members of the society
are to develop their own personal capacities, i.e. they
should not simply respond but be active and informed members. The second is that democracy is not justified in terms
of social justice, but rather that democracy is based upon

freedom from political power and, therefore, every individual must know how the actions of government affect him and
that his interests have been taken into account, and this
requires access to government information. The liberal fears
government, is suspicious that it is following interests
which are not his and that it threatens his private sphere
of life. He is not solely concerned with the consequences of
government, its policy, but with its structure, its limitations. He is not interested in whether a particular policy
has majority support and is unwilling to adopt a 'wait and
see' approach to government; consultation and reason must be
applied before it is too late. He fears that if he is not
constantly on his guard government will encroach upon that
area of his life which is sacrosanct. The liberal is not a
pragmatist, but a man of principle, whose principles are
under constant threat. Secrecy in his eyes is evidence that
government is trying to upset the balance between its power
and his private domain.[6] Sir Isaiah Berlin expresses this as
follows:

> But whatever the principle in terms of which the area of
> non-interference is to be drawn, whether it is that of
> natural law or natural rights, or of utility or the
> pronouncements of a categorical imperative, or the sanc-
> tity of the social contract, or any other concept with
> which men have sought to clarify and justify their con-
> victions, liberty in this sense is always liberty *from*;
> absence of interference beyond shifting, but always
> recognisable, frontier.[7]

The liberal then gives the State no separate existence,
recognises no political danger which the government or party
may be under from the electorate, and therefore gives it no
right to secrecy. To the liberal, secrecy is usually seen as
evidence of a too powerful government, one which is seeking
to aggrandise itself, to turn government into an 'imperial
presidency'. Whether it is legitimate to see secrecy as
evidence of 'despotism' or of power is one of the central
issues, but there is no question that this is how it is seen
by most American political scientists. Corresponding to this
fear of government secrecy about policy matters is the fear
that government will enter that sphere of life which is
legitimately private. Friedrich, in many of his works,[8] has
argued that democracy is characterised by that which is
public being public and that which is private being private,
whilst totalitarianism is characterised by that which is
public being secret while that which is private is public.

BUREAUCRACY, WEBER AND SECRECY

In almost all of the discussions of government secrecy, the
following quotation is produced or referred to: 'The concept
of the official secret is the specific invention of bureaucracy, and nothing is so fanatically defended by the bureaucracy ...'[9] It is a persistent argument that bureaucrats have
an interest in secrecy and that this interest is one of the
main reasons for the existence and perpetuation of government secrecy. However, this claim implies that those who are
formally in control of the bureaucrats are either not in
fact in control of the bureaucrats, or that they too have an
interest in secrecy. In a democracy, however, it is the
politicians who are the ones with the legitimate authority,
and if the bureaucrats are producing the high level of
secrecy a change in policy will require the recapturing of
authority by the politicians.

If in fact the politicians are in control, then the change
in policy can be achieved simply by them exercising their
authority over the bureaucrats. Another problem is to try to
identify what reason people have for believing that bureaucrats have an interest in secrecy. The main basis of this is
the belief that secrecy increases the power of bureaucrats.
Secrecy is said to increase the power of the bureaucracy
because it insulates them from any form of control and,
therefore, allows them to pursue their interests unmolested.
Max Weber argues that bureaucrats believe that they are
superior to politicians and the 'people', due to their expertise, objectivity and rationality. They have a desire to
eliminate politics altogether, as it is seen as being based
upon bias, prejudice, conflict, irrationality, party and
special interests, whereas the bureaucracy sees itself as
objective, impartial and as representing the general
interest. Max Weber's solution to this problem is to re-
assert the importance of politics as the realm of action, as
in fact being concerned with conflict and struggle and as
requiring recognition that politics can only be eliminated
at the expense of the strength, coherence and stability of
the State.[10]

Politics is, therefore, inherently a struggle between men
for the opportunity to win popular support and to implement
personal policies, this opportunity being dependent upon
continuing, and inherently unstable, personal support. The
politician gains a position of authority, not by means of
examinations and rules of selection, but by a struggle for
allegiance and support. One fact which must be kept in mind
is that Weber was talking about the problems of the control
of bureaucracy within a particular situation, the transition

from monarchy to democracy. Weber argues that the political
situation of Germany and Russia at the turn of the century
was such that the authority of the traditional ruling group
had been eroded and that no new class of people existed who
saw it as their duty to participate in political life and
to ensure that politics was healthy and energetic - the
middle class in both those countries he felt was weak and
tended to run from power rather than welcome it. Weber
argued that the weakness of those states was due to the fact
that neither the monarch nor Parliament any longer had
effective control over the bureaucracy. This led to the
'rule of officials', the making of policy by bureaucrats who
were responsible for policy-making. For Weber, the bureaucracy was incapable of performing a policy-making function
because the making of policy involved making judgements concerning the consequences of policy for the degree of support
enjoyed by the State. Policy-making also involves the making
of value choices which, although the bureaucracy could claim
would be made on the basis of the general good, would in
fact be based upon the values of the class with which the
bureaucracy identified. The bureaucracy would gain power
without having to justify acting according to its values,
nor would it have to listen to the values and aspirations of
any other group when making policy, as the position of the
bureaucrat is not subject to popular control. A situation in
which the bureaucracy was only formally under control without this actually being the case would lead to the isolation
of the bureaucracy from social change and the new demands
to which the State is ever subject.

What remains uncertain, however, is whether Weber would
see secrecy as an evil if it was instituted by politicians
and not by bureaucrats. Weber's desire for strong leadership
can be seen as supplying a justification for secrecy if the
leader controls the flow of information as part of the
creation of strong and effective leadership. Of course,
Weber sees the leader as being constrained by the continuing
need to be popular and it is this struggle for authority in
a democracy which would provide the limitation upon the
degree of secrecy. This constraint is missing from the
bureaucratic desire for secrecy, which is no doubt why Weber
fears it more. Weber also indicates that he is aware that
secrecy is encouraged by struggle and competition for
office. He gives a series of relationships in which there is
potential competition and describes these as creating a
tendency towards secrecy - foreign affairs, diplomacy,
defence and political parties.[11] Unfortunately Weber, having
apparently made a clear statement that hostility gives rise
to secrecy, then confuses the issue by explaining the

secrecy of political parties by referring to the growth of the party bureaucracy.[12] Weber, in fact, fails to provide any clear statement of what the various causes of secrecy are, what the interrelationship between them is or how they rank in importance in explaining official secrecy. Weber could have provided considerably greater clarity if he had analysed the structure of political authority and how the political system institutionalised the struggle for office. Weber's analysis fails to provide a clear picture of how a political system may create interests in secrecy, not only for bureaucrats but also for politicians.

CONCLUSION

This summary of the literature shows that the main problem of the analysis of government secrecy is that much of it remains on the level of making value judgements and that such an approach fails to provide an explanation of the flow of information which exists in different democratic political systems. Although the values dominant in a political culture are part of the explanation, the more important part is the structure of authority which creates both the interest in secrecy or disclosure and the authority or lack of it to further that interest. It is to the analysis of the development of official secrecy and the institutional framework within which the development took place that this study now moves.

3. British Government and Secrecy

There are certain aspects of British politics which have been accepted as valid and have only been questioned in very recent times, namely the sovereignty of Parliament, the oppositional nature of politics and the idea of ministerial responsibility. Most of this chapter will attempt to explain the level of secrecy as being a consequence of these foundations of British democracy. I will then show that the attack upon secrecy has come about at the very time that these institutions are regarded, or are coming to be regarded, as inadequate.

THE SOVEREIGNTY OF PARLIAMENT

The idea of the sovereignty of Parliament is best expressed in two ways. The first is that in disputes regarding the legitimate powers of government, Parliament has the right to legislate so as to bring its interpretation of its powers into effect. There is no matter upon which Parliament cannot legislate, and no Parliament can be bound by the actions of its predecessors; thus each and every Parliament is sovereign. The second is that Parliament must not be subservient to any other body and nor must any of its members be bound to any other body; Parliament can be influenced, but cannot be subordinate, in its duties as legislator.

The first of these ideas is expressed in the fact that the courts have no right to review the legislation which Parliament chooses to enact and to declare the same unlawful, that no other body can pass laws except by delegation and authorisation by Parliament, and that Parliament cannot create a vacuum by binding itself against the possibility of legislation on a particular topic.

The second of these ideas is expressed in the fact that no other body can pass laws or exercise authority over Parlia-

ment and that parliamentary privilege would be breached if
some outside body or person were to attempt to threaten or
bribe a Member of Parliament in relation to his parliamentary duties. The main aspect which is considered to be a
contempt of Parliament is an attempt to instruct an MP on
how to vote upon a specific issue or to get an MP to use his
influence in such a way as to benefit a particular person or
organisation in return for some particular benefit accruing
to the MP.

The importance of the above for present purposes lies in
the suspicion which exists under British constitutional
arrangements of extra-parliamentary bodies, in terms of
their power to legislate or to influence legislation either
before it is passed or in the process of its implementation.
The conception of democracy which exists within Britain is
one in which the elimination of outside interference in the
activities of Parliament has been seen as a part of the path
to full parliamentary democracy. This desire to eliminate
outside influences related mainly to the removal of the
powers of the crown. However, all governments consult with
outside interests, especially at the level of administration
and after a Bill has been drafted but not yet finally
decided. Despite this it is accepted that there is such a
thing as the public interest which only the government
represents and which no other 'interest' can legitimately
oppose. Politics is therefore not a matter of consultation
and negotiation between various groups, of which the government is one; rather, it is a system in which the government
claims for itself legitimate authority and to which all
other groups are subordinate. These groups are allowed a say
in order that the government can protect itself against
error, either political or factual, rather than implying a
real transfer of decision-making authority. The result of
these attitudes is that democracy has not traditionally been
defined as implying the participation of extra-parliamentary
interests who thereby acquire certain *rights*, whether statutory or conventional, to government information. The information which they do receive has been at the discretion of
the government and has been determined by the government's
perception of its rights and duties as the sovereign authority and not by consideration of the rights of extra-
parliamentary interests in a pluralist democracy.

OPPOSITIONAL POLITICS

The oppositional nature of British politics is best described as a system of election whereby the ability of the

electorate to influence, or indeed determine, the actions of
government, depends upon the electorate being offered a
clear choice between two contrasting and opposing political
programmes.[1] It is further exemplified by the limited form
of cooperation between the government and opposition. This
lack of cooperation between the government and opposition is
seen as being important in so far as it ensures that the
responsibility for the actions undertaken by the government
should be clearly and unambiguously assignable to the party
in office. This leads to the situation whereby a change of
government means that the incoming party does not have
access to the papers of the preceding party in office. It
also means that the survival of the government depends upon
the support of the party in office by its own members in the
House, especially where the government majority is small.
This situation produces a high degree of party discipline,
especially as loyalty to the party is an important factor in
achieving government office. The oppositional nature of
British politics is expressed in the 'winner takes all'
principle and in the majority vote principle applied to each
seat in each constituency. Seats in the chamber are not
allocated by the percentage of votes received by each party
in the country as a whole, but by the number of seats in
which each party gained the highest number of votes cast.

The consequence of the above is such that any information
which the government possesses is seen as potentially an aid
to the opposition party in their efforts to criticise the
government and to replace its political programme with their
own. Given that cooperation is seen as blurring the lines of
responsibility, the clarity of which is held to be an essential characteristic of meaningful elections and to the
rational exercise of the individual elector's vote, the
desire of the government to release information to the
public becomes coloured by the fact that such information
will be released only for the purpose of enabling the party
in office to achieve its responsibilities.

Each individual MP does not attempt to work out his own
strategy, but is directed by means of the common strategy of
the party in office - back-bench 'freedom' has been of
little constitutional importance since Bagehot's description
of the British Constitution was published in 1867. This
means that the members of the party in office sitting on
committees will be reluctant to pursue and produce information concerning those activities of the government which
are politically sensitive and these, of course, are the
very issues in which most members of the public are likely
to be most interested. This is not to say that they cannot
perform some tasks but it is unreasonable, if one accepts

that the basic style of British politics is oppositional, to expect them to be aggressive and 'independent' critics of the government, or to be important revealers of information which the government wishes to keep secret. It is also a consequence of this style of politics that the civil service must serve a House which does not agree as to what the basic objectives and means of achieving them are, and therefore each new government will expect that its civil servants have not become identified with the policies of the preceding government, and especially that they have not become publicly so identified. Civil servants then must remain anonymous politically and this means that the advice they offer to an incumbent government should not be available either to the public at the time or to the new incoming government at a later date.[2] The most important point deriving from the above is not that information will not be made available, but rather that the essence of the British style of democracy is the clarity with which it purports to draw the lines of responsibility. This precludes a high level of cooperation between the main parties and, therefore, requires a 'defensive' attitude by the party in power as to the amount and quality of information that it chooses to release. It is also clear that the electorate under the British system is said to exercise its choice primarily on the basis of the record of what the government has done, or what the public believe the party will do if it is elected to office. There are few legal or constitutional obligations on the British government to consult the electorate, other than the holding of elections - public influence ultimately lies in the fact that the government must go to the country on the basis of the record of what it has done.

MINISTERIAL RESPONSIBILITY

The idea of ministerial responsibility derives from the fact that the activities of the State are carried out both by elected representatives and by non-elected officials and that a democracy requires that some mechanism exists such that the activities of both should be a consequence of the system of representation. In Britain this takes, or has taken, the form of a hierarchy of administration at the top of which sits an elected representative, the Minister. The legitimacy of the actions of all those subordinate to him derives from the fact that they are under the authority of a duly elected government, of which the Minister is a part. Ministerial responsibility further implies that the actions of those under the Minister are not the actions of indepen-

dent officials, but the actions of subordinate members of a
hierarchy, and that therefore they should not be exposed to
criticism for what they have done or to praise for their
achievements; they are rather the instruments of the
Minister. This means that these non-elected officials are
not directly accountable to the House since they are not
considered to be independent with legitimate authority of
their own. This leads to a situation in which the civil
servant is unable to answer any charges made against him in
the House and it is, therefore, considered unfair that he
should be criticised as a named individual by the House; he
is anonymous. If errors have been committed, provided they
are errors of policy or interpretation of policy, and not
simply errors of an isolated and individual kind, they are
considered to be the errors of the Minister himself.[3] If his
cabinet colleagues feel that such errors are politically
embarrassing then the Minister is likely to resign. In terms
of the traditional constitutional relationship between
elected representatives and non-elected officials, the
secrecy with which civil servants operate is meant to be a
reflection of their subservience to the Minister and, therefore, a symptom of their democratic control. The argument is
as follows: if civil servants' views become part of public
knowledge, then their views are inevitably bound to become
part of a public debate about the merits of these views;
this would also mean the possibility of a civil servant
appealing to the public against a decision by a Minister
rejecting his advice. It has traditionally been felt that
it is more important that the possibility should exist of
the civil service offering bad service and the Minister
accepting the same, than allowing the possibility that the
civil service should be able publicly to compete with the
Minister for political and public acceptance of its views.

It seems reasonably certain that these are the only two
realistic choices - once the civil service becomes free to
make its recommendations public it will not stop being partisan, expert, biased, establishment-orientated or whatever
else it is accused of being now. Although publicity may
assist the Minister to detect these faults it will also inevitably mean that the civil service, if its advice is
rejected or criticised on these grounds, will seek to defend
itself and will use all the resources at its disposal to do
so.

THE HOUSE OF COMMONS

Despite the incentives which the above political arrange-

ments create for a high level of secrecy in British politics
there are several institutions which can affect the extent
to which the government reveals the information at its disposal.

The first of these must be the House of Commons itself.
The House is able to extract information primarily from the
Ministers of the cabinet, but the way in which this information is extracted leads mainly to the production of
justifications of what the government is doing in the fields
of legislation or administration. The degree of detail contained within these explanations is not, however, determined
by anything other than the needs of the government itself.
This may be considered an exaggeration, but it is one which
has come to be accepted as the basic rule even by those who
thought at one time that the level of information available
to the House could be increased by the creation of select
committees, by augmenting the work of the standing committees and generally by attempting to 'revitalise' the
back-bench MP. All of these moves are agreed to have foun-
dered upon the realities of political life, mainly party
discipline. It was argued in the 1960s that the House was no
longer able to scrutinise the executive by means of the
traditional weapons of question time, debate and the existing parliamentary committees.[4] It was felt that government
had become so complex and so large that errors were being
made. These errors were considered to have been of three
main types: carelessly drawn legislation; maladministration;
and the pursuit of ill-advised or irrational policies.
These errors were to be corrected by increasing the level of
scrutiny which legislation received in parliamentary committees, by the introduction of the Ombudsman and by the
setting up of parliamentary committees which would have the
task of investigating the implementation of policy and the
basis of it. The problem with all of these solutions was
that they were constrained by the fact that the government
of the day sought to limit them as soon as they entered
areas of controversy, those matters seen as being related
to the standing of the government and its party, and that
these were precisely the areas in which the exercise of the
role of 'examiner' was held to be most necessary. In other
words, the more nearly these 'solutions' approached the role
of independent investigator seeking to influence matters of
political controversy, the more did they discover the
reality of where power lay - not with them but with the
cabinet and government. There was no sanction which they
could apply to a government refusal to allow investigation
to be free ranging. The only sanction was to bring down the
government and this would not necessarily have the effect of

forcing the government to hand over some of its powers to
back-benchers. It could not have that effect until all back-
benchers refused to support any cabinet which did not agree
to abdicate some of its power, or a new political realign-
ment took place such that a 'new' political party considered
that such an issue could win votes. Neither of the existing
major political parties feel that such a constitutional
change is a necessary item of a political programme if it is
to win mass support; they have not seen this as a major
election issue.

Although there may be considerable political will amongst
the back-bench MPs to challenge the power of the executive,
they have little possibility of achieving their aims. This
can be seen in two ways, one of which is expressed by S.A.
Walkland and one by Michael Ryle, both of whom are members
of the Study of Parliament Group and both have been associated with proposals for reforming the House of Commons. In
1977 they edited *The Commons in the Seventies*, in which the
reforms introduced in the 1960s were subjected to an analysis of how far-reaching their consequences had been. Both of
the editors considered that the reforms had not been as
effective as had been predicted in the 1960s, but their
interpretation of why this occurred is different. Michael
Ryle argues that many of the reforms and expectations concerning what the House of Commons could do were based upon a
misconception of the function of the House in that some
people sought to make the House into the controlling or
governing body, whereas he argues that its true function is
to act as the 'sounding board of the nation'. Ryle lays
great stress upon the ability of the House politically to
embarrass a government or a Minister either by raising
issues which are of public concern but which have not been
satisfactorily dealt with, or by scrutinising the actions of
the government so as to force it to be continually anxious
that it may be caught out and its standing with the electorate damaged. It is the government's constant fear of loss of
political credibility which ultimately justifies the concept
of 'government by the people'. Ryle also admits that this
fear need not necessarily be produced by the House having
access to information which the government possesses.[5] It
can be produced by having access to the political temper of
the nation and to problems which may be causing concern, but
of which the government is unaware. The power of the back-
bencher can, therefore, lie in his superior ability to make
political judgements concerning the 'mood of the people',
and it is to this that all governments through the ballot
box are responsible. This is not to underestimate the extent
to which Ryle argues that the scrutiny function of the House

should be improved, but he does at least allow that political judgements and not just the rationality or efficiency of government can cause the rise and fall of governments.

The rationalist method of dealing with government is based upon the notion that there are right and wrong answers to each separate problem and that the task of the government is to do all that is rational to arrive at the correct answer in each case. The acceptability of each solution will be tested as the decision is made through consultation and participation. The logical conclusion of this 'rationalist' politics is a permanent coalition government on which sit the 'best' men who consult with other best men - the politics of consensus taken to its ultimate. And yet it is, in my opinion, the politics of consensus upon which rest many of the desires to alter the constitutional framework of Britain. The basis of such a politics is: (1) the fragmentation of issues; (2) the application of technical considerations to each isolated problem; (3) open government with a high level of consultation and participation, with the object of arriving at the 'best possible solution'; (4) an opposition which comes to mean the activities of the individual citizen taken in isolation and exercised by means of the law; and (5) the politics of manipulation in which the only matter to be discussed is how to manipulate the existing framework with no attempt to justify or change the distribution of power within society. Evidence that this is the case can be seen from the essay, 'Whither the Commons', by the other editor of *The Commons in the Seventies*, S.A. Walkland, who states:

> It is now doubtful whether either of the main parties is any longer capable of performing the representative function. What is urgent for the country as a whole and Parliament in particular is a realignment of politics to produce a lasting and more compelling consensus.[6]

The need for this is to be found in the fact that experiments in parliamentary reform are seen as having failed, in that power has not shifted from the executive, and that this has been caused by 'single party majority government', the 'electoral basis', 'interventionist politics', and that 'ideological differences between the parties became essentially incapable of resolution'.[7] I think that Walkland is right in that the full introduction of the reforms that he would wish to see are inhibited by these factors, but wrong in arguing that modern British politics is composed of parties with clear ideological differences which are incapable of resolution. This may appear to be the case if one

examines the utterances at election time, but surely not if
one actually examines the policies undertaken by the parties
in office.

Parliament, it is felt, has failed to expose the government and lay bare the information upon which government
policies are based, and this is because such a tactic would
be seen by most members of the cabinet as a usurpation of
its right to govern. If the select committees get information, they are not simply going to be content with criticising the actions of the government in the past, but will
undoubtedly attempt to influence future government policies
based upon their accumulated past expertise and information.
What happens if the recommendations of such committees are
ignored by the 'government' or by the cabinet? Who is to
take the responsibility for such policies if they are based
upon such recommendations, especially when these committees
are all-party committees? These are fundamental questions
which imply an alteration in the whole constitutional basis
of British political life.

THE COURTS

In the case of America and Sweden, the role of the courts
will be seen to be an important basis for the introduction
of Freedom of Information Acts and, therefore, the role of
the courts must be understood if one is to judge the extent
to which the introduction of a British Act would be part of
an already existing trend, or whether it would be difficult
to accommodate. The main basis for judicial reticence to
expose the workings of the government in the course of suits
by individuals to set aside actions of the government is the
doctrine of crown privilege. The main basis of this doctrine
is that the courts have no authority to expose documents
which, in the opinion of a Minister, should not be disclosed
on the grounds that to do so would be against the public
interest.[8] The main developments in this field have been
concerned with the question of whether a Minister's statement to this effect is final or can be reviewed by the
courts. The issue, then, is who has the authority to determine what is, and what is not, in the public interest: the
courts or the Minister? The most famous case, which stated
that a signed statement by the Minister that disclosure was
not in the public interest was final, is that of *Duncan* v.
Cammell, Laird.[9]

On 1 June 1939 the submarine 'Thetis' sank whilst undergoing submergence tests with the loss of 99 lives and with
only 4 survivors. The dependants of the men sued the ship-

builders for negligence and sought production of certain
documents in the possession of the shipbuilders. The appel-
lants argued that the opinion of officers of the State that
the production of these documents was against the public
interest should not be final and that the judges should
determine the public interest after examining the documents
in private. It was obvious that many of the documents were
crucial if a proper decision on the question of negligence
was to be made. Viscount Simon, LC, argued on behalf of the
House of Lords that the question to be answered was whether
the court had the authority to review a claim by an officer
of the crown that documents should not be disclosed, and
what procedure must be followed if such a claim was to be
accepted. Viscount Simon argued that the precedents in such
cases had been that the crown could not be forced to reveal
documents, and stated: 'When the Crown (which for this
purpose must be taken to include a government department,
or a Minister of the Crown in his official capacity) is a
party to a suit, it cannot be required to give discovery of
documents at all.'[10]

Viscount Simon stated that there were two tests if the
claim of public interest in non-disclosure was to be
accepted as valid.

> This test may be found to be satisfied either (a) by
> having regard to the contents of the particular document,
> or (b) by the fact that the document belongs to a class
> which, on the grounds of public interest, must as a class
> be withheld from production.[11]

Viscount Simon argued that a signed statement by a Minister
stating that a document came into either of the above categories was final.

This view was overthrown in the case of *Conway* v. *Rimmer*
in 1968.[12] Two new principles were introduced in this case;
one was that the courts did have the right to inspect the
documents, for which crown privilege was being claimed, and
also that claims of privilege based upon the need to protect
a class of document would be more likely to be questioned
than a statement that a particular document, because of its
specific content, should not be disclosed. The government
had been under pressure to restrict the number of occasions
on which privilege was claimed before the case of *Conway* v.
Rimmer, and a statement had been made by the Lord Chancellor
Viscount Kilmuir, to the House of Lords in 1956 that privilege would no longer be claimed for reports relating to
accidents at work, medical records, statements made to the
police (except by informers), and factual reports relating

to government contractors.[13] However, this did not exclude
the possibility that these documents might fall into a
'protected category' and did not include interdepartmental
minutes and memoranda containing 'advice'. The main argument
centres upon whether special protection must be accorded to
the workings of government, such that candour will not be
forthcoming if an official knows that his statements may
become public, over and above that accorded to the private
sector in which there exists only a qualified privilege for
certain statements connected with the promotion or appointment of personnel. The privilege is qualified in that it
does not protect malicious statements, but only those made
in good faith.

The argument used by the Attorney General, Sir Elwyn Jones,
on behalf of the government in the case of *Conway* v. *Rimmer*
was that: 'The essential basis of "class" claims is that
absolute freedom of communication between public servants
must be maintained. Such communications must be unin-
hibited.'[14] This point arose because the case concerned an
action by a probationary police constable against his
superior for malicious prosecution in connection with the
theft of a torch, for which the constable was acquitted.
Both parties to the case desired that the reports written
by the Chief Constable should be made available, but the
crown sought to prevent this. The court argued that the
knowledge that one's reports could be used in a court case
did not prevent candour in the private sector and therefore
would not in the public. The argument used by the crown was
that immunity from disclosure and lack of accountability
were two sides of the same coin. The court rejected this
argument. One of the considerations taken into account by
the court was that crown privilege is a more serious matter
the more the activities of the State increase, and that one
could not allow 'unbridled' claims of privilege to prevail
when the State was the subject of so much activity. The
courts saw themselves as 'protecting' the public from the
executive. This change in attitude reflects the belief that
the public do require protection from the State.

The courts have also interpreted the importance of natural
justice in a more extensive way (the cases of *Ridge* v.
Baldwin and *Anismic Limited* v. *Foreign Compensation Board*).[15]
This is part of a relatively recent trend to 'judicialise'
the process of administration which parallels developments
in Sweden and the USA which have been related to freedom of
information. The usual ground for judicial control of the
executive has been *ultra vires*, the doctrine of an action
being beyond due authority. This has not entailed the
requirement that a complete record of the decision with all

the pertinent facts be made available to the courts or the
parties concerned; it has largely been concerned with
whether the decision is within the powers of the authority
and whether the reasons given for the decision are reasonable. Nor is it part of natural justice that reasons for a
decision need always be given. The notion of quasi-judicial[16]
has affected the degree to which the courts have protected
the citizen, especially in relation to 'natural justice'
which involves the twin principles of a 'right to be heard'
and that one should not be judge in one's own case, or more
particularly that the judge should be disinterested and un-
biased, in that it has been applied only to certain kinds of
decisions, namely those which could be characterised as
'judicial'. It is recognised by most commentators that for
a period of about forty years this meant that wide areas of
government action were considered to be beyond the reach of
the concept of natural justice.[17] The implication drawn by
the courts was that the government was not acting in a
judicial manner unless there was an express requirement laid
down in legislation to act in a judicial manner; the courts
refused to infer that 'judicial' decisions were being made
from an examination of the nature of the decision itself,
and in particular whether it affected the rights of citizens. Such an interpretation would have made the concept of
natural justice similar to the American requirement that due
process be observed when the decision involved 'life,
liberty or property'.

The main reason offered for this reluctance on the part of
the courts to assert themselves has been explained by the
spill-over effect from the emergency powers taken by governments in time of war, by the increasing regulation of these
matters by statute which led the courts to believe that
where Parliament had not provided for court review it was
deliberate policy to exclude these rights, and by the increasing sensitivity on the part of the courts to the
developing constitutional principles of ministerial responsibility and civil service anonymity. However, the
distinction between an administrative decision and a 'judicial' one is difficult to draw and the courts are in the
process of redefining it.

The British courts have tended to confine themselves to
considering questions of law rather than investigating the
accuracy of the facts upon which administrative decisions
may be based. The courts have recently asserted the right to
quash executive decisions because of obvious factual error,
e.g. that the decision is so bad that it is impossible that
all the facts were examined.[18] This power to quash decisions
which are in error of fact is particularly important because

of the requirement in the case of tribunals that reasons
for the decision be given. This means that any facts which
are given in the decision may be challenged as in error.
This has been further extended by the 'no evidence' rule.
This rule is based upon the principle that if a decision
requires that certain evidence be present, certain facts
ascertained, then if these facts are not present the
decision can be set aside. This occurred in a case in 1971[19]
involving a decision by a Minister to include a particular
property of good condition in a compulsory purchase order,
despite the recommendation of an inspector after an inquiry
that it be excluded from the order. The Minister had this
power only if the inclusion of the property was reasonably
necessary. The Court of Appeal held that there was no evidence for this necessity, and so quashed the order.

The courts invoked the same principle in the Tameside
case[20] in which the Appeal Court overthrew an order of the
Minister of Education to the Tameside Authority that they
had to introduce a plan for comprehensive education, which
had already been approved. John Griffiths, Professor of
Public Law at the University of London, argued in an article
in the *Sunday Times*[21] that the judges had made a 'political
decision' in that they had sought to make a judgement concerning whether disruption was involved or not and that they
should not attempt to make such decisions, for which they
were not competent. Griffiths argues that this is a dangerous precedent in that judicial intervention was based upon
overruling the judgement of a Minister and, therefore,
usurping a function of the Officers of the Crown who are
responsible to Parliament and the electorate for the
decisions which they make, whilst judges are responsible to
no one. This is an important point to bear in mind when
considering the consequences of introducing a Freedom of
Information Act which would allow judges the right to determine whether the release of certain information was or was
not in the public interest.

In conclusion, the courts in this country have not sought
to use principles such as that of natural justice to argue
that participants in a dispute with government have the
right to see all the documents held by the authority; they
are, however, taking a more active role in 'protecting' the
citizen from the actions of government by making the conditions which are necessary for the lawful use of State
authority more stringent.

A major reason for judicial quiescence until present
times of judicial assertiveness is due to the belief that
the British civil servant and Minister were incorruptible
and that the Northcote-Trevelyan reforms had led to a

'rational' and 'responsible' civil service. This meant that
the best interests of the citizens were served by allowing
the administration a high degree of autonomy - not until the
1960s and 1970s has the reputation of the service come under
serious attack. Judicial intervention is a reflection of the
belief that ministerial responsibility has ceased to be
effective, that the civil service has become too large for
its decisions to be overseen by the Minister or Parliament,
and that therefore some outside body is necessary if the
civil service is to be 'brought under control'.

THE CROSSMAN CASE

In 1975 the courts became involved in a 'cause célèbre',
which if not equal to that of the Pentagon Papers in the
coverage and 'objectivity' of the revelations, was certainly
seen by the government as striking at one of the pillars of
the Constitution, namely, cabinet secrecy. The case concerned the diaries of a British Labour Party MP, Minister
and Leader of the House.[22] The diaries span the years from
1952 to 1970, but it was the publication of the first volume
of the diaries which he kept as a member of a Labour cabinet
between 1964 and 1966 which formed the basis of a court case.
In July 1975 a case was heard before Lord Widgery, the Lord
Chief Justice, on an application for an injunction by the
Attorney General against publication of the diaries in book
form and against the publication of any further extracts
from the diaries in the newspaper, the *Sunday Times*. The
Attorney General applied for the injunction on two grounds:
one was the protection of the public interest, and the other
was based upon confidentiality. Lord Widgery was not impressed with the argument on grounds of public interest, it
being very general, but he took the argument from confidentiality seriously. The Attorney General argued that there
were clearly established conventions governing the publications of ex-Ministers concerning their time in office: the
general rule was that permission had to be obtained from the
Secretary of the Cabinet before publication could proceed
and that this had not been obtained in this case, either by
Crossman before his death or by his executors. The Attorney
General did not seek to bring an action under the Official
Secrets Act or any statute, but based his claim upon the
common law of confidentiality. There did not exist then, and
there does not exist now, any statute in this area. Lord
Widgery, however, clearly summarised the areas within which
cabinet secrecy deserves protection, these being:

(a) disclosure of individual views of members of the
cabinet in defiance of the principle of collective
responsibility; (b) disclosure of advice given by civil
servants still in office; (c) disclosure of discussions
relating to the promotion or transfer of senior civil
servants.[23]

Lord Widgery argued that where information involved national
security there would be a clear need to protect the public
interest, but that no such issue was involved in this case.
He went on to argue that disclosure of the views of individual cabinet Ministers can be protected by the courts, and
that the maintenance of the doctrine of collective responsibility is in the public interest but that in his view the
disclosures contained in diaries of ten years ago did not
'undermine' the principle of collective responsibility, and
therefore he denied the injunction. The press and the
Attorney General both felt that they had achieved something
in that publication was to proceed but, on the other hand,
it had been clearly stated that the courts would protect
cabinet secrecy in certain circumstances, even though not in
the present ones.

One consequence of the Crossman case was the setting up by
the Prime Minister of a Committee of Privy Councillors to
consider the principles governing the publication of ministerial memoirs in April 1975, with Viscount Radcliffe as
Chairman.[24] The report claims that it was First World War
memoirs which created the first real breaches of cabinet
confidentiality and that the problem reappeared at the end
of the Second World War.[25] In 1946 the Prime Minister, Mr
Attlee, circulated a memorandum to the cabinet which laid
down two main principles guiding publication of information:
the first was that it should not injure foreign relations or
otherwise be useful to an enemy; and the second that it
should not be 'destructive of the confidential relationships
on which our system of government is based'.[26] These relationships are described as being between Ministers themselves, between Ministers and their advisers and between
Ministers and outside bodies or persons. The reason given
for allowing any publication of government information by
Ministers is that they, unlike civil servants, are responsible for policy and that their actions may have been
subject to public comment, the defence of which will require
them to make reference to matters which were at the time
secret. It is obvious from the report that despite the
possibility of common law preventing publication, the basis
of restraint will remain as obligations to colleagues or ex-
colleagues and that these, allied to pressure to inform the

Cabinet Secretary and, if necessary, the Prime Minister, are the only reasonable deterrents.

The courts are not the only bodies to have the right to participate in disputes between the citizen and the government, and it is to these other institutions that I move, namely the Parliamentary Commissioner for Administration (popularly known as the Ombudsman) and Tribunals and Inquiries.

THE PARLIAMENTARY COMMISSIONER FOR ADMINISTRATION

The Parliamentary Commissioner for Administration (PCA) was introduced as an extension of the right of a Member of Parliament to aid his constituents in certain complaints they may have against the administrative actions of the government. The PCA's right of investigation is limited to matters of maladministration, but within that area he has the right to see all documents concerned with a case, except those which relate to the cabinet or to cabinet committees. He is also restricted to matters which are not privileged according to the rules of the High Court, for instance advice which a solicitor may have offered to a client. He is not, however, bound by the rules of crown privilege, nor restricted in access by the Official Secrets Act, although he himself is subject to its provisions; this means that he has access to information normally seen only by government ministers and senior officials. However, this does not necessarily mean that all the information which is so available to the PCA becomes public knowledge, in that a Minister of the Crown may certify that the release of certain information is prejudicial to the safety of the realm, or is against the public interest, and he is bound by that certificate.[27] The Commissioner's investigation must, under the PCA Act, be in private so that it is only the report of the Commissioner which can lead to an increase in the amount of information available to the public.[28] It is of the essence of the position of the PCA that he is given this unrestricted access because it is known that he will not abuse his position - he is given access to secrets denied to others because he is not, as a court of law would be, obliged to make these public. His value does not stem from the fact that the public have access to the information upon which the PCA based his report, but because he has the status of an 'outsider'. A decision by the PCA has the respect which a judgement by the government in its own case does not have and yet, unlike the courts, which would have a similar respect, he is not obliged to work in the open. This creates a

strain upon the PCA in that he can only defend himself
against a criticism of being a 'government' man by showing
in his report that he has done a thorough job, and yet he
can only keep the active cooperation of the government by
not going so far in winning the respect of the public that
he wins their trust at the expense of losing the trust of
the executive.

The fact that the PCA is part of the 'British tradition of
secrecy' rather than an 'exposer' of secrecy can be seen in
the fact that the Ombudsman is obliged to sign the Official
Secrets Act and also that he cannot be called as a witness
in any court proceedings, except in so far as these may
relate to a breach of the Official Secrets Act, or in connection with an alleged offence of perjury, or in connection
with a court examination of a claim by the PCA that a person
is in contempt for unlawful obstruction of his investigations. The PCA is also excluded from investigating matters
relating to foreign affairs, the investigation of crimes,
matters relating to commercial transactions and contracts,
issues of personnel, as well as information and documents
relating to the cabinet or committees of the cabinet.

The right of a Minister to give notice that certain documents and information shall not be communicated for any
purpose, including the making of a report, is based upon the
principles enunciated in the case of *Duncan* v. *Cammell,
Laird*, principles which have since been overturned by the
House of Lords in *Conway* v. *Rimmer*. The basis of crown
privilege as now stated is that certain documents contain
information, the release of which is immediately identifiable as being against the public interest (most obviously
information relating to national security), and also that
certain documents fall within a category which must be protected, not because the specific information contained in
the documents is damaging but because the release of this
class of document would impair the proper working of government (for instance, advice given to a Minister by civil
servants). This aspect of the rules governing the work of
the PCA may be one of the reasons explaining why the work of
the PCA has had little impact upon the public.

If the PCA does his work privately, as he is required to
do by the Act, then he is unlikely to be of much interest to
the news media. The PCA is also likely to be inhibited in
his use of publicity by the fact that the civil service may
become less cooperative if it is felt that the PCA is giving
information to the public unnecessarily, especially if it
includes the naming of names.

The number of cases of maladministration exposed by the
PCA is relatively small, and the number of cases which have

led to the exposure of serious abuse of executive powers even smaller.[29] In two cases the PCA has been a former high-ranking civil servant, which has the advantage that the PCA knows Whitehall, but has the disadvantage that he may be more keen to win the esteem of his peers than of the public at large. His 'reference group' is likely to be his ex-colleagues rather than the media, in which case the PCA is unlikely to be a media-hungry investigator out to expose the civil service. The PCA is responsible to a House of Commons 'oversight' committee, the Select Committee on the Parliamentary Commissioner, which has encouraged him to take a wider definition of his role than had been taken by the PCA by personal inclination. One could say that this was somewhat hypocritical, in that many of the House committees have been equally reluctant to take a broad view of their investigative powers, but at least the Commissioner is not subject to party discipline. The Select Committee has encouraged the PCA to take the view that some decisions are so bad that they can only have been the result of maladministration, and also to criticise departmental and non-statutory orders. The PCA does not, however, have a special right to comment upon the operation of statutes or the interpretation of them; moreover, he is still largely confined to examine procedures rather than the quality of decisions made, and is still under an obligation to remain apolitical so that he is not seen as part of the 'opposition', as a tool of the opposition.

TRIBUNALS AND INQUIRIES

The Tribunals and Inquiries Act 1958 set up the Council on Tribunals and Inquiries, which has the duty to receive complaints against the workings of the same and also to oversee the procedures of these bodies; the Act also requires that the Council be consulted before new procedural rules are adopted. In particular, it has attempted to give expression to the recommendations of the Franks Report upon Tribunals and Inquiries especially in connection with the principles of openness, impartiality and fairness. It is a requirement of natural justice that the parties to appeals be given 'adequate' knowledge of the case to be answered. There is, however, no requirement that they be given access to all documents,[30] and the courts have protected the right of the executive to refuse to disclose certain information, as well as protected the right to refuse to produce the relevant documents.

In some cases there are statutory rules which require that

certain reports be made available, for instance the reports
of inspectors following upon inquiries in connection with
compulsory purchase orders (Compulsory Purchase by Ministers
[Inquiries Procedures] Rules 1967).[31] The courts have allowed that release of certain information may not be in the
public interest, for example medical evidence which would be
distressing to the party, aspects of national policy and
information supplied in confidence to the government. There
is, however, a general rule that no information which may be
detrimental to the party can be withheld without giving the
party an opportunity to correct, refute or comment on the
information.[32] Since 1971 there has also been a duty upon a
Minister to disclose the reasons for his decisions in connection with the holding of a statutory inquiry, or where
the person concerned could have asked for the holding of
such an inquiry.[33] A similar duty is required of statutory
tribunals.

Before describing the development of official secrecy in
Britain in the following two chapters, there is one common
misperception which must be cleared up. It is that the
Official Secrets Act is the 'cause' of secrecy in Britain.
The Official Secrets Act prohibits the *unauthorised* release
of official information, but it does not explain why those
authorised to release information do not do so. There is
also a very great difference between citizens possessing a
statutory right to information, or there being institutions
which can force the release of information held by the
government (or perhaps more clearly, the executive) and the
simple absence of legislation prohibiting unauthorised persons from releasing information. The elimination of the
Official Secrets Act from the statute books will not necessarily, or by itself, lead to a situation in which the amount
of information available automatically increases.

4. The Development of Official Secrecy in Britain

This chapter is concerned with the development of official secrecy in Britain. It will cover not only the Official Secrets Act but also other rules such as those covering the political activities of civil servants which have a bearing on this issue. My main contention will be that official secrecy arose at the time when democratic reforms were being introduced and that this raises serious doubts as to the truth of the proposition that secrecy and democracy are in opposition to each other.

GOVERNMENT ADMINISTRATION IN NINETEENTH-CENTURY BRITAIN

The term 'official secret' indicates that secrecy in government is related to the development of the notion of office and the duties attached to office. The most important development in relation to public office in the early part of the nineteenth century was the removal of crown influence from office-holding, and the advent of parliamentary control of office-holding and office-holders. The first of these is generally agreed to have occurred by 1832.[1] The importance of this change is that it gave rise to parliamentary and, therefore, public scrutiny of the actions of civil servants and raised issues of how this accountability was to be expressed. It is between 1832 and the 1870s that the position of civil servants in relation to Parliament is determined and the convention of ministerial responsibility takes hold.

It is important to recognise that the role of civil servants changed considerably during this period and not simply in terms of the elimination of patronage and the development of competitive entry, but in terms of the participation of officials in the formation of policy and their participation in political life.

Civil servants were not the anonymous, unknown, 'statesmen in disguise' figures of modern times, but publicly known and accepted statesmen. Their political views were often well

known, they expressed their views in publications, and they
were often appointed because they had well-known views on
matters of policy. The evolution of the civil service is
obviously connected to the development of democracy. This is
especially so when one considers that accountability of
administrators to an elected body is one of the requirements
of a democratic polity. The problem which one has to explain
is how official secrecy developed with the evolution of a
democratic or constitutional bureaucracy. It will be my contention that official secrecy in Britain was one of the
mechanisms used to enhance the control of elected representatives over unelected administrators. This does not imply,
however, that countries without official secrecy are ones in
which elected representatives do not control bureaucrats.
The important point is that officials should not be able to
determine what government information is released, and that
this decision should be made by those with political authority, in accordance with the law and the demands of political life. There *is* a lack of control by elected representatives where the degree of openness is a product of
arbitrary civil service leaks. The problem to be explained
is why, in Britain, the arbitrariness was eliminated by
adopting a high level of secrecy and not openness. The major
reason is that Parliament sought to bring the civil service
directly under its supervision in order to eliminate competition to its authority, and a consequence of this was
that information became part of the political process, part
of the struggle for power, unlike Sweden, where administration was hived off, or America, where political authority
was not centralised to the point where this level of control
was possible. The British Parliament had the authority to
exercise this degree of control and secrecy was one of the
ways in which its supremacy was exemplified.

By the 1830s, crown patronage had largely been eliminated
from both the House of Commons and the civil service, but
this did not mean that one had a civil service of a contemporary kind. It was a civil service still appointed, at
least at the senior levels, by politicians, and one in which
a substantial proportion of administration was carried out
by means of Boards, administrative bodies not directly
answerable to Parliament and not headed by one person, a
Minister, who enshrines that responsibility.

Political patronage is important, not only for its relationship to the problem of 'expertise' but also to the
problem of the political views of civil servants being known
and acknowledged as a basis of appointment. Appointment of
civil servants who shared the same political views as the
party of government was seen as being one way to ensure that

the civil servants would act in accordance with government objectives.[2] However, by the 1830s the civil service was already a permanent civil service, so conflicting requirements existed; on the one hand, a civil service which was responsive to the Minister and shared his views, and on the other, a civil service which was neutral and could serve masters of various political persuasions. Patronage became something which was seen as a short-term expedient, but one which, in the long term, damaged the credibility of politicians and made future dealings with civil servants more difficult, rather than easier.

Autonomy of administration will be seen as being one of the major factors in explaining the openness of Swedish government, so it is obviously necessary to discuss the degree to which British administration was also autonomous. In the 1830s a substantial amount of administration was undertaken by Boards which were not responsible to a Minister; although the Board may have had Members of Parliament upon it, they were not necessarily in a majority, and parliamentary supervision of their workings was often very slight.[3] The use of Boards was part of the system of administration which had existed prior to parliamentary supremacy in government and had been favoured by the crown because it avoided the development of powerful Ministers who could oppose the crown, and increased the number of appointments available for crown patronage.[4] However, parliamentary responsibility for administration made the position of these Boards anomalous, although the Boards of the pre-reform period were continued and even after 1830 new ones created, partly because of tradition and partly to avoid the creation of positions subject to the political patronage of Parliament. Many of the activities of these Boards were also such as to be relatively minor; they were, therefore, of little interest to Parliament and of little political importance. However, this was by no means always the case. The most often quoted example is the case of the Poor Law Commissioners whose duties were of such a sensitive nature that Parliament tried to comment on their activities and resented the fact that the administration of the Poor Law was not under parliamentary control. The general principle followed in the latter half of the nineteenth century was that administration was satisfactory only in so far as it was under the responsibility of a Minister and was therefore subject to parliamentary supervision. The Boards were held in low esteem because responsibility for a decision was not clear and accountability was difficult to enforce, the consequence being that some of the Boards were turned into Ministries, and most others made subject to the authority of a Ministry.[5]

The process of institutionalisation of secrecy in Britain
is associated with the development of democratic political
institutions. The most important development was the extent
to which the administrative process became intimately connected with the political process, with the survival of
governments.

THE DEVELOPMENT OF CIVIL SERVICE ANONYMITY

The first part of that process I shall examine is the
development of the relationship between the civil service
and Parliament. To use Parris's terms, the changeover from
zealots to professionals or the change from specialists to
generalists is the crucial development.[6] The period from
1830 to 1870 saw the development of ministerial responsibility and the creation of a permanent civil service
characterised by being divorced from politics. I mean by the
latter phrase that it was a service which no longer took
part in the public process of policy-making, it was no
longer part of the political forum. This meant that it was a
service which was not responsible for the decisions made and
it was not accountable for the decisions taken. It was excluded from the political process by not being able publicly
to state its views and insist upon them being taken into
account. Its role became that of adviser not participant.
This is not to deny that advisers do not have influence
(indeed, it would be a rather odd sort of adviser who had no
influence), but they have no authority in that they are not
able to appeal to the body politic and to attempt to capture
public opinion. It is by means of influencing an elected
representative who does have that authority that they operate, but one must not forget that should their advice be
rejected, they have no recourse to the public. Making the
advice of civil servants public would not only make them
liable to scrutiny, but also liable to praise as reposi-
tories of good advice, and to have lost one form of influence, uncriticised advice to Ministers, but gained another,
participation in public discussion.
    In order to show that civil servants were not the self-
effacing anonymous persons we now think of, I offer the
following examples from the Board of Trade, and the Council
for Education.
    In the case of the Board of Trade, two joint secretaries,
J.R. McGregor (1840-7) and G.R. Porter (1847-52) both published articles and books in support of Free Trade.[7]
Political considerations and McGregor's Whig sympathies
played a part in his appointment, and his party affiliations

were no secret. In a letter to Lord Russell,[8] McGregor
claims to have made his party affiliations equally clear to
his Conservative masters, and when told by the new Conservative administration of Peel that they had no confidence in
McGregor because of his partiality on the issue of Free
Trade, he stood his ground and refused to resign: this led
to the Conservatives being 'more reserved and discreet in
their relations with the officials of the Board of Trade'.[9]
McGregor and Porter did not feel that holding a senior civil
service post was any obstacle to taking a particular point
of view and publicising it; rather they felt that they had a
duty to promote the public interest.[10]

In the case of the Committee of the Privy Council for
Education, the most outspoken 'zealot', to use Parris's term,
was Dr Kay, or Dr Kay-Shuttleworth as he became. Kay-
Shuttleworth was appointed as Secretary to the Committee in
1839.[11] He was a well-known Radical in middle-class circles
- he wrote pamphlets on education and organised the Man-
chester Statistical Society. When he was appointed to the
Committee, he already had a considerable reputation, important political connections, well-known views on education and
was considered an expert on such. Kay-Shuttleworth made
public speeches, expanded his department and encouraged the
Inspectors to take an active part in the shaping of policy
by holding an annual conference, and by publishing their
reports in full. Not only was he a 'zealot', but all the
Inspectors could be so classified in that they were all men
of substance and of independent views. The average age of
the Inspectors on appointment was thirty-six, and they were
men of high scholarship and religious standing. The Inspectors did not hesitate to criticise educational policy, to
ally themselves with specific causes and even publicly to
vote against the Council's policy at their annual conference.
In 1859, Sir Robert Lowe, then Vice-President of the Council,
stopped the annual conference and also attempted to stop the
full publication of the Inspectors' reports, intending to
publish only excerpts chosen by his office. This led to the
Inspectors drawing up a grand remonstrance, which was signed
by almost all of them, against this censorship and arguing
in the same vein as did some Members of Parliament, that:

> most of the inspectors were men who had already won their
> spurs in the fields of literature and science. If their
> united opinion should ever be opposed to the policy of the
> Department, their full opinions should be placed before
> Parliament.[12]

Lowe was defeated and the reports continued to be published

in full; that is, Parliament wished to have each individual
Inspector responsible to it. In 1861, however, Robert Lowe
instructed the Inspectors that their reports were only to
contain descriptions of schools and practical suggestions
rather than general comments on educational policy, as otherwise the reports would be returned to them for amendment.

The famous Lowe scandal occurred in 1864, when it was
claimed that Lowe was censoring Inspectors' reports without
their knowledge or consent. Robert Lowe denied this, but
documents were circulating in the House and being quoted
which could only have been supplied by civil servants in his
own department, and which showed that censoring had occurred.
Robert Lowe found their behaviour 'base', but Lord David
Cecil argued:

> I do not believe that in the service of the Crown any
> loyalty is due to the Heads of Departments as against
> the House of Commons. The Heads of Departments and the
> Departments themselves are alike subject to our juris-
> diction; and if persons employed see what they deem to
> be abuses they do no wrong in laying them before the
> representatives of the people.[13]

It was subsequently established, after Lowe's resignation,
that officials in his department, contrary to his instructions, had been censoring the reports but, due to his very
bad eyesight, he had not been aware of this. However, the
main issue was one of who was to be responsible to Parliament, and both Lowe and Palmerston argued that Parliament
could not have responsibility divided, that is, expect the
policy of the department to be Lowe's and for him to be
responsible for it and to have officials in his department
interfere with this policy. The issue of ministerial responsibility was effectively settled in 1864.

GOVERNMENT CONTROL OF STATE PAPERS

At the same time as this development, the government took
an increasing interest in memoirs, letters and diaries which
had been kept by government officials, and in particular
those of diplomats.[14] The government concern was over the
sale and publication of these and it applied for court in-
junctions to prevent this occurring. All the cases that I
have been able to trace relate to foreign affairs, and the
concern with these is greater in the period 1830 to 1870
than with civil servants writing in the newspapers about
domestic matters. This reflects a more traditional concern

with allegiance and with treason than with the modern concern with bureaucratic official secrecy. According to the
Foreign Office papers, the first case dealing with 'modern'
documents is that of a proposed sale of the manuscripts of
Lord Hanley in 1833. The papers were to be sold at auction
and they referred to foreign relations between Britain and
Bavaria, Denmark, Austria and Prussia covering the period of
1777-89, during which time Lord Hanley was engaged on a
series of foreign missions. The Foreign Office considered it
'unadvisable' that they should be sold and raised the
question of how the sale could be prevented. The Foreign
Office was advised that the problem was whether such papers
could be said to belong to an individual, to be his property
and therefore to be disposed of as he would. On the basis of
claiming that the government had property rights in the
papers, the Foreign Office informed the auctioneers that it
would seek an injunction against their sale. The auctioneer
then withdrew the papers from the sale, but Palmerston
pressed that the injunction be continued with, in order to
establish the question of who had rights over the documents.
The case was heard in the Court of Chancery, where an injunction was obtained and subsequently the papers were
delivered up to the Foreign Office. One result of this,
apart from establishing a precedent, was that other book-
sellers and auctioneers wrote to the Foreign Office for
permission to proceed with sales of this nature. However,
this did not end the problem.

In 1862 the Foreign Office came up against a lady with a
degree of persistence which engaged the Foreign Office, and
even a Prime Minister, in correspondence for seven years.
In 1862 Lady Jackson wrote to the Foreign Office offering to
sell to them the papers which had been in the possession of
her late husband, who had been a diplomat in Berlin. The
papers consisted of dispatches between London and Berlin
between 1772 and 1800 and she offered them to the Foreign
Office for the sum of £3000. The Foreign Office wrote to her,
warning her not to sell the papers, and that if she did so
an injunction would be sought. However, Lady Jackson was
living in Paris and she had the papers with her. The British
Ambassador in Paris was then requested to investigate the
legal position in France as to whether they could be recovered there. The British Ambassador said that it might be
possible for them to be recovered legally, but he enclosed
a letter from a French adviser suggesting the possibility
of seizing the papers. This was not done, but Lady Jackson
was spied upon, and her hotel address in Paris discovered,
as was the fact that she intended to return to England. The
British Ambassador sent a telegram to the Foreign Office

with her date of return and also a note of her forwarding
address in England, which she had left with her hotel in
Paris. On her return in 1864 the Attorney General sought an
injunction against Lady Jackson and the Court of Chancery
granted it.

Lady Jackson then offered the papers to the Foreign Office,
who asked to inspect them in order to determine which ones
were official papers and which private, as these she could
retain. Legal action was continuing in that the Foreign
Office was seeking an Attachment Order. She requested that
it be discontinued and if they did she would give them all
the papers, and they should be good enough to recompense her
for the inconvenience she had suffered in looking after the
papers for all these years only to find that they were not
her property after all. The recompense she received was £800.
In 1865 she then applied for a pension on the grounds of her
husband's service, but this was refused; she then applied
for an additional gratuity to the one she had been given,
but this too was denied. In 1866 she again applied for a
pension but was again denied. However, this determined lady
had one last card. In 1866 she wrote to the Foreign Office
saying that on her return to Paris she had discovered that
there were still some more papers and that the Foreign
Office could have these for £1000. She hinted that if she
was not paid for these she would sell them to the French.
The Foreign Office simply wrote back refusing. However, in
the Foreign Office papers, doubts are expressed as to the
existence of the papers. The Foreign Office evidently felt
confident that the arrangement arrived at in 1864 covered
all papers in her possession and that the courts would uphold recovery of any that might exist. Lady Jackson made one
last attempt to extract money in that she applied to the
Prime Minister in 1869 for financial assistance from the
Royal Bounty, but this too was refused.

An important case occurred in 1865 concerning the Buckingham and Grenville papers. These papers contained official
diplomatic correspondence relating to the Peace of Fontain-
bleu of 1762, secret letters, and minutes of cabinet
meetings of 1809. The Foreign Office was in doubt about the
official nature of the papers, but they considered the
possible sale of these papers would be of considerable damage and would breach the Foreign Office rule that no documents from 1760 onwards were available for public inspection.
The Attorney General applied to the Court of Chancery on the
grounds that these papers were the property of the government and that their sale and publication would be 'detrimental to the public service'. The auctioneers returned the
papers to the bookseller who had commissioned the auction

and asked that the writ be withdrawn. The bookseller then returned them to the then Duke of Buckingham. The Foreign Office asked to be allowed to inspect the papers, but after this no more was heard of the sale.

The importance of these cases is that they show government, and particularly Foreign Office, concern with the existing arrangements whereby many diplomats and ministers considered that they had the right to dispose of their letters, correspondence and diaries as they saw fit. They considered their papers to be their property and, provided they were not engaged in treason or theft, the government had no, or certainly not sole, right to limit the spread of the knowledge which they had, including access to the actual papers themselves. This was a view which governments were no longer willing to countenance in that it implied a personal system of government by which independent men gave service to the crown: the terms of that service were a matter of individual judgement and did not derive from official rules. The government was attempting to establish the view that information and papers acquired in the process of government service belonged to the office and not to the individual, and that rights of disposal over these belonged to the government in whose service the official had worked. The only basis that the government could operate upon, however, was property, especially so, as in many cases the actual authors of the papers were dead and therefore could not be considered to be in breach of faith or to be acting treasonably.

THE CONTROL OF THE UNAUTHORISED RELEASE OF OFFICIAL INFORMATION

A related series of cases, and ones which also mainly involve foreign affairs, are mid-nineteenth-century leaks, i.e. the unauthorised release of official information. The leaks which are discussed below are ones which took place before the existence of any Official Secrets Act. One of the most famous of these was the appearance in *The Times* of 1847 of correspondence relating to the Congress of Vienna of 1814/15. The matter in *The Times* consisted of correspondence between Lord Casterlaugh and representatives of Imperial Russia over Poland. The Foreign Office sought legal advice on whether further publication of the letters could be prevented, but were advised that in this case the question of ownership was difficult to determine and that without a claim based upon property, nothing could be done. The Foreign Office examined their copy of the correspondence and discovered that the letters were retranslations of letters

from the French and were therefore difficult to trace. The
Foreign Office was unable to prevent publication as *The
Times* refused to cooperate.

In 1858 Gladstone set out to the Ionian Islands as an
emissary of the Colonial Office to investigate the desire of
the islanders to join with Greece. Confidential dispatches
of 1858 and 1857 relating to the issue were printed in the
Daily News: the contents of these appeared to prejudge the
case and were therefore an embarrassment to the Colonial
Office.[15] Other newspapers assumed that the dispatches had
been leaked by a member of the cabinet, but this was denied.
Inquiries were instituted in the Colonial Office and led to
a William Guernsey, who had removed printed copies of these
dispatches whilst visiting the Sub-Librarian of the Colonial
Office, with whom he was friendly. He had then sold these
dispatches to the *Daily News*. Guernsey was arrested and
committed for trial on a charge of larceny, but his Defence
Counsel claimed that an important element of a larceny offence was missing, namely to deprive the owner permanently
of the article in question. The judge in his summing up
stated to the jury that the *Daily News* had acted quite properly in publishing the papers. Despite the fact that the
Attorney General stressed the potentially serious consequences of the act and the defence admission that the act
was unjustified, Guernsey was acquitted.

A similar case occurred in 1878 when a young copy clerk,
Charles Marvin, sold details of a secret agreement which had
been arrived at between Russia and Britain prior to the
Congress of Berlin, to *The Globe* newspaper.[16] Marvin had
been a temporary copy clerk in the Treaty Section of the
Foreign Office for one year. He was charged with larceny,
but was acquitted on the grounds of insufficient evidence,
although *The Globe* was criticised by the judge for its part
in the affair. There was no real doubt that Marvin sold the
papers to *The Globe*; the question was whether this constituted larceny.

One consequence of this affair was a tightening up of the
rules on civil servants acting as newspaper correspondents.
This had been commented on before but had not actually been
prohibited. The Foreign Office took a very serious view of
this affair in that the leak concerned matters of immediate
contemporary relevance and yet no legal punishment was in-
flicted.

There were a few other leaks concerned with announcements
appearing in the press before being given to Parliament; for
example, the results of a medical enquiry and a proclamation
by General Gordon, but none on the scale of Marvin or
Guernsey.

During this period then, one had three types of cases creating anxiety for the government: publication of correspondence to and from Ministers and diplomats, public statements
by civil servants especially in the press and magazines, and
leaks. The government response to these events was related
to the doctrine of ministerial responsibility, the development of a permanent civil service staffed by 'officials',
and the rise of political parties as the main instrument of
parliamentary authority. By the 1870s the government had
established that civil servants were not individually responsible for what they said or did and that the House could not
hold civil servants directly responsible for their actions.

MINISTERS, CIVIL SERVANTS AND PARTY

In order to show the difference, I will examine the position
in the 1870s in relation to ministerial responsibility,
party unity in Parliament and civil service discipline.
Henry Parris contrasts the controversy over the Lowe case
with the clarity of the Scudmore one.[17] This was a case of a
Post Office official, Frank Scudmore, who diverted funds
from one branch of the Post Office to the one with which he
was concerned, namely the telegraph. Scudmore was impatient
to create a national telegraph scheme and when the money
allocated to the purpose ran out he diverted funds. When
this was discovered, Scudmore freely admitted what he had
done and claimed responsibility for it. The House of Commons,
however, stated that 'This House has nothing to do with Mr
Scudmore. He is not responsible to us.'[18] Although Lowe
resigned his office, and Scudmore's chief did not, no one in
the House was in any doubt that Ministers were responsible
to it and that civil servants were not. In *The English Constitution*, first published in 1876, Bagehot argued that
Parliament is incapable of administering or of supervising
administration directly, because administrators would be too
weak and Parliament too powerful. It would 'poke fun at it
[administration] till it makes it impossible ... The incess-
ant tyranny of Parliament over the public offices is prevented and can only be prevented by the appointment of a
Parliamentary head, connected by close ties with the present
Ministry and the ruling party in Parliament.'[19]

    1867 was also a year of reform with a further extension of
the franchise which gave the final impetus to the domination
of party politics.[20] The more Ministers' actions were related to the success of a party at the elections and ministerial actions became associated with party success, the
more did information become a tool of party politics. The

Public Secrets

consequence of this is that information is not simply a
neutral commodity linked to rational decision-making, but a
part of the political process, an element of victory and
defeat. One would therefore expect that the greater the
element of party government, the more secrecy one would find.
The Official Secrets Act starts when party politics becomes
finally dominant. The figures supplied by Professor Beer
establish the level of party consensus as follows:

Table 1

Party Unity 1860-94 — Coefficients of Cohesion

Year		Liberals	Conservatives
1860	All Divisions	59.8	57.3
	Whip Divisions	58.9	63.0
1871	All Divisions	71.7	76.0
	Whip Divisions	75.5	74.0
1881	All Divisions	82.0	82.9
	Whip Divisions	83.2	87.9
1894	All Divisions	86.9	94.1
	Whip Divisions	89.8	97.9

Source: Samuel A. Beer, *Modern English Politics*
(London: Faber and Faber, 1969, p.257).

Not only does the level of party unity increase in general,
but it is not until 1881 that one has a universally higher
level of unity on a whip vote than one without. Moreover, by
the end of the nineteenth century, most legislation was
introduced by the government and not by Private Members'
Bills. The nature of legislation had changed such that Bills
were less likely to be concerned with local, or indeed private matters such as enclosures, naturalisation, setting up
of turnpikes, canals and harbours. Another important change
was that legislation increasingly included powers of delegation, rule-making and inspection, which further increased
the authority of the executive.[21]

THE CIVIL SERVICE AND OFFICIAL SECRECY

The first major step towards a modern civil service was the
setting up of the Civil Service Commission in 1855 as a
result of the Northcote-Trevelyan report. The Commission was

set up by an Order in Council and had the duty of examining those to be appointed to any junior situations in the civil service. This was an attempt to reduce the level of patronage in the service, but as those to be examined still had to be nominated by the department concerned, many posts were competed for by one candidate only. At least the examination eliminated the stupid or sick.

An important step towards an Official Secrets Act occurred in 1873 with the issuance of a Treasury Minute on the 'Premature Disclosure of Official Documents'. The minute is concerned with 'certain cases which have recently occurred in which information derived from official sources has been communicated without authority to the public Press, apparently by members of the civil service'. The Lords Commissioners of the Treasury stated that they considered such offences to be of the 'gravest character' and that where they have the power to dismiss the offender, they will do so. They also stated that this offence was one to which most civil servants would not stoop and that the service itself would wish to check these practices which injure its reputation for fidelity and honour. Two points are to be made: one is that there is no whiff of espionage involved in the anxieties expressed and, secondly, the press is specifically mentioned. The relationship of the minute to what has been said earlier is that it shows the civil service mentality as in the process of creation, in the appeal to the ethics appropriate to a profession of anonymous, silent, dedicated men who know their position and know that publicity has no part of it. These are the ethics of officials, of bureaucrats, who are divorced from political life, from the public arena, and to whom that arena is dishonourable, liable to contaminate and lead astray anyone who is foolish enough to have links with it. This can be seen even more clearly in a Treasury Minute of 1875, which specifically attacks the links which some civil servants openly have with the press, and the publishing world in general. Again, it complains of the unauthorised communication of official information to the press, and issues a caution to any 'gentleman' who has connections with the press. It states that any 'gentleman' with such a connection will be held liable for any breach of official confidence committed by a writer or correspondent of the periodical with which they are associated, and that they render themselves liable to instant dismissal. This rule is to apply to all offices under the authority of the Treasury. A periodical, *The World*, stated that this rule would apply even if civil servants write on the arts or music, and a letter was sent to the Treasury asking for clarification: the Treasury did not reply, implying that any connection with newspapers was suspect.

A further minute was issued in 1884 in response to the
premature release to the press of documents about to be
released to Parliament, and in particular General Gordon's
proclamation of 1884. The minute specifically mentions that
the timing of the release of the documents may be just as
important as the release of matters still under discussion.
It also clearly states for the first time, the nature of the
offence which is grounds for dismissal, namely 'the publication, without authority, of official information'. It also
states that no distinction will be allowed to be drawn
between one kind of unauthorised release and another. The
danger of release is a general one and cannot, it is claimed,
adequately be guarded against if distinctions are allowed to
be drawn between the degree of danger involved. In its all-
embracing phrase 'official information' and its refusal to
draw a distinction between the need to protect some kinds of
information more than others, it clearly shows the way to
future Official Secrets Acts.

Before going on to discuss the four developments of the
Official Secrets Act, it is worth noting that the Larceny
Act of 1861 (Victoria c 96 530) made it a felony for anyone
in government or public office to 'steal or ... unlawfully
or maliciously to cancel or obliterate, injure or destroy ...
the whole or any part of any original document in any wise
relating to the business of any office or employment under
her Majesty ...'[22] This Act, however, does not cover the
release of information and, as the government had discovered
with the Marvin case, a conviction under the Act was difficult to obtain.

THE OFFICIAL SECRETS ACT OF 1889

By 1887 the Admiralty was drafting an Act to make it an
offence to 'improperly divulge official information'; the
Admiralty informed the Treasury to this effect. The immediate stimulus for the Act was the case of an Admiralty
draughtsman named Terry, who had sold a set of warship plans,
possibly to a foreign power. Terry admitted that he had sold
information and the Admiralty felt very strongly that dismissal was inadequate and that it 'should be possible to
punish such a grave offence'. The Secretary of State for War
agreed with this view, but felt that it was an issue which
affected the whole public service and he would therefore
prefer the Treasury to deal with it. This correspondence
took place in July of 1887.

The Treasury agreed that a bill was necessary and agreed

to draft one. The first draft of the Bill dealt with the defacing of documents and with their release without lawful authority, or in disregard of orders. However, in November 1887 the Treasury wished to broaden the offence to the 'illicit communication of information' and not simply information which took a documentary form. This draft, however, did not include spying and was intended to deal with the release of information irrespective of whether a foreign power was involved or not. The Foreign Office wrote to the Treasury in December of that year suggesting that the Bill include spying, and this was incorporated into the Bill which was laid before Parliament. The War Office was also concerned with the difficulty of proving intent in these cases, and this was dealt with by making it an offence to enter a place with intent and without lawful authority to steal documents. This was considered to make it easier to obtain a conviction in that it was easier to prove that someone did not have authority to be in a particular place, than to prove theft *per se*. These changes in the Bill meant that its short title was changed from 'Breach of Official Trust' to the Official Secrets Act. The Bill specified that its intent was to prevent the disclosure of documents or information by means of spying or breach of official trust. The Bill was divided into two sections, section one dealing with spying, and section two dealing with the obligations of office in respect to information.

The Bill was presented to Parliament in 1888 but was subsequently withdrawn. However, the Bill was represented to Parliament in the 1889 session and, after the various amendments, was passed into law. The major amendments were that contractors undertaking work for the government were to be covered by the Act, explicit reference to spying was removed, incitement to commit an offence under the Act was made an offence, and the permission of the Attorney General was required before prosecution could be undertaken.[23]

Clause 2(3) of the 1889 Act made persons engaged in government contracts which included an obligation of secrecy of the same standing in relation to the Act as crown officials; that is, it was an offence for any such person to commit any of the deeds prohibited by the Act. This section was added as a result of the case of Mrs Champion, who, in May 1889, incited someone in a printer's office to steal certain papers which contained proofs of the civil service examinations. She was charged with larceny, but since the judge directed the jury that it was only an offence if she had intended permanently to deprive the owners of their property, she was acquitted. The cabinet instructed the Parliamentary Counsel to include some measure in the Bill which would prevent this recurring.

The 1889 Bill had a relatively speedy and unobstructed
passage through both Houses. Certain points were raised, however, and two of the more interesting were as follows. A
member of the Commons, Dr Cameron, pointed out that no
exemption was given for information given to Members of
Parliament by officials. Before a reply could be given,
however, a motion of adjournment came before the House and
was passed. What Dr Cameron said, however, is indeed the
case and, furthermore, Members of Parliament were liable for
prosecution if they incited a civil servant to give them
information without lawful authority, or if they passed on
information concerning defence matters which they knew to
have been obtained illegally. The second point was raised by
Sir G. Campbell, who thought the Bill inadequate since it
punished only the 'poor clerk' and not the real offender,
the receiver of stolen goods, the press, 'The people who
obtain secrets and publish them for profit'.[24] This statement is not quite accurate since Section 1(b) makes it an
offence to pass on information obtained unlawfully, and this
would seem to cover the press, though I am unaware of any
prosecutions which occurred under this section. Mere receipt
of information, however, was not an offence.

Cases Brought Under the 1889 Official Secrets Act

The first serious case under the 1889 Act occurred in 1892
and was *R. v. Holden*. A lance corporal stationed in Gibraltar
received a letter from a former quartermaster in the Royal
Engineers asking for information concerning fortifications
and gun positions in Malta and Gibraltar. The lance corporal
reported these overtures to his superiors and Holden was
arrested. It was alleged at his trial that Holden was associated with a foreign agent in Paris, for whom he was obtaining the information. Holden was charged with a misdemeanour,
which carried a maximum sentence of only one year, and not
with a felony.

As a result of this case, the War Office suggested that
because of the difficulties of proving that a foreign power
was involved, the distinction between a misdemeanour and a
felony should be abolished. This was resisted by the
Treasury, who argued that the distinction was necessary if a
proper balance of punishment was to be maintained, and that
if one could not prove that someone was communicating with a
foreign power, one should not punish him as if he were. The
Act failed to satisfy the government in that it failed to
end anxieties that the unauthorised release of information
had ended.

The Home Office was disturbed by a claim made by the
London editor of a provincial newspaper, the *Echo*, that:

> Gentlemen in the Home Office, Foreign Office, India
> Office and other great departments of State are con-
> tributors to these London Letters. Good prices are paid
> for contributions. Five pounds are often paid, or even
> £100 have been paid for great secrets.[25]

The Home Office sent round a note warning of the gravity of
the offence, but assuring its officers that it did not
believe it happened.

The case of *R.* v. *Holden* was cited by the Secretary of
State, Campbell-Bannerman, in 1895 when he expressed his
dissatisfaction with the existing Official Secrets Act to
the Treasury. He again suggested that the distinction between a felony and a misdemeanour be removed, and again this
was resisted by the Treasury who stated that the Act was
deliberately wide and covered many trivial cases which ought
not to have the possibility of penal servitude for life
attached to them. The War Office also wrote to the Treasury
in 1895 concerning the inadequacy of the 1889 Act, citing an
incident which occurred when Frenchmen were found photo-
graphing fortifications. They were arrested, but the arrest-
ing officer had no power to do so under the Act since the
approval of the Attorney General was required. The War
Office asked that the Act be amended, giving summary power
of arrest with the Attorney General's consent coming at a
later stage. In January 1896 the War Office wrote to the
Treasury asking that the Official Secrets Act be amended in
the following ways: that the penalty for misdemeanour be
increased to two years, that commission of an offence under
Section 1 be prima facie evidence of intent to communicate
with a foreign power, that power of summary arrest be
granted, and if there be insufficient evidence to convict on
felony it should be possible to convict on the lesser charge
of misdemeanour. A Bill was drawn up and approved by the
cabinet at Easter 1896 and incorporated most of the features
desired by the War Office, except for the clause making
certain actions count as prima facie evidence of intent to
communicate with a foreign power. The War Office further
claimed that without these changes the country was 'practically unprotected against spying'. This Bill was presented
to Parliament, but was withdrawn.

Despite the existence of an Official Secrets Act, leaks
continued to occur and continued to exercise the government.
For instance, there was a leak concerning the introduction
of pensions in March 1899, and although a civil servant was

interviewed no charges were pressed, although a further
reminder of the ban on press interviews without the permission of the Head of the Department as per the Treasury
Minute of 1884 was issued. In 1901 another internal enquiry
was instituted concerning a premature leak of an announce-
ment concerning metropolitan police pay. Nothing was discovered, but another warning was issued concerning the duty
not to disclose information, and again relationships with
the press were particularly mentioned.

OFFICIAL SECRECY PRIOR TO 1911

In March 1903 the War Office again submitted proposals for
the tightening up of the Official Secrets Act and, in particular, they objected to the necessity to obtain the consent of the Attorney General which could mean that a spy
could come to Britain, photograph fortifications and escape
before the Attorney General's consent to arrest had been
obtained.

The second element they pushed for was that the onus of
proof should be changed. The 1889 Act required that one
'wilfully' communicated the information; it also required
that the State prove that it was not in the interest of the
State that such communication took place. In 1908 the government again tried to amend the Official Secrets Act. The
major force of the amendments was that the publisher of
information whose disclosure was unauthorised would become
liable to penal sanctions although, in line with the 1889
Act, only if publication was not in the interest of the
State. Lack of parliamentary time and fierce opposition by
the press led to the Bill being withdrawn.[26] It was at this
time that German spy fever became general and provided the
overt justification for the 1911 Official Secrets Act. However, before going on to discuss the 1911 Act, I should
point out that in my view it has been established that the
Act was not a consequence of spy fever; rather it was the
culmination of a prolonged government campaign to eliminate
leaks by civil servants. The legislation in this area was
 much more concerned with civil service discipline than with
foreigners sketching fortifications. There is certainly none
of the anxiety concerning 'infiltration' of ideologically
motivated spies into government service.

The important question, however, is what interpretation
one places upon these attempts to restrict legally the flow
of government information. As I stated in Chapter 2, one can
see these as part of an attempt by the State to subvert
democracy, as part of an attempt by the British establish-

ment to limit the application of democratic principles and
to stifle any notion that democracy implies participation or
sharing of power. However, there is another interpretation,
which is that governments saw democracy as implying that the
traditional civil service view of itself as part of government must be ended and that it must be brought under the
control of those who had been elected, and that part of that
control was the creation of an Official Secrets Act. In one
interpretation such actions are part of an anti-democratic
plot, and on the other they are part of a democratic system
of government *given* a certain structure of responsibility.
Other systems of responsibility may not require or permit
such a form of control. What this chapter is attempting to
show is that a particular method of ensuring the control of
the civil service evolved in Britain, ministerial responsibility, and that this provided both the incentive and
authority to the cabinet to institutionalise a high level of
government secrecy.

OTHER CIVIL SERVICE RULES RELATING TO INFORMATION

Apart from the OSA, there are other rules relating to government information. In 1884 the Home Office issued a confidential memorandum to its factory inspectorate stating that
they should not divulge the contents of their reports to
parliamentary committees, nor to courts of justice. A
further and more detailed memorandum was issued in 1896
which stated that 'privilege' should be claimed for all
documents relating to inspectors' reports, and that as far
as possible they should decline to give opinions or evidence,
unless subpoenaed; and that in that event they should report
the matter to the Home Office. They should decline to give
documents, and restrict themselves to verbal comment, and in
the event that documents are requested they should report
the matter to the Secretary of State. The main reason given
for this was that their report would inevitably be seen as
biased, as favouring one side or another and that this would
affect the reputation of the inspectorate.

In 1914 a Treasury Memorandum was issued on the question
of the production of official documents before select committees of Parliament. The production of documents before
parliamentary committees was not new in that the Public
Accounts Committee was set up in 1861 with the task of moni-
toring government expenditure. The Committee had available
to it a staff of auditors responsible to the Comptroller and
Auditor General. By a statute of 1866, all departments were
required to render detailed accounts, which were then scru-

tinised by the auditors, and on the basis of this were made
the subject of committee investigations. The Committee had
to establish its right to all documents at a fairly early
stage in its history, when the War Office attempted to deny
documents to the Comptroller and the Committee had to intervene and insist on its right.[27] This is not to say that the
Committee ever got more than it asked for. The 1914 memorandum attempts to establish certain principles governing
relationships with select committees. The issue of access
arose in connection with a Select Committee on the Marconi
Wireless Telegraph Company in which the Committee called for
certain papers from the Admiralty and the Treasury. These
papers were refused to the Committee as they were considered
by the government to have a bearing on war arrangements and
therefore could not even be produced in private session. The
Committee also requested certain papers which took the form
of internal memoranda, and these were refused on the grounds
that they did not necessarily reflect the view of the department and were written as suggestions or advice; their release
would have a 'far reaching effect upon the efficiency of the
great Departments of State'.[28] The argument was that the
frankness with which even the most junior member of the
civil service felt able to express himself would be inhibited, and that the government would therefore suffer. Also
it was suggested that if these written memoranda were to be
produced this would tend to encourage the giving of advice
in a verbal form to the detriment of efficiency (with perhaps the not too veiled threat that this would also affect
the efficiency of Select Committees!). It was also argued
that if these memoranda were to be revealed, then the
Minister would be placed in an intolerable position in that
he would find himself having to justify his acceptance or
rejection of that advice.

Also in 1884 the Treasury issued a minute on the political
activities of civil servants. The minute stated that any
civil servant seeking to stand for Parliament must resign
his position. The minute argued that although it was difficult to define an acceptable level of activity in theory, in
practice it worked well; the only form of political office
which civil servants could aspire to was membership of local
parish councils, although this rule was relaxed in 1912 when
they were also allowed to stand for membership of local
councils at the discretion of the head of department. A
report presented to the cabinet in 1912 on civil service
discipline by Sir G. Murray stated that 'overt political
activity' by civil servants is 'undesirable'. This view was,
and indeed still is, based upon the requirement that those
who advise and administer cannot be seen as impartial if

they are actively engaged in political life. It is argued
that even though civil servants may be capable of being
politically committed in public and impartial at the office,
this would not be believed by the public and that, therefore, the service would become tainted. Wade and Philips
argue that: 'It is recognised that the political neutrality
of the civil service is a fundamental feature of British
democratic (i.e. constitutional) government.'[29] This remains
the accepted view.

In 1903 the rules governing public access to official
records were formalised. Prior to this it had been a matter
for the individual department as to what public records were
made available and to whom and up to what date. A cabinet
committee was set up in 1903 to investigate the situation,
and it discovered that there were wide discrepancies between
departments. For example, the Admiralty and the War Office
refused access after 1830, the Colonial Office - for the
most part - after 1802, the Foreign Office after 1780, the
Home Office after 1778 and the Treasury winning the race
with no documents released to the public after 1759. As is
obvious, there is no pattern in terms of the modern conception of defence or national security explaining the
various department rules; if anything, the reverse seems to
be the case, with the War Office being most liberal. One can
only speculate as to the reasons for this, but it seems to
be the case that the older departments, the ones with the
closest links to the crown, most clearly exemplify a pre-
democratic attitude of denial of access. In 1903 the rules
were formulated such that internal memoranda, foreign
relations, privacy of the individual, secret service and
'scalping and other such atrocities in war' were not to be
released. This list conforms very closely to most freedom of
information act or secrecy law exemptions. Obviously government was being modernised!

In 1958 a Public Records Act was passed which stated that
most records would be made available after a period of fifty
years; however, in 1967 the Act was amended such that records
would be released after a lapse of thirty years. The Acts
provide, however, that under certain circumstances certain
papers need not be revealed for a period of up to 100 years.
The Lord Chancellor has responsibility for public records,
although there also exists an Advisory Council which inter-
prets the Acts and advises on procedures for release. The
criteria used to decide whether a particular paper ought to
be withheld for longer than thirty years are hard to define,
but they include: a request by the Lord Chancellor and
Minister; if they may cause distress to living persons or
their descendants; or information received in confidence; or

papers likely to prejudice existing security or foreign
relations.[30] The arguments used in favour of such a rule are
that it removes civil servants from the area of political
controversy until the controversy has become simply one of
historical interest. Further, in the absence of such a rule,
inhibited or self-conscious advice could be offered, and
Ministers might otherwise be encouraged to write for the
record rather than dealing with the problems confronting
them. Although there is no immediate link between the Official Secrets Act and the Public Records Act, except that
any document released under the Act can no longer be the
subject of an Official Secrets Act prosecution, the thinking
underlying each is similar.

In June 1977 a document was circulated to those civil
servants in the Ministry of Defence whose duty it was to
decide which records were to be kept and which destroyed and
released by the Ministry in March 1978.[31] The guidelines for
the preservation of records contained few surprises and were
concerned with the following categories of record: those
which show the reasons or authority for decisions; establish
precedents; relate to legal claims or titles; reports of
committees and other such groups; diaries or other logs and
records which relate to matters of 'interest' and famous
persons.

One last area which must be brought up to date concerns
the rules governing civil servants, diplomats and military
officers publishing their memoirs or diaries, the subject of
much earlier anxiety and court action. In 1910 the Foreign
Office was worried by publications by diplomats; for example,
the ex-Ambassador to Vienna, Sir Horace Rumbold in the
National Review, and Sir Henry Elliot, ex-Ambassador to
Constantinople in *Nineteenth Century*. The Foreign Office
proposed to the Treasury that although these cases might be
liable to prosecution under the Official Secrets Act, they
could be punished by having their pensions removed. The
Treasury thought that this would probably not be possible
because the pension was not discretionary but statutory. In
1910 a minute was published by the Foreign Office entitled
'Publication of Information by Civil Servants'. It refers to
previous practice which, it claims, was that officials
should apply for permission before publishing or giving a
lecture on the subject of their work, but the writer of the
minute was unable 'to find any formal rule to that effect'.[32]
The Foreign Office wrote to the Admiralty, War Office and
India Office to find out what their rules were. The War
Office and Admiralty replied that Kings Regulations and
official instructions required prior approval for any publication, and the India Office that the Governor's Servants

Conduct Rules prohibited any public comment in writing, or otherwise, upon matters likely to become the subject of public discussion. The War Office also pointed to the existence of a Treasury Minute of 1891 which stated that:

> Every civil servant, before publishing a handbook or other work compiled or prepared from public sources to which he has had access in his official capacity, must obtain from the head of his department leave to make use of the official records, and assent to the terms on which the work when published shall be supplied to the Controller of the Stationery Office for the use of the public service.[33]

This rule however seems as much concerned with copyright as it does with official secrecy. However, it is another part of the chain which shows that the Official Secrets Act should not be seen in isolation but as part of a wider concerted effort to control the public activities of civil servants.

ORIGINS OF THE 1911 OFFICIAL SECRETS ACT

The Official Secrets Act was not rushed through in response to fears of war or German spying, but as part of a deliberate policy to control the civil service, and to restrict access to public information, with foreign countries simply being one of the groups from which the government preferred to withhold information. One point which is of vital importance if the Official Secrets Act 1911 is to be understood is that it deals, as do all other such Acts, with the *unauthorised* release of information; that is, it does not explain, in and by itself, why any government does not *choose* to release information. There must after all be some persons who are in a position of authority to release the information; otherwise what is the point of talking about its unauthorised release? However, the arguments which any government uses to justify a law which prohibits the release of certain information by subordinates is likely to find those arguments convincing reasons as to why it should not release such information itself. If a major reason for the creation of an Official Secrets Act is that civil servants and Ministers are so closely intertwined that it is impossible to have civil servants release certain official information without this leading to an involvement in politics, then it is also impossible for Ministers to release certain information which they have without this also leading the civil servants into politics.

In March 1909 the Prime Minister, Asquith, set up a Subcommittee on Foreign Espionage of the Committee of Imperial
Defence. The Committee was set up to report upon the nature
and extent of espionage and the best ways of dealing with it
and, in particular, whether the Admiralty, War Office,
Police, Post Office and Customs could be brought into cooperation. The Committee's conclusions fell under two main
headings: (1) a need to amend the Official Secrets Act; and
(2) to set up a 'Secret Service Bureau'. The Committee felt
that the 1889 Official Secrets Act was inadequate in that:
it did not punish newspapers for publishing secret information; to obtain a conviction the government had to testify
to the truth of the material published; that arrest should
be made easier; and that powers of search should be granted.
The Subcommittee in its report to the cabinet emphasised
that German espionage was a serious threat. Colonel Edwards
of the General Staff gave these figures to the Committee:

Table 2

German Espionage	1908	1909 (3 months)
Cases of alleged reconnaissance	27	7
Individual Germans who have come under suspicion	16	15
Houses occupied by succession of Germans who have come under suspicion	4	9
	47	31

The Committee noted that Colonel Edwards stated that *none* of
these cases was reported by the police and that he was 'in-
debted for information regarding them to private individuals'.[34] The Committee was also informed that certain investigations had been carried out by the police but no details
were given. The Committee, on the basis of these unsubstan-
tiated reports, stated that 'there is no doubt in their
minds that an extensive system of German espionage exists'.

The Subcommittee's recommendations to amend the 1889
Official Secrets Act were amendments concerned only with
espionage and not with the press, the reason being that
earlier attempts to legislate on the press had created such
opposition in 1908 that they did not wish to risk the new

Bill. They recommended that legislation on this topic should be introduced, but later and in a separate Bill. They also recommended that the new Bill be introduced by the Secretary of State for War, rather than the Home Office, as this would excite less opposition since it could be presented 'as being a measure of precaution of great importance to the national defence'[35] - an unnecessarily complicated manoeuvre given their belief. However, the Committee also knew that the 1911 Act had implications far beyond catching spies and that to have had these discussed might have jeopardised the Bill. The government then took advantage of a war situation, but the war did not bring official secrecy into existence.

5. Official Secrecy in Britain

This chapter is concerned with the 1911 Official Secrets Act and amendments to it, and with the position of the civil service in the political process. The reason for considering the Official Secrets Act and the political position of the civil service in the same chapter is a continuation of my main thesis that the balance between secrecy and openness is determined by the relationship between elected representatives and officials. The first part is divided into three main sections: the 1911 Official Secrets Act and the cases which determined important questions of interpretation; the subsequent amendments of the Act in 1920 and 1939; and the system of D notices. The second part, the discussion of the role of the civil service, will include the issues of loyalty, developments in the restrictions upon political activity, the criticisms which have been made of the structure of political control of the civil service and the demands for open government. This section will consist of a discussion of the type of complaint made against the system of ministerial control in the 1920s and 1930s, namely delegated legislation, and the criticisms made in the 1960s concerning the failure of the civil service to modernise itself. The importance of these issues is that as the civil service becomes seen as no longer clearly under the control of elected representatives, the more will demands be made for greater openness of government as an alternative or supplementary form of control. The discussion of the Franks Committee Report and of recent demands for reform will, therefore, be dealt with after the discussion of the civil service so that the above link will be clear.

THE 1911 OFFICIAL SECRETS ACT

The main differences between the Act of 1911 and previous legislation in this area were that the 1911 Act was clearly concerned with spies and not simply with the unauthorised

disclosure of information by civil servants; the Ac\
the burden of proof under Section 1 to the defendant\
requirement that Section 2 offences be against the in\
of the State or public interest was removed, and the n\
receipt of unlawful information was made an offence, as was
its further transmission.

Section 1(1) of the 1911 Act requires that the person
intends to act in a manner which is 'prejudicial to the
safety or interests of the State' and secondly, must involve
a prohibited place or material which would be of interest to
an enemy in order to constitute an offence. The short title
of this section of the Act is 'penalties for spying',
although recent cases have shown that this section can be
used to punish persons who are not in fact spies. The Act
states that it is not necessary to establish that the action
itself had consequences which were prejudicial to the State
and that a conviction can be obtained on the basis of circumstance, conduct or character appearing to show the purpose
was so prejudicial.

Section 2 of the Act concerns the wrongful communication
of information, and this includes any information of an
official character, irrespective of its nature and irrespective of any purpose; the offence is communicating information without authorisation or to an unauthorised person,
or retaining any document contrary to duty. Section 2 also
makes it an offence to receive information knowingly, or
having reasonable grounds to believe that the information
was communicated in contravention of the Act, unless one can
prove that receipt of the information 'was contrary to his
desire'. It is also an offence further to communicate
information received in contravention of the Act, meaning
that one can have a potentially unlimited chain of offences.
Section 2 is, therefore, a 'catch all' section in that it
prohibits the unauthorised release of any official information by anyone to anyone, and its receipt by anyone from
anyone. According to this section, a government gardener
commits an offence if he tells another gardener what roses
he grows, as does any civil servant who tells his family,
over dinner, what he did that day.

The Act does not define the term 'authorisation' nor the
phrase 'his duty to communicate it', so any civil servant
is placed in an ambiguous situation unless he has been instructed by his superiors as to what he is authorised to
release. ⌐ ⌐n then there is still the question of who his
superior is, who can issue that instruction, whether it is
Parliament, the Minister, the head of the department or
senior civil servants. In their evidence to the Franks
Committee,[1] civil servants stated that, in practice, senior

civil servants are self-authorising though responsible to
the Minister for any errors of judgement they may make; in
other words they are self-authorising provided they are
cautious and do not embarrass the Minister. The ability to
make these kinds of decisions is one aspect of office which
civil servants learn - if they do not learn it they are unlikely ever to become senior civil servants. The uncertainty
of the Act makes for caution. It also has the effect of
providing an excuse for denying information on some occasions and releasing it on others, since no other party can
convincingly state that any interpretation of the Act is
clear. The Act does not, therefore, create the rule of law
but allows political decisions to be made depending upon
what the Minister and his civil servant interpret as being
suitable for release. In practice then Ministers are self-
authorising, senior civil servants are also authorised to
release information within conventions laid down by departmental practice and the Minister, and the lower the civil
servant the less likely he is to have the authority to
release any information, other than what his duty requires
him to release.

Further sections of the Act define 'prohibited place', the
main elements of the definition being that it is any place
related to defence and any place which affects the supply of
materials and supplies of energy, and generally any place so
declared by the Secretary of State. It is also an offence to
incite someone to commit an offence under the Act, or to
harbour anyone who has or is about to commit an offence
under the Act. The Act also gives powers of arrest and
search, the latter requiring the consent of a Justice of the
Peace, unless a Superintendent of Police considers it to be
an emergency. The Act also states that any prosecution
requires the consent of the Attorney General, although a
person may be arrested and detained in custody without this
consent.

The position in 1911, then, was that the government had
succeeded in its efforts to have a comprehensive Act on
official secrecy which attached criminal sanctions to civil
servants leaking information and which brought the press
under the Act by making the receipt of such leaked information an offence, as was its further publication.

Early Prosecutions Under the 1911 Official Secrets Act

The immediate use made of the 1911 Act was to prosecute
those considered to be German spies. Most of the early prosecutions were under Section 1 and not Section 2 and most
were prosecutions of German nationals.[2] There was consider-

able spy fever preceding the First World War and almost all
people with German names or of German origin were suspect,
many of them being under surveillance by the new intelligence service. One case which established certain interpretations of the Act occurred in 1913 and concerned an ex-naval
gunner named Parrott. Parrott was found guilty of communicating with the enemy, although the defence argued that much
of the evidence depended upon suspicion alone. The case was
taken to the Court of Criminal Appeal which upheld the conviction on the grounds that the jury were entitled to infer
actual communication from the circumstances, and that the
onus of proof was upon the defendant to show that his
actions were for a purpose not prejudicial to the State.

A case occurred in 1919 in which an attempt was made to
argue that Section 2 only referred to information which was
useful to an enemy.[3] A prosecution was brought against a
clerk in the War Office who had passed information concerning contracts for officers' clothing to a firm of tailors.
A magistrate at a Metropolitan Court dismissed the case on
the grounds that no secrets useful to an enemy were involved. However, the Attorney General sought a Bill of
Indictment and the case was heard in the Old Bailey at which
the judge argued that there was no justification for inter-
preting the Act in such a way; it was clear that any and all
information was covered by Section 2 and not just secret
information useful to an enemy.

THE 1920 AMENDMENTS TO THE OFFICIAL SECRETS ACT

Government anxieties concerning the control of information,
however, were not ended with the passing of the 1911 Official
Secrets Act. The government considered the powers which had
been granted under the First World War Defence of the Realm
Regulations to be too useful to allow them to disappear with
the end of the war.[4] To forestall this the War Office Emergency Legislation Committee proposed a National Security Bill
which would have replaced the 1911 Official Secrets Act and
would have combined the powers granted by the Defence of the
Realm Regulations with the provisions of the 1911 Act. The
main elements of the proposed National Security Bill were to
make it an offence to impersonate an officer of the crown,
to misuse a passport or other permit, to communicate with
foreign agents and wilfully to neglect or refuse to disclose
to the authorities any information concerning an offence
committed under the Act. Sir C. Mathews of the War Office,
who had prepared the Bill, wrote to the Admiralty in September 1918 saying:

That the provisions of the Bill are of so drastic a
character as to make it certainly desirable, and perhaps
imperative, to present the measure to Parliament whilst
the war is still in progress.

Even the Department of Naval Intelligence considered the
Bill to be 'revolutionary' and was relieved to note that
despite the powers granted under the Bill, the maximum sentence was not to exceed life imprisonment. The Department
further considered that the provisions may be appropriate to
war but not to peacetime. The Home Affairs Committee of the
cabinet decided to set up a Departmental Committee to consider the Bill with the objective of redrafting the proposals as a set of amendments to the 1911 Official Secrets
Act rather than as a new act. This was done and the 1911
Official Secrets Act was amended in 1920.

 The Official Secrets Act as amended created new offences
relating to the unauthorised use of uniforms, falsification
of reports, forgery, impersonation, falsifying documents,
retaining documents contrary to duty, communicating secret
pass words, interfering with a police officer or a member of
HM Forces in the vicinity of a prohibited place and communicating with foreign agents. In the last case the Act provides a very wide test of what constitutes such communication; it includes visiting the address of, possessing the
address of, or associating with a foreign agent. The only
defence is that the accused must prove his ignorance of any
connection with foreign agents. The Secretary of State also
has the power to require the production of telegrams sent
to or from any place out of the United Kingdom by any private cable service. The Act also requires the registration
and regulation of accommodation addresses, including that a
record be kept of all persons using such addresses and a
note of forwarding addresses and a record of receipt of any
package, its date of post mark and its date of collection or
forwarding. Section 6 of the Act, which was altered in 1939,
required that every person gives on demand to a chief of
police any information relating to an offence or suspected
offence under the Act and makes it a misdemeanour to refuse
to do so. Section 7 also makes it an offence not only to
incite someone to commit an offence, or to attempt to commit
an offence, but also to do any act *preparatory* to the commission of an offence.

These measures are certainly potentially devastating in
their impact upon civil liberties and political activity.
For instance, the definition of 'foreign agent' is not related to war, and is defined as being someone who is reasonably suspected of being employed, either directly or in-

directly, by a foreign power to undertake acts prejudicial to the safety or interests of the State. Who defines the interest of the State, its safety, indirect employment, reasonably suspect? The State itself, of course; the courts have not challenged government statements on these issues. For instance, in 1935 a turf accountant was prosecuted under the section on accommodation addresses, with no question of any official information being involved.[5] One of the few provisions of the National Security Bill not incorporated in the 1920 Amendments to the Official Secrets Act, was the offence of 'procuring, offering or supplying money, intoxicating liquor or any sedative narcotic or stimulant to any of H.M. Forces or officials, with the purpose of obtaining information prejudicial to the safety of the State'.[6] Perhaps it was felt that this clause was unnecessary since no officer or gentleman would ever be tempted to indulge himself!

On one thing the cabinet were right: they anticipated that in 1918, unlike 1911 and 1889, there would be considerable opposition to the amendments. The government presented the amendments as being concerned with espionage and as a response to a world in which spying had become ever more sophisticated. Much of the opposition was to the incursions upon ordinary rights which the amendments contained, and which were felt to be inappropriate to a peacetime society. However, the opposition was not sufficient to persuade the government to withdraw or to defeat the amendments. The main reason for this was that the government argued very strongly that the new provisions related to Section 1 of the 1911 Act and were concerned with spying. For instance, when anxieties were raised concerning Section 6, the duty to give information, the Attorney General stated that this was intended against spies and spying. This however was a total misrepresentation of what the section actually stated, since it obviously did refer to any offence committed under the Official Secrets Act, and therefore included Section 2 offences.

CONTROVERSY AND THE AMENDMENT OF 1939

Anxieties concerning the powers granted under the 1920 amendments were sufficient to cause the Newspaper Proprietors Association to send a memorandum to the government objecting to the wide and drastic powers of search and interrogation, and to the range of new offences created. The Attorney General replied that the powers were necessary and that people could rely on the fact that they would be sparingly used. However, the government was sufficiently sensitive to the criticisms to set up a departmental committee to investigate whether any of the criticisms were justified. The committee's conclusions simply repeated the view already expressed by the Attorney General that all the powers were necessary, but the government felt that something had to be done. It therefore issued a memorandum stating that the powers of questioning granted under the amended Official Secrets Act would only be used where the mischief had already occurred, and with the consent of the Attorney General.

A famous case, which involved a Member of Parliament, occurred in 1938. Duncan Sandys discovered details of the anti-aircraft defences of London whilst an officer of the Territorial Army and when he sent these in a letter and draft parliamentary question to the Secretary of State for War, he was sent for and interviewed by the Attorney General. Sandys was asked how he had obtained the information. He claimed that he was threatened with a prosecution under Section 6 if he refused to answer. This was to be denied by the Attorney General, but Parliament set up two Select Committees to investigate the affair and to report on whether parliamentary privilege had been violated. The embarrassment which this created led to the government introducing an amendment to the Official Secrets Act restricting the powers of questioning to offences under Section 1. This became law in 1939.

This reform was not undertaken without misgivings on the part of the government. The Home Secretary stated to a cabinet committee on the Official Secrets Act that it was dangerous to exempt Members of Parliament who were often in touch with senior civil servants and that 'unauthorised information might occasionally slip out accidentally'.[7] Sir W. Fisher, Permanent Secretary to the Treasury, felt that such cases were not a serious danger, although the committee concluded that Members of Parliament were covered by the Official Secrets Act, subject to questions of parliamentary privilege.

Almost all of the prosecutions under Section 1 have been cases of espionage or cases related to defence. However there was a contrary instance in 1962 when six members of the anti-nuclear Committee of 100 were convicted on charges of conspiring to commit an offence under Section 1, namely to enter a prohibited place. The case was taken to the Court of Criminal Appeal and the House of Lords, where it was ruled that espionage was not a necessary part of the offence and that they were not entitled to offer evidence that their purpose was not one prejudicial to the State. The government decided what was prejudicial in cases involving national defence.[8]

THE OFFICIAL SECRETS ACT AND THE PRESS

Between the wars four cases out of seven under Section 2
involved the press; since the Second World War there have
been only two cases out of twenty-three involving the press,
and in one of these cases the defendants were acquitted. The
largest category of cases since the Second World War involved the release of information by a member of the police
or the post office to criminals.[9] In the last ten years two
cases have occurred which created considerable public and
media interest in the operation and scope of the Official
Secrets Act; the Biafra case and the ABC case.[10] These cases
created such opposition to the Official Secrets Act that
they require a fuller discussion.

The Biafra case concerned the publication of a confidential report written by Colonel Scott, the Defence Adviser at
the High Commission in Lagos, Nigeria, during the time of
the Biafran war.[11] Scott gave a copy of the report to
Colonel Cairns, a member of the international team of ob-
servers, who sent a copy to General Alexander, who gave the
report to a newspaper correspondent; the newspaper for whom
the journalist worked then published the report. Only four
parts of the chain were prosecuted under the Act: Cairns,
the journalist, the editor of the newspaper and the newspaper publisher. The prosecution obviously accepted General
Alexander's claim that the report had been given in confidence to the reporter and was never intended for publication.
The four defendants were acquitted and the judge remarked
in his summing up that:

> This case, if it does nothing more, may well alert those
> who govern us at least to consider, if they have the time,
> whether or not Section 2 of this Act has reached retire-
> ment age and should be pensioned off, being replaced by a
> Section that will enable men like Colonel Cairns, Mr.
> Aitken, Mr. Roberts and other editors of journals to deter-
> mine without any great difficulty whether a communication
> by any one of them or a certain piece of information
> originating from an official source, and not concerned in
> the slightest with national security, is going to put them
> in peril of being enclosed in a dock and facing a criminal
> charge.[12]

The ABC case involved two journalists and a former member of
the Army Signals Corps.[13] The basis of the charges was that
one of the journalists had collected information concerning
signals intelligence for a purpose prejudicial to the safety
and interests of the State, information which may be useful,

either directly or indirectly, to an enemy; that another
journalist had aided and abetted him in this; and that the
former Army man had communicated information to these men.
These charges were brought under Section 1 of the Official
Secrets Act since they involved defence, prejudice to the
State and usefulness to an enemy. However, the charges under
Section 1 were dropped due to defence submissions that much
of the material was already available from public sources,
and due to the judge's remarks that he found the charges
under Section 1 to be 'oppressive'. The three men were then
charged solely with offences under Section 2 of the Official
Secrets Act relating to the unauthorised communication of
official information, which has a much reduced maximum sentence of two years as opposed to the fourteen years under
Section 1. The two journalists were found guilty under
Section 2 and were given conditional discharges, and the
ex-Army man was also found guilty but was given a six month
suspended sentence.

The most interesting aspects of the case were its connection with technological surveillance of the communications
of foreign nations, the judge's remarks and the public attitude towards the case. Given the fact that the government
had had the Official Secrets Act under review for some time,
it is perhaps surprising that the prosecution took place at
all. In my view it was because of the involvement of technological intelligence-gathering that the government considered the 'risk' of a prosecution to be worthwhile, since
many experts in this area consider technical surveillance to
be the single most important source of covert intelligence-
gathering. The prosecution was also, in my opinion, influenced by the fact that British signals intelligence is
linked to similar activities of the American, Canadian and
Australian governments under a pact known as the 'SIGINT
Pact'.[14] In such circumstances any reluctance on the part of
the British government to prosecute in this area may have
affected relations with the intelligence agencies of these
other countries, particularly the USA. In the event, however,
the prosecution failed to establish that the men had
seriously threatened the intelligence-gathering capacity of
the UK signals service. The judge in the case did, however,
state: 'The law will not tolerate defectors or whistle
blowers from our intelligence service who seek the assistance of the press or other media ... to publish secrets.'[15]

The judge also affected the case by influencing the
charges and by the sentences he gave the defendants. Much of
the press and the defendants themselves considered the sentences to be of a token nature and to be a judgement on the
advisability of the prosecution and indeed of the Official

Secrets Act itself. The public reaction to the prosecution
was outspoken and organised. A campaign was formed by the
magazine for which one of the defendants worked as a journalist. The trial itself was picketed throughout the proceedings
and the defendants held some 150 meetings throughout the
country to explain their case.[16] After the trial was over
the press commented variously that the case was a 'rebuff',
'official ineptitude' and a 'Whitehall farce' (*Telegraph*,
Guardian and *Sunday Times* respectively). It was generally
argued in the press that the case had effectively 'finished
off' the Official Secrets Act.

THE SYSTEM OF D-NOTICES

In 1912 a system of voluntary cooperation was established
between the press and the government in relation to the
publication of defence matters and the Services, Press and
Broadcasting Committee was formed.[17] The Official Secrets
Act obviously provided the background to the system of
voluntary censorship, although the government was concerned
that the reporting of defence matters should not simply be
restricted by prohibiting the use of unauthorised information but that any information, however come by, should be
subject to questions of the public interest as defined by
the government.

The Committee issues 'D' (or Defence) notices, but the
notices have no legal standing and are not obligatory, nor
is there any penalty attached to non-observance, except in
so far as some Act such as the Official Secrets Act may be
involved. A D-notice takes the form of a formal letter of
request which is circulated to editors of newspapers, of
broadcasting and of some periodicals, likely to publish defence material, advising against publication of certain
defence-related material. The subject of a D-notice may
cover 'naval, military and air matters, the publication of
which would be prejudicial to the national interest'.[18]

D-notices, although concerned with military matters, can
include more general matters, provided they can be shown to
be related to military matters; no attempt is made to draw
rigid guidelines as to what is meant by 'military matters',
and it is left to the particular circumstance and negotiation. This is not to say that there are not occasions on
which the press feel that the D-notice has been issued for
reasons of politics and convenience, and the Radcliffe
Report emphasised that because the system is voluntary such
anxieties should be treated seriously, and that D-notices
should only be issued where the matter is genuinely military

and likely to prejudice security. There had for instance
been considerable press opposition to a D-notice issued in
July 1961 which seemed to prevent any publication of information related to new weapons and armaments.[19] The Report
largely accepted the criticism made by the press that this
was unnecessarily restrictive in scope. The Report also
considered what benefits the government and the press
receive from the system. It is fairly obvious what the
government obtains in that it has a method of influencing
the press in secret and without having to pass a censorship
law whose use would then be subject to scrutiny in the
courts. The government attempts to convince the press that
certain subjects should not be published with the minimum of
positive information, with the minimum of disclosure and
without the intervention of the courts. The more difficult
question to answer is what the press receives from such a
system. The press in Sweden or America does not have such a
system and in neither case would it be willing to accept
such restrictions; indeed in both countries such action
would be unconstitutional and, therefore, there is no legal
basis for such a system. In the case of Britain, the
Official Secrets Act provides by its all-embracing formulae,
a situation in which the publication of almost any information which is derived from official sources, but is not
part of an authorised release, may be made the subject of a
prosecution. It is the uncertainty as to what the government
will interpret as a sufficiently serious breach of the
Official Secrets Act as to require prosecution that gives
the press the incentive to cooperate. It is obviously in the
areas of defence that the government is most likely to consider breaches of the Official Secrets Act as serious and
likely to prosecute, and that the press therefore has most
to gain. This is not to deny that the press may not be motivated by a responsible attitude to the public interest and
matters of national security, but this attitude cannot
explain their cooperation because, in so far as they have
such an attitude, there is no need for the cooperation.
Their motive then is fear of the uncertainties which stem
from a wide-ranging Official Secrets Act. The D-notice system is unlikely to disappear with the liberalisation of the
Official Secrets Act if the alterations in the OSA still include criminal penalties, as the uncertainty of prosecution
relating to those matters will continue.

LOYALTY

In 1948 the Treasury issued a memorandum on civil servants

'vital to security', concerned with the existence of Communists in government service.[20] The memorandum gave Ministers the responsibility of deciding which posts were concerned with security, and which officials were associated with the Communist Party in such a way as to raise doubts about their reliability.

In 1953 it was stated that 17,000 civil servants out of one million had been investigated and that 148 had been suspended. Subsequently 28 were reinstated, 69 transferred, 9 were on special leave and 23 were dismissed.[21] The rule was that a civil servant should be transferred to non-secret work where an adverse finding had been made, and only where this was not possible or where the civil servant had not resigned was the result dismissal from the service. The fear was related to the post-war spy scares involving the Gouzenko revelations in Canada[22] and by the case of Dr Alan Nunn May, a British scientist, who had been involved in the wartime research on nuclear weapons and had admitted handing over information to the Russians. The new aspect of these cases was that they involved ideological switches of allegiance and were not necessarily associated with any outward or public act. As far as governments were concerned this was a new form of treachery and one which was insidious and highly dangerous.

In 1955 a Conference of Privy Councillors was set up as a result of the defection of two senior foreign office civil servants, Burgess and Maclean. A report was published in 1956 which offered only a summary of the main findings and criticisms; the government stated that the public interest prevented full publication.[23] The report stated that Communists and their sympathisers were the main danger to security, and not penetration by foreign agents. The report also emphasised the importance of defects in character when making security assessments, since such defects could lead to entrapment by foreign agents; the defects included homosexuality, drunkenness, addiction to drugs and 'loose living'. The Privy Councillors recognised the distasteful aspect which investigation of these factors involved and the reluctance which many civil servants would feel to inform heads of departments of character defects of fellow civil servants. The report, however, felt that the security of the State justified this as a necessity. The report also recommended that in cases of doubt the decision should go against the individual concerned, even to the extent of suspecting the reliability of someone who may not be a Communist himself but may be married to one.

In 1961 the government set up another committee to review security procedures under the chairmanship of Lord Radcliffe,

as a result of the Portland spy case and George Blake. The
report takes a different view of the main threat posed to
British security from the 1955 report in that it sees the
main threat as coming, not from the Communist Party as such,
but from the various Russian, or Russian affiliated, intelligence services.[24] However, the report has little to say
about how this actually affects the uncovering of 'spies'
and, apart from recommending the strengthening of the organisational aspect of departmental security, the major part of
the report is concerned with the system of positive vetting.
This system was introduced in 1952 and involves the detailed
investigation of civil servants in particularly sensitive
positions. The normal basis of the purge system is what is
known, that which is already on file in the department or in
the files of the security service. Positive vetting involves
a field investigation, the use of two referees, the filling
in of a questionnaire and a check on the files of the security services. It is claimed that this procedure was introduced in consultation with the United States, who felt that
British security arrangements had been suspect, given the
cases of May and Fuchs, a nuclear scientist who had worked
in both Britain and the United States.[25] The Americans were
particularly worried about the passing of information about
nuclear weapons to the Russians, and one of the requirements
imposed by the Americans for continuing to inform the
British about nuclear developments was a tightening of security. The report states that, on the whole, the system of
positive vetting is effective.

There is no doubt that the above procedures fall far short
of what would normally be expected were a punishment, which
denial of promotion or dismissal undoubtedly are, to be in-
flicted by the State upon a subject. However, for my purposes the important issue is what such a loyalty programme
can tell one about the position of the civil service and its
relationship to political power. The most striking contrast
between the British programme and that of the USA is that in
Britain this programme never developed into a public issue,
except in so far as anxieties were expressed about the justi-
fiability of what the government was doing. Here there was
no political influence to be made out of proclaiming that
the civil service was full of Communists. British politicians
were able to define clearly the limits of the problem and
successfully managed to claim that they were in control of
the situation. As far as the British government was concerned, the problem of loyalty was a matter of acts of
espionage or preventing such acts, and at no time did the
government consider it necessary to introduce oaths of allegiance or the like. The government was interested in

actual damage to the State and managed to contain the spread
of the idea that the potentiality of influence by Communists
was unlimited, and that one Communist or Communist sympathiser was one too many.

If one believes that political authority has passed to the
civil service, then its nature, loyalty and devotion to a
certain 'way of life' become the only means of ensuring that
the political decisions which are taken are 'representative'
or in the interests of the people. Where this is not the
case and it is accepted that politicians are in control,
then the politicians will resist any attempt to raise a hue
and cry about the loyalty of the service, since this is an
attack upon their power, upon their claim to be in charge of
the civil service. An attack upon the civil service would
have been an attack upon the whole edifice of ministerial
responsibility and this would have been against the interests
of the government and the official opposition.

The secrecy with which these investigations were conducted
did affect the civil liberties of civil servants, but it was
also part of the screen by which civil servants were removed
from political attack.

POLITICAL NEUTRALITY AND THE CIVIL SERVICE

At the same time as the anxieties concerning loyalty arose,
the rules on the political activities of civil servants were
undergoing modification. The main pressure for these changes
came from the civil service trade union organisations and
were a reflection of the increasing size of the civil
service, which meant that a very large number of officials
were not engaged in anything other than routine administration or industrial work. A committee was appointed under
the chairmanship of Mr J.C. Masterman, which reported in
1949.[26] The essence of the report was that the civil service
should be divided into two categories, those who would be
subject to no political restrictions at all, and those who
would be subject to a ban. The first category referred to
industrial workers, the 'manipulative' grades of the Post
Office and a number of minor grades such as messengers. The
second category included all but a few of the non-industrial
or clerical service. These recommendations, however, were
opposed by the civil service staff organisation as being unnecessarily restrictive, and the government decided to set
up further negotiations between the Treasury and the staff
organisations. A report was issued in 1953 which created a
third class of civil servant who would be intermediate between the two earlier proposed categories.[27] This inter-

mediate group would be allowed to engage in all political
activities, except parliamentary candidature. The basic rule
is that within the lower grades of clerical staff, those
whose contact with the public is remote will be given
greater freedom.

Those given freedom are allowed to stand for Parliament
and to be reinstated if they do not succeed, hold office in
political parties, speak in public on matters of political
controversy, write letters to the press on political matters
and engage in canvassing. These things are therefore excluded to those in the restricted category. The percentages
in each category were considered to be 62 per cent complete
freedom, 22 per cent to be free, except as parliamentary
candidates, and 16 per cent to be banned from national politics.[28] Of course all civil servants must resign if they are
elected to the House.

The arguments presented as to why these bans are necessary
are obviously part of the traditional ban upon the holding
of office under the crown and a consequence of the anonymity
rules. The Masterman Report argued that an impartial service
was necessary and that public confidence could not be sustained if civil servants were to have complete freedom to
announce their political allegiance by engaging in political
life. It is also the case that civil servants would inevitably find the Official Secrets Act difficult, if not impossible, to obey if they were to become part of the
political process in which charge and counter-charge is made.
It would be extremely difficult for them not to use information obtained by virtue of their office to make political
comments and judgements, and such a threat to ministerial
monopoly would not be tolerated by a Minister who, of course,
makes the rules by which civil servants operate.

THE NEW DESPOTISM: DELEGATED LEGISLATION

From the period of nineteenth-century reform until the
Fulton Committee, the civil service came under very little
attack. Indeed, British commentators felt they could safely
claim to have the finest service in the world.[29] It was a
service staffed by men of the highest intellectual calibre,
men of Oxford and Cambridge, and men of wide, humane and
liberal sympathies. The senior civil servant was also someone who was a generalist, able to handle many different
situations, who had cultivated administrative expertise
based upon experience and not theory. He was a man of cultivated impartiality, able to serve masters of many persuasions
and was universally agreed by those in power to be submissive

to the will of elected representatives. It was a service
which was, compared to most others, lacking in corruption.
In fact, the whole constitutional arrangements were considered to be satisfactory, if not even exemplary.

There was only one anxiety which came to prominence in the
late 1920s and 1930s and that concerned the use of delegated
legislation. Delegated legislation basically consists of
authority granted to Ministers in Acts of Parliament, to
make such rules as may be necessary to carry out the principles established in the Act proper. Such rules could not
be made except in so far as they were seen as subsidiary to
the main enabling law. The practice of delegating to the
Minister or administrative body the right to make such rules
was not an invention of the 1920s; indeed, the practice had
been rationalised with the Rules Publication Act of 1893,
which ensured the publication of the rules and helped to
create unified procedures. However, in the 1930s it was felt
that the power exercised by Ministers to make rules was so
great as to undermine the democratic principle that laws
should only be made by the elected assembly. This view was
most forcefully expressed by Lord Hewart, the then Chief
Justice of England, in his book *The New Despotism*. Lord
Hewart felt that too much delegation had taken place, not
only to Ministers, but in effect to civil servants. To
investigate Lord Hewart's criticisms, a Committee on Ministers' Powers was set up which reported in 1932.[30] The
conclusion of the report was that there was no bureaucratic
conspiracy to undermine democracy and that without the
power of delegation the quantity of work which Parliament
had to achieve in order to satisfy the public demand for
government action would simply not be met.

There is a constitutional difference between delegated
legislation and parliamentary Bills in relationship to the
amount of information made public. In the case of delegated
legislation there is no restriction upon showing the full
text of the proposed regulation to any interested parties,
although the question of whether this is desirable is still
a matter for the government to decide. Professor de Smith
summed up the situation as follows: 'None the less, prior
consultation with advisory bodies and organised interest
groups is a more conspicuous characteristic of delegated
legislation than of parliamentary legislation.'[31] Apart
from the difference in legal requirements between the two
types of legislation, the main reason for the difference in
degree and form of consultation is that delegated legislation is normally concerned with details of administration
which are not of general, but rather of special interest.
A high level of consultation is also desirable so that the

Minister can respond to new contingencies. As a threat to
democracy, delegated legislation is a dead issue. The advan-
tages of flexibility and efficient administration which this
allows are so great that opposition in principle to this
practice no longer exists.

INEFFICIENT DESPOTISM: THE FULTON REPORT

However by the 1960s such objections as the above to the
power of Ministers and civil servants pale into insignifi-
cance compared to the blast of criticism heaped upon the
civil service.[32] The British government was considered by
many to have failed to achieve that which so many required
of it - the modernisation of Britain. This was expressed in
terms of finding a new role for Britain with the Empire gone,
and in the desire to match other Western industrial countries
rate of economic growth. Underpinning these criticisms was
the belief that the government had responsibility for these
matters and, therefore, a failure to modernise was a failure
of government. Many of the criticisms also took an institutional form in that it was felt that this failure was not
a consequence of any particular party; both the Labour Party
and the Conservative Party had had periods of office, and
yet the problem or crisis had persisted. Many commentators
therefore felt that reform of Parliament, the civil service,
the law and constitution, and elections, were preconditions
for success. One must state at the outset that compared with
many other European countries these criticisms did not take
the form of the rise of 'extremist' political parties, or at
least none that was able to win any seats in Parliament, nor
did it - in the British mainland at least - lead to significant terrorist movements. The British political system is
still remarkably stable and peaceful. The demands for reform
did not come from the major political parties, although
individual members of these parties spoke in favour of one
sort of reform or another, nor was it a major election issue.
    In the mid to late 1960s the demands for reform were
particularly centred upon economic policy, and in particular
the policy of intervention in the field of wages with 'stop-
go' policies of domestic restraint and balance of payments
crises. The Treasury was held to blame for this situation in
that it was considered that Ministers had been badly advised
and that the Treasury was not professional enough, a fre-
quent 1960s complaint against the civil service. For example,
Mr Sears, a former civil servant, argues that 'The senior
officers of the Treasury see their function chiefly as that
of curbing extravagance and strengthening the pound, rather

than modernising the economic structure and promoting its development'.[33]

The difficulty was, and indeed is, that the problem can be identified - namely the need to modernise industry and industrial relations - but that governments continue to fail to solve it. The attempt by governments of all parties to 'manage the economy' has led, and still does, to doubts being expressed over how efficient, well trained and expert the civil service is to undertake this relatively new task of management.

The other element adding to anxieties about the civil service was the area of foreign policy. This undoubtedly can be traced to the Suez crisis of 1956. Many British modernisers were critical of the action in that they saw it as being the product of outmoded Foreign Office ideas of world political realities. British ideas of its position in the world were also shaken by the realities of nuclear arms, which again reduced Britain to a state of effective military dependence upon the United States.

These criticisms led in 1966 to the government appointing a Committee of Inquiry into the Civil Service, under the chairmanship of Lord Fulton, after whom the report is known. The report was extremely critical of the existing structure and methods of the civil service, the major criticism taking the form of a condemnation of the failure of the service to modernise itself. Many aspects of the service which had been seen as part of its virtues, were seen by the Committee as outmoded and inimical to efficient government. The civil service was criticised for being too heavily dominated by people from Oxbridge and from the higher stratum of British society, too hierarchical, too inflexible to outside influence, too generalist and not specialist enough, amateurish, lacking in skilled managers, failing to provide a career structure for all but a few of its members and too secretive.[34] The major thrust of the criticisms was that there existed a new age, an age of technology, of planning and of professionalism and expertise, and that the civil service had failed to recognise this and adapt to it.

Before going on to discuss what the report says about secrecy, it is important to recognise that in 1980 the technocratic dream of the Fulton Report is not the dominant myth of our time and that the focus of attention has moved to trade union influence, electoral reform, devolution and the virtues of consensus government; in 1980 fear of government seems more dominant than efficient, white-hot government.

The Fulton Report criticises both the level of secrecy and the tradition of anonymity. It argues that: 'the administrative process is surrounded by too much secrecy. The

public interest would be better served if there were a
greater amount of openness'.[35] The main reason for so arguing was that the impact of government was so great that only
full discussion and consultation could guarantee good
quality decisions. The report also makes a passing reference
to how this is healthy for democracy. However, it soon
returns to safer ground with an emphasis upon decision-
making. The report recognises that secrecy is necessary during the process of formulating policy, but sees no justification why 'some of the material and some of the analyses'
upon which the policies are based could not be released.
The report goes on to argue that British governments are apt
to give too much weight to the difficulties of openness,
and points to the Swedish case as an example of a democratic
society with a high degree of openness. The report suggests
a Committee of Inquiry to investigate the possibility of
getting rid of unnecessary secrecy and of revising the
Official Secrets Act.

The report also comments upon the anonymity of civil
servants, their unwillingness to associate themselves with
particular policies and to argue the case for them in public.
It is recognised that by convention Ministers are responsible for policies, but the report argues that this convention is one which is only applicable to a situation in
which government undertakes a limited range of tasks: it is
inappropriate to a situation in which it is known by everyone that departments are so large and make so many decisions
that it is objectively impossible for the Minister to know
everything that his department does. The Committee felt that
if this was the case then it was better to recognise the
fact and to make civil servants answerable in public for the
decisions which, in many cases, they actually take. In other
words, the Committee felt that ministerial responsibility
was a fiction and that it would be more realistic to recognise the limitations of Ministers than to continue a pre-
tence.

The result of the Fulton Report and the government paper
was the setting up in April 1971 of a Committee to investigate Section 2 of the Official Secrets Act under the chairmanship of Lord Franks.

SECRET DESPOTISM: THE FRANKS REPORT

The main comment made by the Franks Report[36] on the Official
Secrets Act is that Section 2 is a catch-all provision in
that it fails to distinguish between degrees of secrecy or
between different degrees of sensitivity of the positions

occupied by civil servants. It also comments that the Act
does not define 'authorisation' or the 'interest of the
State' as reasons for communication of information. The Committee found that in fact authorisation was often implied,
in that it flows from the nature of the particular post;
senior civil servants have a wide sphere of personal discretion, whilst Ministers are self-authorising. The Committee found it extremely difficult to assess the impact of
Section 2 on the extent to which information is not revealed.
The civil service witnesses and the press tended to argue
that it did inhibit the free flow of information. Ultimately,
however, if the Minister is self-authorising, then the
reason for secrecy can only be that the Minister or the
cabinet have decided not to authorise the release of information and this is the reason for secrecy. What Section 2
does do is make civil servants cautious where no clear
departmental guidelines exist as to what they can and cannot
reveal, but again the absence of such guidelines must be
seen as a political decision.

The Committee considered three alternatives in relation to
Section 2: retention, removal or replacement. The arguments
put forward in favour of retention were that any half-way
position was likely to produce as many ambiguities and difficulties of knowing whether particular information came within
a new Act or did not, and that the catch-all nature of
Section 2 was not a great problem because of the requirement
of the consent of the Attorney General to any prosecution.
Those in favour of removal accepted that any half-way house
would be unsatisfactory, but saw this as a case for abolition, and argued that Section 1 was sufficient protection
for national security, the only category which should be
protected by the criminal law. The view taken in the report
is that a half-way house is an improvement in that it would
narrow the catch-all basis of Section 2 and provide a list
of information, not necessarily solely of a national security nature, requiring the protection of criminal sanction.
The Committee recommended the replacement of Section 2 with
an Official Information Bill which would protect the
following categories of information: defence or internal
security, foreign relations and that relating to currency;
likely to assist criminal activities or impede law enforcement; cabinet documents; information entrusted to the
government by a private individual or concern. It should
also be an offence not to return a document clearly marked
'Secret' to the crown which has 'innocently' come into one's
possession. The offences should not only apply to active
crown servants or contractors, but also to those who have
retired or otherwise altered their position. However, the

Committee proposed that it should no longer be an offence
merely to receive official information, although it would be
an offence to communicate information which had been
received in contravention of the Act without the authorisation of the crown.

There was a great deal of interesting evidence presented
to the Committee, but perhaps that by the Home Office and
the press was the most interesting of all. The main
anxieties expressed by the Home Office concerning any alteration of Section 2 were (1) that civil service discipline
was not a sufficient deterrent to small but important categories of civil servants, namely those who are motivated by
financial gain or ideology, those who are temporary, those
not envisaging a career in public service, those who have
retired and particularly those who do not have a pension,
and (2) that any attempt to formulate a list of prohibited
categories suffers from the difficulty that any such list is
likely either to be too specific and therefore lacking in
flexibility, or so general as still to leave considerable
ambiguity of interpretation. The Home Office and the
Director of Public Prosecution were reluctant to admit a
defence that disclosure was in the public interest, since
the courts would become involved in making what would, in
effect, be political decisions. It would thereby remove
responsibility from the Minister for safeguarding the information placed in his care. The press felt that abolishing
Section 2 was the only desirable goal since any replacement
of Section 2 would still not remove the danger that the
government would use any list of categories of protected
information to protect the interests of governments rather
than the interests of the nation. The press felt that any
Secrets Act was likely to be used to cover up incompetence
and inefficiency, and that in the unlikely event of a government being able to eliminate these, there would be no need
for an Official Secrets Act at all. This debate highlights
many of the issues underlying the argument on democracy and
open government, and particularly whether secrecy is only
justified in terms of protecting the nation and whether in
a democracy there is any justification for protecting the
political process, for protecting politics, from the public.
As a comment on this problem, it is notable that the Franks
Committee proposals did not include protection for internal
working papers, minutes or advice offered to Ministers. Only
cabinet documents are listed because of the need to arrive
at collective political decisions. The implication of this
is that the Committee accepted the reality of cabinet responsibility, but not that of ministerial responsibility.
The belief that ministerial responsibility is now a myth is

one of the major reasons why open government is considered
to be necessary.

ELIMINATING DESPOTISM: OPEN GOVERNMENT?

In recent years there has been considerable agitation over
the question of reform of the 'British tradition of
secrecy'.[37] Although much of this has centred upon the
reform of the Official Secrets Act, the discussion and
pressure have been of much wider import in that many of the
reform proposals have sought to replace the Official Secrets
Act with a Freedom of Information Act which would provide
statutory right of access to large amounts of government
information.

There is not the space to deal with all of the proposals,
but I intend to take Justice and the Outer Circle Policy
Unit as showing the two main strategies of those involved in
the campaign for reform. The two strategies are wholesale
versus gradual change and they are based upon two contrasting judgements as to the degree of political and constitutional meaning which remains in the notion of ministerial
responsibility. Those demanding immediate and total reform
premise their demand upon the view that ministerial responsibility is no longer (if it ever has been) adequate as a
mechanism of controlling the civil service. Those advocating
a more gradual approach base their view upon the notion that
existing arrangements give Ministers too great an incentive
to block any but the most pragmatic of changes.

In June 1978, Justice, a branch of the International Commission of Jurists, produced a report entitled *Freedom of
Information*. The basic recommendation of the report is that
the government should issue new guidelines regulating the
disclosure of information, and that these should be policed
by the Parliamentary Commissioner. The main reason why
Justice did not advocate legislation such as a Freedom of
Information Act was that an evolutionary approach was more
likely to be acceptable to any foreseeable government and
that such an approach would allow all the parties likely to
be affected by disclosure to develop a pragmatic basis for
making decisions.

The Justice Report does not require that all documents
relating to a particular matter be disclosed, but that as
much information as is 'reasonable and practical' be made
available. This decision is to be made by the Minister in
accordance with a set of guidelines to be drawn up by the
government as a whole. The policing of these arrangements is
to be carried out by the Parliamentary Commissioner. These

proposals were premised upon the view that:

> ... Parliament is in control of the actions of adminis-
> trators through the mechanism of ministerial responsi-
> bility and this committee does not feel that the country
> is willing to overthrow this principle, which could be a
> consequence of a British Freedom of Information Act in
> its most widely proposed form.[38]

The Outer Circle Policy Unit is an independent body funded
by the Rowntree Trust, which attempts to bridge the gap
between research and policy-making. The Unit has produced a
Bill which is not simply a Freedom of Information Act, but
also covers penalties for the wrongful disclosure of information. The Unit has produced what it considers to be a
practical Bill tailored to British circumstances. The main
arguments produced as to why such a Bill is necessary are:

> ... we are sceptical of the claims made for the value of
> the present relations between civil servants and Ministers.
> We think that it would have a salutary effect on Ministers
> if they knew that the impartial, balanced and well in-
> formed advice of the civil servants was shortly to be
> available to the public; and salutary for the civil ser-
> vants to know that what may sometimes be partial, incom-
> plete and ill-formed advice would be made public too.
> Ministers would remain responsible to Parliament but it
> would be a Parliament much better equipped to hold them
> to account than it is now. Indeed, much of the point of
> public access is to alter the balance between an enor-
> mously expanded permanent civil service, the small number
> of politicians who are supposed to be in charge of it and
> Parliament to which they in turn are supposed to be
> answerable.[39]

The Bill grants access to all official documents, except for
certain classes of documents which are made exempt. These
are: defence and security, foreign relations, information
otherwise protected by statute, law enforcement, individual
privacy and cabinet documents for a period of five years.
Internal minutes and other such advisory documents are not
exempted, but access to them may be deferred in accordance
with normal and proper administrative practice, or in the
public interest provided an event or time is specified after
which they will be released. Enforcement of the provisions
of the Bill is not given to the courts, but is to be super-
vised by the Parliamentary Commissioner for Administration
(the Ombudsman). The Bill is certainly comprehensive and

sensible, but acceptance of the Bill does depend, first,
upon agreeing that the existing constitutional arrangements
for the control of administrative and government decision-
making have broken down, and secondly, that such an Act is
the most effective method by which this breakdown can be
remedied. The Outer Circle Policy Unit is characterised by
a 'rationalist' approach, one which sees information as
being true or false, biased or fair, complete or partial.
The rationalist approach underestimates the difficulty of
making decisions which are purely 'rational' and underestimates the impact the attempt to make government and
administration 'rational' might have upon the authority of
politicians to govern and to be effective. The Bill also
underestimates the extent to which the rationalist approach
requires increasing legalism and a system of administration
which reflects this.

Whilst this 'outside' agitation has been proceeding, the
government itself has not been idle. The last Labour government made two main moves, one in relation to administrative
practice and the other to produce a White Paper on the subject. On 6 July 1977, the then Head of the Civil Service,
Sir Douglas Allen, sent a memorandum to all Heads of Department entitled: 'Disclosure of Official Information'. The
main thrust of the memorandum is that in accordance with the
Prime Minister's wishes, as stated to the House in the address of 24 November 1976, a change of policy should take
place such that as much as possible of the factual and ana-
lytic basis of major government policy be released. The
memorandum further recommends that in future factual background material should be kept separate, as far as this is
possible, from the advisory part of submissions to Ministers.
The advisory element, it is stated, is not to be published.
Sir Douglas Allen makes it clear that part of the reason for
this change of policy is so as to avoid the government
having to adopt a Freedom of Information Act, which he calls
'formidably burdensome' and an 'expensive development'.
There is no mention in the memorandum of the Official Secrets
Act and the problems of authorisation associated with it,
although since the memorandum was sent to Heads of Department, presumably the implication is that such Heads are
authorised, indeed encouraged, to disclose as much information as possible.

In July 1978, the government published a White Paper on
the Official Secrets Act which caused uproar in Parliament
and disappointment in the press and other interests pressing
for reform.[40] The White Paper was solely concerned with
Section 2 of the Official Secrets Act and did not propose
reform for Section 1, the section normally used only against

spies. The White Paper generally follows the recommendations
of the Franks Committee on the Official Secrets Act which
reported in 1972. The government proposes an Official Information Act which attaches criminal sanctions only to
specific categories of information, namely: defence and
internal security, international relations in so far as they
involved serious injury to the national interest, law and
order information which is likely to be helpful in the commission of crime or would impede prosecution, and confidential information concerning individuals or firms. The
proposed legislation would also remove the mere receipt of
unauthorised information from the Act, such that it would no
longer be a criminal offence. Apart from the fact that no
positive steps to provide for the disclosure of information
are mentioned in the proposed Act, disappointment was also
expressed that the categories of information protected by
criminal sanctions remained wide and relatively undefined.
For instance, defence information will be protected whether
or not it is classified as secret. Some Members of Parliament and the press were also anxious that the new Act would
simply make it easier for the government to prosecute civil
servants for leaking information, by making the law on
official secrets less odious and more 'respectable'.

In March 1979, the government produced two documents on
open government, one a discussion document, a Green Paper,
and the other a report on disclosure of information in other
countries.[41] The tenor of both documents is that British
constitutional practice means that open government can only
be gradually introduced in Britain. The Green Paper states:

> In the Government's judgment further steps designed to
> achieve greater openness must be fully in accord with our
> constitutional tradition and practice which have developed
> in this country. Nothing must be allowed to detract from
> the basic principle of Ministerial accountability to
> Parliament; and the prime aim of any new measures must be
> to strengthen Parliamentary democracy and the public con-
> fidence in it. The Government believes that these objec-
> tives will best be achieved by gradual development, which
> build on existing arrangements, and which are capable of
> adjustment and modification in the light of experience.[42]

The rest of the document makes it clear that what the above
means is no statutory right to government information will
be introduced in the foreseeable future. However, the Green
Paper also makes it clear that the government is aware that
there is considerable pressure for the introduction of a
more liberal policy on disclosure of government information

and that this demand must be met. One factor which may have affected the government's willingness to make any concessions may have been the fact that it was a minority government and one in which back-bench Members of Parliament had greater influence than normal. A strong majority government may not see the demand as quite so 'irresistible'.

Both documents make it clear that the government sees a Freedom of Information Act as burdensome and expensive and that it would undermine existing constitutional arrangements.[43] The Green Paper therefore proposes that the solution is the adoption by the government of a Code of Practice, similar to the measure proposed by the Justice Report, which would guide ministerial decisions on what information ought to be disclosed.

What is of most interest is that, up to the present, all the reports and statements which successive governments have made on this issue have always been more liberal than the previous ones. This trend exists despite government statements that greater disclosure undermines other aspects of the existing constitutional arrangements. Existing constitutional arrangements give the government both the incentive and the authority to control the flow of information, but the government has no defence against those who wish to introduce greater disclosure *because* it undermines existing arrangements. Few of the proponents of a British Freedom of Information Act state this objective quite so bluntly, but the assumption seems to be that ministerial accountability is a myth and that the executive is no longer capable of managing a large and complex bureaucracy. The proponents of freedom of information are then following the pattern of argument to be found in America and Sweden; that open government is a necessary part of the system by which the citizen can challenge and scrutinise the actions of government, and that the legislature and the courts can no longer be relied upon to perform this function adequately.

The conclusion is that the British government will move slowly and minimally in the direction of greater disclosure, but that the most serious issue is whether a British Freedom of Information Act is sufficient compensation for the demise of the convention of ministerial responsibility. I am sceptical of this claim.

6. American Government and Secrecy

This chapter is concerned with an analysis of secrecy within American government, its sources and consequences but not with the legislation on this issue which will be discussed in the following chapter.

POLITICAL CULTURE

As stated in an earlier chapter, American political theory has been very much in favour of open government, seeing democracy as requiring a well-informed public, and arguing that any restriction on the free flow of information between government and the public is a step, and an important step, on the road to despotism. The argument reflects the spirit of rebellion, the absence of inherited political privileges or duties, the deliberate creation of a system of government at a time when governments were objects of suspicion and the placement of the individual, his liberty and his rationality, at the centre of the political process.

There are, of course, conflicting attitudes towards exactly what powers government should have, but the dominant ethos is one, and was one, of suspicion of government. The experience of the colonists was of an executive power which had a foreign source, governors and judges being appointed by the crown, whilst colonial assemblies were elected. This in a large part explains why they considered, in Professor Corwin's words, 'that the "executive magistracy" was the natural enemy, the legislative assembly the natural friend of liberty'.[1] It is also clear that in theory, in the terms of the available justifications for actions, secrecy is suspect. There are very great difficulties within American culture in justifying keeping any 'public' matter from the public. It is considered that this means that some action against the public interest is being undertaken, as evidence that representatives or officials are attempting to usurp their positions and escape public accountability. There is no feeling that the public is not a uniform body, that the 'people's right to know' may lead to the struggle for particular preference and the neglect of the general interest and no fear that politics must be protected from the people - this kind of paternalism has no place in American political culture.

Secrets, however, are related to evil-doing on a personal moral plane, as well as at the level of politics. It is perhaps no accident that it is an American sociologist, Goffman, who has analysed 'impression management' and 'stigma', the idea that we all have a secret identity which, if revealed, would discredit our public persona.[2] This fear of exposure is a particularly American fear, very much related to the stress on equality and the uniformity of the criteria of judgement. None of the above arguments implies that secrecy does not exist in either American public or private life - it is simply to suggest that the culture of the society makes it difficult to give a legitimate or acceptable defence of the secrecy which does, in fact, exist. This means that, whenever secrecy is under attack, it tends not to be able to call upon any traditional set of justifications and both government and the individual are on the defensive.

THE CONSTITUTION

The description of the American political system, in so far as this is necessary for an understanding of the level of secrecy in American government, is complicated by the existence of a written constitution. This problem is particularly important in the realm of secrecy because of the demands which are made for information by the legislature on the executive in the name of the constitution and the refusals of the executive to supply that information, also in the name of the constitution. They argue that the very performance of their respective constitutional duties requires that they be supplied with, or refuse to supply, certain information. However, certain consequences of the constitution are quite clear.

The major one for the present study is the separation of powers. In Britain there is no question that Parliament is sovereign, those who are head of the executive are also those with the support of the majority in the principal House of Parliament and the judiciary have no right of scrutiny over the laws which Parliament decides to pass. In the United States, the situation is quite different. Those who constitute the executive are not members of the legislature

and, furthermore, they are prohibited from being so. The
courts have a constitutional duty to ensure that the laws
which are passed do not infringe the provisions of the
constitution.

The consequence of the separation of powers has been to
create a situation in which the legislature cannot learn of
the effect and viability of its laws by implementing them -
this function is assigned to a separate branch of the government. As a result, the legislature requires to be informed
rather than the information being a consequence of the
exercise of its responsibilities. This means that the problem of information is quite different between the USA and
Britain. Of course, the problem that British Cabinet
Ministers have in keeping themselves informed about how the
policy which they enacted is in fact being implemented, and
what the consequences of the policy have been, is similar to
the problem that the executive has in the USA, but there is
less need for a further step in the British case to pass on
this information to those who propose, discuss and enact
legislation.

The major problem then of the American system is to work
out the interrelationship between the public's right to know,
the congressional right to know, the presidency's right to
independence as a separate power, the control by the presidency of the bureaucracy, and the need for certain activities by their very nature to be secret. These are problems
because the framework of responsibility within the American
political system is unclear. In fact, the separation of
powers does not correspond to a separation of lines of
responsibility. This is best seen in the congressional right
of 'oversight' and in the overlapping 'publics' to which
members of Congress and the President are responsible.

RESPONSIBILITY AND ACCOUNTABILITY

It will be the major argument of this chapter that it is
precisely because responsibility is so difficult to locate
that there is such an emphasis upon freedom of information.
The argument is this: if responsibility is difficult to allo-
cate, if the centre of power is unclear, then this creates
a situation of uncertainty. This uncertainty is resolved by
an 'open' system of government. The problem of responsibility can be seen in the method of congressional and
presidential elections. The President is elected for a fixed
term of office and one which does not directly coincide with
the elections to Congress. The consequence of this system of
fixed periods of office and staggered elections is well put

by Malcolm Shaw, so well put that I shall quote him at considerable length:

> This brings us once again to the question of responsi-
> bility. It is sometimes asserted that party government
> is responsible government while government by individuals,
> as in the United States, is not. It is true that there
> is a dimension of responsibility present in Britain which
> is absent in the United States. When parties seek endorse-
> ment in a British general election, it is usually clear to
> the voters who is responsible for the actions of the
> Government since the last election. It is - assuming that
> two-party competition is in effect - the incumbent party.
> Thus there is a direct line of responsibility between, on
> the one hand, the governing party and, on the other, the
> national electorate. In this situation people know, to the
> extent it is possible for them to know, what they are
> voting for - or against.
> In the United States this kind of responsibility can
> rarely be said to exist. Because of the system of stag-
> gered elections, it is not always possible to link a
> period of office with a party. Should different parties
> be in control in the White House and Congress, the problem
> is compounded. Even a President up for re-election follow-
> ing a four-year period, during which his party had majori-
> ties in both Houses of Congress, may have had a recalci-
> trant Congress. Under these circumstances, can a whole
> party be held responsible for what has been going on in
> Washington? Are voters justified under such circumstances
> in taking an identical view of all candidates of the
> President's party or of the 'opposition' party? Clearly
> the answer is no.[3]

Another aspect of this divided responsibility relates to
whether the executive is to be responsible to the 'people'
or to Congress. This problem can be seen in the arguments
concerning whether the 'public's right to know' is dis-
tinguishable from a congressional 'right to know'.

This dilemma can be seen in the fact that the President
is most likely to reveal secret information to Congress
when Congress is least likely to reveal this information to
the public, and yet Congress is most likely to press for
information when it has strong public support for its investigations and when it will, therefore, be obliged to reveal
the information in order to retain the public support. When
Congress and the President are in agreement that certain
information should be kept secret, then the public right to
know cannot be enforced,[4] and Congress will then seek to

distinguish the congressional right from the public right,
and yet Congress uses the justification of the 'public right
to know' when it is politically expedient to do so in order
to condemn executive secrecy. There is no clear centre within American politics where the justification of this right
can be adjudicated; no one has clear *political* responsibility to make this decision. The conflict between the executive and Congress is a matter of legitimacy and the public
right to know is used as a tool of debate. This is especially so when one considers that constitutionally Congress
has the role of executive supervision, and yet only the
President is elected by the nation as a whole so that both
sides have a basis for claiming to represent the 'public
interest'.

This problem can be seen in the congressional right of
impeachment and the debates over executive privilege.

IMPEACHMENT

Article II, Section 4 of the Constitution provides that 'The
President, Vice President and all civil officers of the
United States, shall be removed from office on impeachment
for and conviction of, treason, bribery, or other high
crimes and misdemeanours'. If, however, these words are
interpreted in a sufficiently wide manner then the executive
and, indeed, the judiciary, become responsible to Congress
almost as the Ministers are in a parliamentary system. Certainly the power of impeachment was an important mechanism
in the struggle of the English Parliament to achieve control
over the King's Ministers.[5] However, impeachment as a means
of controlling Ministers was gradually replaced by the vote
of confidence in the House of Commons and thereby the
Ministers became responsible to the House rather than to the
crown. Impeachment, then, is only of political significance
if it is undertaken for breach of *duty* rather than for the
commission of specific statutory offences. Raoul Berger
argues that the ability of Congress to impeach does not
depend upon the commission of specific criminal offences,
for example, bribery and corruption.[6] Berger wishes to argue
that an impeachable offence is a 'great offence' but not
necessarily a criminal one.

This argument is not only important in terms of a general
discussion of the clarity with which the lines of responsibility are drawn within the American political system, but
is also of relevance to a discussion of what powers of
investigation Congress possesses. Berger argues that the
congressional right of impeachment is an important consti-

tutional basis of the congressional right of investigation.
His argument runs as follows.[7] The framers of the Constitution were impressed with the struggle which Parliament had
undergone to establish its right to scrutinise all aspects
of executive behaviour, to establish itself as the 'Grand
Inquest of the Nation'. The power to investigate was seen as
being a necessary adjunct of the right to impeach. It was
necessary that Parliament be able to gather those facts
which would enable it to arrive at a just decision as to
whether an impeachable offence had taken place. One must be
able to make general enquiries *before* one brings a charge
of impeachment, otherwise one would never be able to bring
such a charge except on the basis of prejudice or specu-
lation. Therefore, given the right of impeachment, there is
a corresponding necessary right of *general* enquiry.

However, if there are difficulties in establishing the
uses and basis of impeachment within the American system,
this is not likely to clarify what the boundaries are between the congressional right to know and executive privilege. The limits of investigation may be clarified if they
can be shown to be related to some specific duty which will
require that certain specific categories of information be
obtained, but if the original right or duty is vague as to
what constitutes a 'great offence', then so will be the
alleged subsequent right or duty of enquiry. The problem
arises again that if impeachment is the likely, or indeed
possibly the only, remedy for gross executive abuse, then
how is one to determine that such abuses do not occur without a general right of enquiry, and how is one to allow such
a right without this threatening the independence of the
executive? These disputes concerning information are not
'accidental' but inherent. They stem from a basic uncertainty in the lines of responsibility.

EXECUTIVE PRIVILEGE

The main argument which has been developed to explain the
effect of Congress upon freedom of information is that based
upon the separation of powers, and the 'conflict' between
the legislature and the executive. Congress has been seen as
the 'people's protector' against a high level of secrecy in
government. There is, of course, a great deal of truth in
this argument but not as much as is often claimed.[8] The conflict between the executive, especially in the figure of the
President, and the legislature is a conflict over representation. The fact that the President is the only person
elected by the society as a whole gives to the Presidency a

basis for arguing not only that he has a duty to ensure that
the laws are faithfully executed, but also that only he represents 'the people'. He therefore has a basis for arguing
that if Congress seeks to impede or obstruct him it is
obstructing the will of the people. This is an argument
independent of the separation of powers, it is an argument
over legitimacy. This means that if the President argues
that certain things must be kept secret in order for him to
act in an effective manner, and Congress seeks to prevent
him from keeping those things which he wishes to, secret,
then it is attacking his claim to represent the wishes of
the electorate, and is proposing a counterclaim that only it
can determine what can be kept secret as only it has the
necessary legitimacy and trust of the electorate. This makes
the argument that this issue can be solved in the courts, by
Congress exercising its prerogative of subpoena and contempt
against the executive as if it were a matter of constitutional law, an inadequate solution. This is not to say
that there are not elements of constitutional law in the
question but its solution, in my view, is fundamentally a
political one.

The arguments concerning executive privilege have occupied
a considerable amount of congressional attention in recent
years. Concern with this issue can be seen as part of the
congressional revival and part of the general attack upon
the 'imperial presidency' which was associated with the
Vietnam War and Watergate. In this struggle for legitimacy,
Congress saw that certain actions which the President had
undertaken had undermined, in most people's eyes, the aura
and sense of legitimacy which it had acquired in the Kennedy
years. As the Presidential claim to represent the people had
sunk to its lowest ever level of credibility, a congressional
claim would therefore have its highest chance of success.
The question is whether the 'people', and Congress in particular, have considered the consequences of limiting
presidential power, if and when a President decides to start
doing things which are considered desirable by the electorate and in which he claims he is being obstructed by congressional action either present or past.

However, it is necessary to examine the arguments concerning executive privilege and Congress, and it is to this that
I proceed. Richard G. Kleindienst, Attorney General to
President Nixon in 1973, defined executive privilege as
follows:

    The doctrine of executive privilege denotes the consti-
    tutional authority of the President in his discretion to
    withhold certain documents or information in his possession

or in the possession of the executive branch from compulsory process of the legislative or judicial branch of the government, if he believes disclosure would impair the proper exercise of his constitutional functions.[9]

It is admitted by all parties to the dispute that this doctrine has been tested in the courts in the case of private citizens, but only recently and to a limited degree in the case of Congress.[10]

The discussion takes two main lines: one is an analysis of the constitutional and other bases of the doctrine; and the other an attempt to establish or to refute precedent for the doctrine. The origin of the term does not, however, lie with the Founding Fathers; it is not mentioned in the Constitution, and its origin according to Raoul Berger is as recent as 1958.[11] The main basis for the claim is the separation of powers. The separation of powers argument is a difficult one because it is an abstruse one. However, the main issue can be put clearly. Congress, it is argued, has the duty to pass laws and as a consequence of this it must know whether it acted wisely, or is about to act wisely; this requires access to executive information and this requirement is not therefore an attempt to administer the laws and to usurp the executive function, but a necessary part of its legislative function. The counter-argument is that the President has a constitutional duty to 'take care that the laws be faithfully executed', that Congress has no right to attempt to usurp this function, that it is impossible to distinguish between information and control, and that as Congress has no right to control it can have no right to information. However, that this argument cannot be settled *by definition* can be seen from the rather tortuous analysis that Raoul Berger falls into when trying to argue against executive privilege and yet defend Congress against the charge of usurpation:

> Where the line between such supervision and actual
> 'control' over administration is to be drawn presents
> the familiar task of drawing boundary lines. But if congressional control over execution of the laws is improper,
> it does not follow that inquiry *after* execution has taken
> place into *how* the laws have been executed is also
> objectionable. The former may trench on the 'exclusive
> province' of the executive, but the power of inquiry is
> beyond dispute.[12]

It seems to me perfectly obvious that denying information to Congress is one very simple way of denying its right to con-

trol. The argument that there is a difference as to when
the inquiries are made, and that this determines whether it
is an attempt to control or inform is the weakest argument
in what is otherwise a remarkable essay.

With most laws there is no time at which they cease to be
in operation and become mere objects of curiosity. If they
are still in the process of administration then any inquiry
can obviously be seen as a potential threat of interference
in the way the law *is* being executed. It is not sufficient
to say that the separation of powers gives to both parties
certain duties which can, if defined in a certain way, be
exercised without the exercise of the one impinging upon the
exercise of the other. One must deal with the actual situation, and when one does it becomes obvious that the desire
that Congress has to protect its constituents and to claim
political credit for the actions of government and the
desire for the President to do so are incompatible. Although
this is a complicated issue, the political element makes it
unlikely that this argument will be settled solely by applying the principles of constitutional law.

This fact has been recognised by certain Presidents, for
example Jackson, Cleveland and Eisenhower. This is not to
say that they did not also give arguments couched in constitutional terms, but as Younger argues, they have a powerful
weapon in the claim that they are the 'tribune of the
people'. He gives the following two quotations from Jackson
and Cleveland respectively:

> Their continued repetition [congressional demands] imposes
> on me, as the representative and trustee of the American
> people, the painful but imperious duty of resisting to the
> utmost any further encroachment on the rights of the
> executive.

> The pledges I have made were made to the people, and to
> them I am responsible for the manner in which they have
> been redeemed.[13]

This emphasis upon the political has also been shown in two
empirical studies of congressional investigations by Scher,
who found that Congressmen saw their oversight function as
being less important than their constituency and legislative
functions, because there is less political credit to be
obtained through this activity than through the other two.
The motivation for taking the oversight function seriously
arises when constituency interests claim that a particular
agency is acting in a way which adversely affects them.
Scher makes it very clear that despite the rhetoric of inde-

pendence which is used to describe certain agencies, what is in fact desired is that these agencies should be independent of the President but not independent either of the interests which they are supposed to be regulating or from congressional influence to try to ensure that such an accommodation with these interests takes place.

> The Congressman, frequently as lawyer participating in the regulatory legislative process, formally accepts a norm that makes regulatory agency orders reviewable by courts rather than by Congressmen. However, his conception of his role as representative reviewing agency behaviour - a conception that associates him with particular group and constituent interests - involves no requirement of self-restraint on his part. Acting as overseer, the norms of the representative prevail over those of the lawyer or the administrator.[14]

Scher's study of a particular agency, the National Labor Relations Board, showed that Congressmen used the opportunity of hearings on the agency to comment on its 'quasi-judicial' decisions, to make it account to Congress for these decisions, and to influence future decisions, using as their basis of criticism complaints by their constituents - all of these actions, in terms of the rhetoric of quasi-judicial independence, are, of course, unthinkable.

What this means is that the lack of self-discipline, because each Congressman's obligations are to his constituents and not a political party or Congress or the President, raises very serious doubts when the rhetoric of congressional rights is used to justify a particular investigation or demand for information. This is not to say that motives are suspect on every occasion, but the fact that the President at least understands the political nature of Congress is bound to lead him, if not constitutional lawyers, to be wary of conceding too much on the basis of principle, rather than public support.

A Presidential claim of executive privilege was recently tested in the courts in connection with the trial of the Watergate defendants accused of conspiracy in the 'cover-up'.[15] The basis of the controversy was a claim by President Nixon that tapes of his conversations with his advisers were subject to executive privilege and, therefore, he refused to release them in their complete form for use in the trial. The tapes had been subpoenaed by the Watergate Special Prosecutor and the case went to the Supreme Court, which determined that the President's claim of privilege in this specific case was too general and that the necessity of the

tapes in this particular case of a criminal prosecution was
such as to outweigh the privilege claimed. There are two
important points about this ruling: one is that it asserted
the right of the courts and not the executive to determine
the limits of executive privilege, and the second that it
did recognise such a right although in the specific case
before it, a criminal prosecution, it did not uphold the
privilege. The decision both pleased and upset those who
were suspicious of the doctrine in that it showed a court
willing to challenge even a presidential claim that his ex-
changes with his confidential advisers should be considered
privileged. The Senate Committee on Watergate had also subpoenaed the tapes and President Nixon had refused to supply
them on the grounds that the proper functioning of his
office required that his discussions remained confidential.
The Committee could have instituted contempt proceedings,
but felt reluctant to do so because of the possibility that
the full Senate would not at that stage have been prepared
to support such a measure. The Committee then decided to sue
for the tapes in the courts. The Committee failed, despite
several court hearings, to win its suit. The reasons given
in the several judgements were that Congress had provided no
statutory basis for the suit; this was rectified by the passing of a Bill. It was then rejected as being too general. It
was argued that the release of the tapes to the Committee
would lead to publicity which might prejudice the trial
about to take place; this was appealed, and although the
Appellate Court upheld the refusal, it was on new grounds,
namely that the Committee had failed to show that its responsibilities could not be fulfilled without access to the
tapes themselves since it had been provided with copies. The
court had again repeated that the President's discussions
were 'presumptively privilege' and that a strong need would
have to be shown for this privilege to be denied. Despite
the legal doubts expressed by constitutional lawyers, the
courts had decided that the President did possess an executive privilege based upon the need for confidentiality of
discussion if he was to be able to carry out the functions
of his office effectively. The courts however had denied
that the issue was a political one and therefore one upon
which they could not rule, but they had recognised that only
in exceptional circumstances would White House discussion
not be protected from Congress, thus recognising the realities of political life.

Before leaving the 'separation of powers' justification
for executive privilege, it is important to recognise that
not all Presidents have sought to use this justification for
refusing information to an equal extent. The most famous

occasion for its usage, and one to which all subsequent justifications have sought to refer, was President Eisenhower's refusal to allow Army Counsel, John Adams, to testify to a Senate Committee investigating the Army-McCarthy dispute. Eisenhower, in a letter to Defense Secretary, Charles E. Wilson, in effect forbade testimony as to the high-level discussions which had taken place over the Army allegations that McCarthy had sought preferential treatment for an ex-employee of his, Private David Schine.[16] The letter stressed the importance of 'candid interchange' within the executive and 'proper separation of powers'. What this statement by Eisenhower showed was that ultimately the executive was under his protection and although Congress may investigate the executive, the Presidency was willing to use the aura attaching to the office to limit the power of Congress. In such a battle, Congress was likely to lose. After the sending of this letter, Eisenhower made a further thirty-four refusals to supply information to Congress, President Kennedy four, President Johnson two, and President Nixon, up to December 1972, nineteen. In trying to explain this variation the major factor appears to be whether Congress was controlled by the party of the President; in the case of Nixon and Eisenhower the legislature and the executive were of different parties, whilst in the case of Presidents Kennedy and Johnson, they were of the same party. As Harold Relyea of the Congressional Research Service, the Library of Congress, states:

> The fact that there is much more conflict over Congressional access to Executive Branch information when the two branches are controlled by different political parties gives substance to the view that 'executive privilege' is a partisan problem.[17]

SECRECY IN CONGRESS

Another aspect of government secrecy is the extent to which Congress conducts its affairs in secret. Following the passing of the Freedom of Information Act in 1966 and the associated spotlight upon secrecy, Congress itself came under attack for holding such a large number of its committee meetings in secret, especially since it was in those meetings that many important decisions were taken. In a study by the *Congressional Quarterly*, some 37 per cent of all congressional committee meetings between 1963 and 1971 were held in secret.[18] In 1970 Congress revised its rule of procedure: most meetings were to be open except where a majority

of the committee voted otherwise. The Senate excluded mark-
up (when a committee formulates the final version of a Bill)
and voting sessions, although the House did not. This re-
organisation had little impact upon the secrecy of either
House, since committees normally voted to close the decision-
making meetings. Until 1971 all the meetings of the powerful
House Appropriations Committee had been secret. In 1973 the
rules were further refined to require that the voting to
close a meeting be in public with a quorum present, including mark-up sessions. This further reduced the number of
meetings held in secret and the House had a somewhat better
record than the Senate. In 1973 the percentage of closed
meetings dropped to 16 per cent and in 1974 to 15 per cent.
The reform also applied to joint House/Senate conferences on
legislation, where again important modifications of Bills
had taken place and where the tradition had been one of
secrecy. The reason for these changes was a feeling that
Congress could no longer operate in a secret manner, given
the many public statements that had been made by Congressmen
on the evils of secrecy. Also many of the younger Congressmen, especially those elected in 1974, considered secrecy to
be part of the congressional 'patriarchical' system. Secrecy
had also been criticised in so far as it permitted special
interests, especially constituency ones, to be 'protected'
at the cost of the national interest.[19] One of the dangers
of these changes is that the system of seniority and committee power, whatever its failings, provided what little
structure and discipline Congress possessed, and their removal may simply mean that it becomes even more difficult
to pass legislation, especially in a hurry. Openness *may*
lead to fragmentation, endless consultation, and little
action.

I was also informed that one consequence of the reorgan-
isation has been a 'fiesta' for lobbyists and that most of
the bargaining is still done in secret, but in off-the-
record meetings. However this is not to deny that some constraints upon 'pork-barrelling' may now exist as a result of
having to justify the basis of these alterations to the Bill
in public, rather than simply having to justify the final
Bill before Congress as previously.

Many congressional investigations lead to majority/
minority reports, and in these situations there is a possibility that the minority will make public statements on what
happened in committee, even if the majority decide not to
release their findings. This raises the question of the
ability of Congress to discipline its own members. As will
already be clear this is difficult to achieve by the mechanism of the party in that the actions of one of its own

members cannot lead to a 'vote of confidence' and the threat
of elections. This means that it can only be done by the
courts or by Congressional Rules. Under Congressional Rules
a Congressman is subject to expulsion if he discloses secret
proceedings, and a Congressional Officer, such as a Staff
Assistant, could be charged with contempt of Congress.[20] In
the Senate there have been only seven votes of censure
against a member in its whole history and only two of these
cases, those of Senator Pickering in 1811 and Senator Tappan
in 1844, concerned breaches of security. In the House of
Representatives, until 1967, there had been only seventeen
instances of members, and one case of a delegate, being
censured, and one of these was related to the disclosure of
State secrets. In fact there is considerable doubt as to
whether a member would be censured for the release of
executive secrets unless the House felt that this was actually damaging to the United States: this is a political
judgement and one which the executive would not necessarily
share.

This is also complicated by the claim of both Houses to
congressional immunity. As Senator Jesse Helms argued in
hearings on congressional immunity, one would expect those
arguing for the broadest interpretation of congressional
immunity to be those arguing for the broadest interpretation
of executive privilege, but as he said, this doesn't seem to
be the case.[21] The main basis of congressional immunity is
Article 1, Section 6 of the Constitution:

> They [the Senators and Representatives] shall, in all
> cases except treason, felony and breach of the peace, be
> privileged from arrest during their attendance at the
> session of their respective Houses, and in going to and
> returning from the same; and for any speech or debate in
> either House they shall not be questioned in any other
> place.

The present position is that the Speech and Debate Clause
covers anything said or written in the course of legislative
duties or functions. The latter extension was granted by the
Supreme Court in the case of *Powell* v. *McCormack* when the
court stated:

> ... it would be a narrow view to confine the protection
> of the Speech and Debate Clause to words spoken in debate.
> Committee reports, resolutions and the act of voting are
> equally covered as are things generally done in a session
> of the House by one of its members in relation to the
> business before it.[22]

This means, then, that in the performance of any duty which
the court considers to be of a legislative nature, the Congressman has complete immunity from any judicial or executive scrutiny. The original purpose of this section of the
Constitution was to protect legislators from being sued for
seditious libel by the executive, having the model of parliamentary privilege in mind and the importance which this
privilege had had in the history of parliamentary supremacy
over the monarchy. If the executive could call Congressmen
to account for any criticisms which they made then it was
felt that, without this ever needing to happen, it would
place an intolerable 'chilling' effect upon the legislature
given the fact that the courage of Congressmen should not be
assumed to be greater than that of the average citizen. However, Congress is anxious that because the courts have
sought to determine what is included and what is excluded
from the 'legislative function', a Congressman may have to
go to court and incur legal costs in defending an action
which seeks court determination of the boundary. These costs,
it is argued, could have a 'chilling effect' upon congressional utterances, even if the case is a 'nonsense'. The
implication behind this view is that Congress, and only Congress, should have the right to determine its boundaries and
against the arguments proposed that these boundaries can be
determined only by the judiciary. There has been an important recent case in which the 'legislative function' has been
a matter for the courts to determine: the Pentagon Papers
and Senator Gravel.

This case concerned the reading of the Pentagon Papers
into the congressional record at a meeting of the Senate Subcommittee on Buildings and Grounds. This reading took place
while publication of the papers was temporarily banned pend-
ing a Supreme Court ruling, and the obvious intention was to
make sure that the papers would be available in case the
Supreme Court ruled in favour of the executive. Daniel Ells-
berg had given the Pentagon Papers to the Senate Foreign
Relations Committee and then to the *New York Times*. A US
District Court found that Gravel could with impunity read
the papers into the record even though they were classified
by the executive as top secret. An interesting issue arising
from the case was the position of congressional staffs, in
this case an aide to Senator Gravel. The court decided that
congressional immunity did extend to congressional staffs if
they were acting as part of the congressional function: a
member and his aide were to be 'treated as one'. The court
did decide, however, that the Senator's aide could be
questioned in order to trace: ' ... the source of obviously
highly classified documents that came into the Senator's

possession and are the basic subject matter of inquiry in this case, as long as no legislative act is implicated by the questions.'[23]

Senator Gravel's acquisition of the papers and his arrangement for them to be privately printed, in the court's opinion, stood on a different footing and was not covered by the Speech and Debate Clause. This ruling gave the government permission to proceed to seek indictments for the alleged arrangements to publish the papers. What these issues raise is whether or not Congress has incompatible expectations *vis-à-vis* the executive and as to whether Congress can legitimately be expected to be trusted and also be an antagonist. It is surely the case that if Congress does not wish to be a partner of the executive, but a watch-dog of executive 'dirty tricks', then it can hardly be expected to be seen by the executive as a *body* which can be entrusted with those things which the executive sees as being secrets and which are crucial to the furtherance of its policies. Congress would then become government and have to take responsibility for these decisions. If that were to happen, its attack upon the executive, based upon the separation of power, would cease to have any meaning. In my view, the American system of government means that there is an inevitable tension between having an imperial presidency or an imperial congress, and all arguments about each other's privileges are simply arguments about political supremacy.

CONGRESSIONAL INVESTIGATION OF THE EXECUTIVE

There is one other aspect of congressional and presidential relations. It concerns the oversight function of Congress. What this means is that it is a necessary part of the legislative process that one not only passes laws but that one monitors their implementation and ensures that the funds which have been allocated for that purpose are being used for that purpose and no other. There is also a duty on those who pass laws to ensure that the purpose for which the law was enacted is actually being achieved. The case for a particular congressional duty and right of oversight is put by Schwartz as follows:

Among the most consequential of Congressional tasks today is that of exercising effective control over administration.

The legal basis of legislative control is to be found in the fact that all exercises of authority by the federal administration must find their source in a Congressional

act. Our law, as will be seen, rejects the notion of
inherent or autonomous law-making power in the executive.
Thus, the officers and agencies of the executive branch
owe their authority and, indeed, their very existence to
delegations of power by Congress.
It follows from this that the administration, in the
exercise of its delegated powers, acts as the agent of the
legislature. But if that is true, the latter must possess
the authority to exercise continuous supervision over
administrative activities. It is a fundamental principle
on the law of agency that a principle retains control over
his agent.[24]

As defined in the Constitution, the duty of the executive is
to carry out faithfully the laws passed by Congress. However,
this does not solve the question of who is to ensure that
this is done, whether by the President, Congress or even
judicial order. The difficulty is that although the Constitution does not give primacy to the legislature, it is the
case that it assigns a specific duty to the executive and
no specific duties to the legislature, only powers. What
this means is that the President has no role of oversight
vis-à-vis Congress, as Congress has no duty which could be
the executive's role to enforce - but Congress can and does
argue that it has such an obligation relative to the executive. This 'oversight' function could have been turned, and
attempts were made to turn it, into a parliamentary system,
despite the separation of powers.
      This problem arose at a very early stage in American
history with President Washington and the St Clair incident.
General St Clair was in charge of some 1500 men on an expedition into Indian territory. The expedition was attacked
with the loss of 600 men and Congress demanded the right to
investigate the 'massacre'. In cabinet discussions reported
by Jefferson on how the President should respond, the question was raised as to whether Congress was trying to act as
a Parliament and make the heads of Departments of State
answerable to it by calling them before the House. Washington
argued that Congress was not a 'council' and he decided that
there were no papers in this case which it could not properly see, but that 'he thought himself not so far subject as
to be obliged to produce all the papers they might call for.
They might demand secrets of a very mischievous nature.'[25]
      The important point is that the Constitution prohibits
simultaneous membership of any two or all three branches of
government. Presidents have been aware of the danger that
Congress may seek to call members of the President's cabinet

and to make them *answerable* to it, and that this must be
resisted if the system of government is not to be trans-
formed.

There is, of course, no question that congressional committees have questioned the members of the President's cabinet and, indeed, any other member of the executive. The only
exception to this has been the White House staff. These are
considered to be confidential advisers to the President and
to be protected by the President. As it is difficult to
imagine the President being subject to a congressional contempt order, then the same applies, so it is argued, to his
personal staff. The difficulty is that the growth of the
White House staff has been considerable and has expanded its
functions to include, under Henry Kissinger, the virtual
running of foreign affairs, although he was not Secretary of
State until some years later. This means that if this
'personal adviser' argument is accepted, Congress cannot
question the person who may, in fact, be responsible for
United States foreign policy.

EXECUTIVE AUTHORITY

The main power which the President has over his subordinates
is the power of dismissal. The only exceptions to this are
the independent regulatory agencies: they are independent
precisely because the President's power of dismissal does
not apply. An executive official can be summarily dismissed
and has no right of notice or hearing, unless otherwise
allowed for in Statute, as this is considered to be necessary to the proper functioning of the executive. The courts
have argued that the President cannot be held responsible
for executive administration if he is unable to ensure that
those who are instructed to carry out his policies actually
do so, and has the right to dismiss them if they do not.

The classic case on this is *Myers* v. *United States* in
which a postmaster argued that he could not be removed except with the 'advice and consent' of the Senate, this being
a condition of his appointment under a congressional statute
of 1876. The Supreme Court, however, speaking through Chief
Justice Taft, an ex-President, argued that as the President's 'selection of administrative officers is essential to
the execution of the laws by him, so must be his power of
removing those for whom he cannot continue to be responsible.'[26] The court argued that the 1876 Statute was an in-
valid encroachment upon Presidential power.

However, Congress in recent years has considerably
increased the amount of legislation on the operation of the

federal bureaucracy in the areas of merit systems, personnel
administration, pay and retirement, rights of employees and
veteran preference. It has been argued that this attempt by
Congress to pass detailed legislation governing the operations of the federal bureaucracy decreases the flexibility
available to the President to too great a degree.[27] However,
the power of dismissal has not been challenged by Congress,
although it has insisted that certain procedures be followed.
This right of the President is reflected in the fact that
almost half a million federal appointments are filled outside the rules of competitive examination - this amounts to
approximately 16 per cent of the federal service. Only some
1384 employees are directly appointed by the President, the
others being appointed by his appointees.

The main contrast between the British and Swedish civil
services and that of America is the extent to which civil
servants change with a change of government, or, to be more
precise, a change of President. The necessity for civil
servants to restrain their public comments in order not to
be identified with particular policies because this would be
embarrassing for a subsequent administration with different
policies is greatly reduced. The President is able to ensure
that those who carry out his policies share his views and
that their public utterances ought to be ones which will be
in accord with his own views. It would be very interesting
to know whether those leaks which are *damaging* to the administration come from lower-level or career civil servants
rather than from those who have been politically appointed.
One would imagine this to be the case, but discovery of such
facts is obviously almost impossible.

In David Wise's book, *The Politics of Lying*,[28] almost all
the leaks that he identifies come from the high echelons of
the administration and are attempts to manipulate the press
in *favour* of the administration. However, whether this
reflects the number of cases which are known and which the
press are willing to reveal, rather than the typical leak,
it is impossible to say.

CONGRESS AND APPROPRIATIONS

One other factor which encourages relative openness on the
part of the American bureaucracy is that Congress controls
bureaucratic finance. This is not to say that all departments do not have to have their budget approved by the President's Office of Management and Budget - they do. However,
if the department feels that its budget has been trimmed by
the President, it has methods of informing Congress to this

effect and of supplying Congress with information to support
its case for more money than the President was willing to
allow to the department.[29] It is a standard joke in Washington that at appropriations time the Navy suddenly releases
reports of sightings of Russian submarines off the coast of
America. Normally, of course, such information is top secret.
The pressure to release information normally kept secret is
also felt by the President, who must convince Congress of
the need to spend large sums of money on defence. This
necessitates the release of confidential national security
information - not necessarily the complete report, but
enough to support the President's case. Congress will then
question members of the administration in order to find out
whether the information they have been given is complete and
whether members of the federal bureaucracy are willing,
under questioning, to reveal more information. This can lead,
certainly in the light of British experience, to quite
extraordinary situations, such as the questioning of the
administration's dismissal of General MacArthur in the
middle of a war and the attempt to discover how the war was
being conducted. The generals in this case were anything but
reticent.

Information also produces confidence in the committee themselves that they are being thorough and makes them feel
confident that the House will see them as being 'tough on
budgets' and as being a hardworking committee not easily
fooled. Information, then, is not solely desired for itself;
indeed one feels that there is too much of it to allow a
balanced view to emerge, but for the purposes of creating an
image of competence, both on the part of the agencies and on
the part of the committee.

Before concluding, there are certain areas of the political
system which must be discussed in more detail: these are the
courts and the press.

THE COURTS

Schwartz and Wade at the beginning of their discussion of
America make the following statement: 'American society,
more than any other, is imbued with legal ideas and dominated by lawyers and lawyer-judges.'[30]

The importance of the law and the extent to which the law
is seen as the protector of the people can hardly be over-
stated. This stems from two basic principles - one is the
separation of powers, the other is the fact of a written
Constitution. The first of these encourages 'legalism' in
two ways. First, through the explicit role which is granted

to the courts as part of the system of checks and balances, and secondly by the fact that the legislature's main mechanism of social control is the law. The Constitution further encourages legalism by the fact that all activities of the other two branches of government are subject to challenge as to whether they contravene the written constitution, a matter which can only be settled in the courts. Law, however, is not just the means by which the citizen obtains redress; the passing of new laws has always been seen as the main means of enforcing the 'will of the people'.

The courts in America have also taken, since the Second World War, a role totally alien to a parliamentary system, that of initiating major social changes, such as the 'desegregation' of the South.[31] This was done by declaring certain actions unconstitutional, such as the racial segregation of schools.

The courts have affected the amount of government secrecy by their attitude towards discovery and executive privilege. In the case of civil suits the courts have ruled on the right of the executive to refuse to disclose information. The Supreme Court conclusively rejected the view that the executive had the sole right to determine what would be disclosed in *United States* v. *Reynolds* (1953). This was a case in which a military plane, carrying both civilian passengers and secret electronic equipment had crashed, and in which the widows of the civilian passengers sought discovery of the Air Force's investigation report. The plaintiffs were in fact denied the report, but the court made it clear that its grounds for so doing were that they had failed to show that the report was relevant and not that the court recognised the right of the executive to deny such a report on the grounds of military secrecy. The court stated: 'the court itself must determine whether the circumstances are appropriate for the claim of privilege'.[32]

However, the court did recognise that there were some circumstances in which it would accept the claim of privilege without even examining the documents *in camera* simply on the basis of the nature of the documents themselves. The reasoning of the courts is that there is no justification for arguing that the courts are unable to keep military secrets which have been entrusted to them by *in camera* inspection and that they are as capable of determining the public interest in disclosure as well, if not better, than the executive.

The main difficulty of these arguments concerns the basis upon which the judiciary are to make such a decision and as to whether a balanced view is always to be expected. It may well be the case that over time a reasonable balance between

privilege and disclosure can be maintained, but whether this
can be guaranteed in every instance is somewhat more debat-
able. The argument of the executive could well be on the
basis that even one error may be of such great importance
that no chance of error occurring can be allowed, and that
therefore a claim of privilege by the executive should not
be subject to judicial review. However, this view has not
been accepted by the courts, and the acceptance of such a
claim would seriously threaten the 'separation of powers'.
The American courts have never allowed a claim of executive
privilege in the way that the British House of Lords did in
the case of *Duncan* v. *Cammell, Laird.*

THE PRESS

It has often been remarked that in American politics the
press is the fourth branch of government. However, as David
Wise notes, this is both a strength and a weakness.[33] The
problem is that if the press is to be privy to government
information and inform the public, then this implies a
relationship of trust between government and the press which
is inimical to its role as an adversary of government. This
dilemma is exacerbated if it is the case that it can only
perform its role as adversary if it receives information
from the government itself. One can argue that this dilemma
can be solved if it can obtain information from the government by compulsory means, for example by the Freedom of
Information Act, which then removes it from obligation to
the government. However, much of the information in which
the press is interested is exempt from disclosure under the
Act and in fact the dilemma has not been resolved. The
extent to which the press is able to obtain information from
the bureaucracy, which the President would rather it did not
obtain, raises the issue of bureaucratic discipline, which
has again been discussed in connection with Congress. However, if the problem with Congress was that the Congressman
is politically responsible primarily to his constituents and
not to the nation, the question of to whom the newsman is
responsible is even more acute. A basic consideration for
any newspaper is after all survival, the selling of newspapers, and whether this is an adequate criterion for the
determination of what information is, or is not, in the
'public interest' is, to me, a dubious one.
    Congress has consistently refused to pass legislation
making it an offence to pass classified information to the
press[34] (unlike the British Official Secrets Act which was
designed with the press in mind, as already shown), and the

only recourse open to the executive in America is internal
discipline. This is made difficult, however, by the fact
that the government does not wish to alienate the press, but
to control the information which it receives, and this means
that it is unwilling to prohibit contracts between the press
and the bureaucracy. The press sees this relationship as a
'game' in which the Presidency tries to use the press, and
where the press tries to exploit the relationship to extract
as much information as possible. Competition between members
of the press also means that newspapers have something to
gain from executive secrecy, that is a 'scoop'. A particular
newsman, favoured by the administration, may be given an
'inside story' because he has proved 'reliable' in the past
and thereby be able to increase his value to his newspaper
and increase the sales of that newspaper.

There is no question that the executive would like to see
greater restrictions placed upon the release of information
by individual bureaucrats, but laws to this effect have been
resisted by Congress, partly because its information comes
from the same 'unauthorised' sources and partly because a
press which is able to embarrass the Presidency is to its
advantage in the struggle for political legitimacy. The main
reason for the existence of the 'leak' however, is not, in
my view, the lack of criminal sanction but the dispersal of
interests within American government, the lack of a centralised system of responsibility. The fact that each area of
the bureaucracy is subject to one particular, and several
interested, committees of Congress means that in the areas
of finance and obtaining permission to grow, the different
departments and agencies of government are in competition
with each other. This means that the release of information
becomes a tactic in this struggle between departments for
the scarce resources which Congress and the nation control.

CONCLUSION

In conclusion, let me repeat my main point which is that
democracy consists in representative government, and that
for its proper functioning it requires that responsibility
can be assigned and those responsible removed - either within the government or the government itself. It has been my
desire to show that responsibility within the American
political system is unclear and that this has led to the
more open system of government. However, I think it is
necessary to note that whether 'open' government is more
desirable than 'responsible' government is not an easy judgement to make. Commentators on the British situation ought to

be wary of judging Britain as being less 'democratic' than America simply because it has a higher level of secrecy, for it seems to me that when one examines the American situation, many aspects of it strike someone looking from a British perspective as thoroughly undemocratic, despite admiration for its more open system of government.

7. Secrecy, the Law and the Civil Service in America

INTRODUCTION

This chapter is concerned with the evolution of the American civil service and with the development of the legislation controlling government secrecy and disclosure. The main argument used to explain the American 'balance' between secrecy and disclosure is the fear that bureaucracy is not being controlled by elected representatives, and that this in turn is a consequence of the fact that the lines of responsibility for such control are not clear. The balance between secrecy and disclosure has not been resolved by giving a particular institution clear responsibility for the balance, but by turning to the law and legal rights to information.

This chapter will be concerned to show that the 1966 Freedom of Information Act was part of a series of mechanisms instituted to control the federal bureaucracy. These include the creation of a 'neutral' federal service, the Sedition and Espionage Acts of 1918, the control of delegated legislation, loyalty, the Administrative Procedure Act, and the Freedom of Information Act. Although some of these may appear irrelevant to an understanding of the balance between secrecy and disclosure, they are all part of the attempt to create an impartial, legalistic and responsive bureaucracy.

Analysis of these issues illustrates a persistent dilemma in American government, the desire to create an efficient and effective federal service without it becoming powerful and usurping the functions of Congress. Congress cannot take direct control of the large bureaucracy it has created, and it will not allow the President to do so either, for he too is not under the control of Congress. The solution has been for Congress to attempt to control the bureaucracy by a system of legal supervision. All of these factors are related to the question of what the political role and position of the federal service ought to be. The issues of neutrality

and loyalty are attempts to define the proper political role
of the bureaucracy, and this will affect the amount of
executive information which can be revealed, since secrecy
is one way of limiting the degree to which civil servants
become part of public, political discussion and debate. This,
however, creates another dilemma, to exclude or limit the
overt political role of the federal service, whilst at the
same time ensuring that it is subject to scrutiny. To repeat
an earlier but important argument, there is no simple link
between the influence of the civil service upon political
decisions and either secrecy or disclosure, and to make a
civil service subject to disclosure laws does not necessarily reduce its influence. Influence is also a matter of
responsibility and legitimate authority.

American attitudes to the federal civil service have been
shaped by two forms of anxiety, one that it will become an
élite, with its own interests and policies, and the other
that it will be corrupt, inefficient and biased in its application of the law by being contaminated by politics. Both of
these views are based upon suspicion and fear and none of
the dominant political philosophies views the executive as
the repository of law and impartiality.

In the early part of the nineteenth century, government
bureaucracy can be fairly described as being concerned only
with details of administration and the numbers of posts involved was small. At the end of the nineteenth century
neither of these statements was true, and the spoils system
was seen as an obstacle to an efficient civil service capable
of carrying out the tasks of administration in an impartial
and expert manner. The spoils system, however, has never
been eliminated although it has been limited. The tension
between the need for a President to have executive officers
who will carry out his policies, and the need for administration to be carried out in an impartial manner, has not
been resolved but compromised. The relevance of these
remarks is that the form of political control over the civil
service adopted by a democratic polity bears a crucial
relationship to the level of executive secrecy found within
it. The relative openness of the American political system
is to be understood in terms of the shared responsibility
for administration, the importance of judicial review of
administration, and the dilemma of creating a civil service
which is firmly under control on the one hand, without this
leading to the centralisation of power on the other. This
tension is the cause of openness in the United States.

NEUTRALITY

The American focus on the neutrality of the civil service
has been upon the selection, promotion and, later, the political activities of civil servants. An attempt has been
made to separate freedom of expression from overt political
identification, and to control the latter without this
impinging upon the former. Whether this attempt has been
successful will be assessed in due course, but the first
point at issue is why this attempt at separation was felt to
be necessary. One of the important factors is the requirements of the Constitution and of the First, Ninth and Tenth
Amendments in particular. These amendments are concerned
with the right of free speech, common law rights and with
the relationship between the federal government and the
states. These amendments raise the question of whether Congress has the constitutional authority to control the political activities of civil servants, since this may affect
constitutional rights. The Constitution specifically deals
with freedom of speech, but not with the right to join, or
participate, in the activities of political parties. It is,
therefore, constitutionally easier to prohibit civil servants from participating in overt political activity than to
place any restrictions upon their ability to express
opinions. Both Congress and the courts have also recognised
that there may be a tension between the need to create an
efficient civil service and the civil liberties of individual civil servants. The resolution of this tension has been
affected by the fact that there exists a fear of the power
of the bureaucracy and that this poses the problem of limiting the political activities of the civil service without
this depriving the nation of access to the information held
by civil servants.

There is also the problem that a President is anxious that
his ability to control the executive branch not be undermined by Congress and the congressional desire to create an
effective executive, without creating an 'imperial presidency'. However this later problem, the prerogative of each
branch, is by no means a simple one in that it was the President rather than Congress which sought the end of the spoils
system. The American political system did not see the neutrality of the civil service as requiring that criminal
sanctions be attached to the unauthorised disclosure of information; neutrality originally referred to the bureau-
cratisation of the federal civil service and, in the late
1930s, to the fear of an overtly partisan service, one
contaminated by ideology. This issue will be dealt with
under the heading of 'loyalty'.

The history of attempts to ensure a politically neutral civil service go as far back as the presidency of Jefferson. Such attempts were unsuccessful because of the nature of recruitment to the civil service, which was based upon the spoils system. Under Article 2, Section 2 of the Constitution, the President is given the power to appoint the officers of his administration. The basis for this appointment is not, however, given and until the Civil Service Act of 1883, recruitment was not necessarily based upon open competitive examinations but upon the personal decision of the President. Ability to appoint people to federal office was 'the spoils to the victor'. The spoils system was justified by Andrew Jackson in 1829 in order to combat the idea, which he said civil servants had, that their offices were their property and to make them more responsive to the 'people', to provide a justification for the removal of incompetents, and to ensure that only those faithful to the President held office. It was also seen by Jackson as being an egalitarian move in that he argued that a far wider range of people were competent to hold office and 'experience' was not as essential as a civil service which was of the 'people' rather than establishment or 'caste-like'.

However, the consequence of the spoils system was to produce a federal bureaucracy which was 'partisan' in that the relationship between support for the party in power and the holding of office was close. Federal employees were not excluded from aiding the party in its pursuit of power, even to the extent of money, in the form of party contributions being solicited from them. Often a political tax was levied, in the form of a small percentage of the salary. Direct political activity in the form of electioneering was also required if the federal employee was to retain his job. Active work for the party was also the surest way to ensure that in the event of an election victory one would receive paid office.[1]

The Civil Service Act of 1883 made certain positions within the civil service open only to those who achieved high grades in open competitive examinations. It also restricted the abuse of the political power of patronage by making the extraction of contributions from civil servants illegal and by making the giving of money by one civil servant to another 'for political purposes' illegal. The Act also prohibited any person in the competitive civil service from using 'his official authority or influence to coerce the political action of any person or body'. Attempts by Presidents to limit the political activity of civil servants grew increasingly strong from the 1870s onwards. However, these efforts were designed to prevent civil servants from engag-

ing in campaigns and from holding office in 'political'
organisations, rather than preventing them from making public statements. How is this situation to be explained? After
all the emergence of a career civil service had very important ramifications within the British political system and
one might expect that a similar desire to restrict the
political activities of the American civil service would
also occur.

In a sense it did emerge; the restriction upon the civil
servants taking an active role in the politics of the nation
is an attempt to restrict the use to which their information
can be put. Making a statement to the press or to Congressmen is quite different from forming a political lobby
against the existing government. The former is a less damaging activity than the latter. One of the reasons for this is
that the individual can be dealt with through internal
disciplinary procedures, whilst if someone is part of an
organisation this becomes a political issue rather than
being one concerned with an individual's breach of trust.

When the first attempts were made to restrict the political activities of the civil service, the constitutionality
of such actions was challenged in the Supreme Court. However,
the doctrine which developed was that no citizen had a constitutional right to government employment and that the
government could make whatever terms of contract it deemed
feasible.[2] Classified civil servants, those not political
appointees, are not removable without 'such cause as will
promote the efficiency of the service', and although the
executive can make whatever restrictions upon employment it
wishes, they must be justified in the above terms.

The next attempt to control the political activities of
civil servants came with the Hatch Act of 1939. Section 9 of
that Act states: 'No officer or employee in the executive
branch of the Federal Government, or any agency or department thereof, shall take any active part in political management or in political campaigns' (5 U.S.C. 118).

In 1947 a case occurred in which a group of federal
employees contested the constitutionality of the Act, and
the Supreme Court upheld its provisions although with some
dissenting members. The Supreme Court held that Congress had
the authority to legislate for the efficiency of the service
and that if it considered a prohibition upon political
activity to be necessary to that goal, then it had the authority so to legislate. The court argued that the prohibitions were limited and that many political activities were
not prohibited:

Expressions, public or private, on public affairs, person-

alities and matters of public interest, not an objective
of party action, are unrestricted by law as long as the
government employee does not direct his activities toward
party success.[3]

It is impossible to imagine the above statement having any
meaning within the British political system since all activities of the government are matters intimately connected with
party. The British Cabinet is drawn from a political party
and is also responsible for administration; it is hard to
imagine what would not be 'an objective of party action' or
unrelated to 'party success' in such circumstances.

The present position is that as described above; namely,
that civil servants must tread carefully in acting to assist
any political party, but there is nothing to stop them expressing their opinions on what their employer is actually
doing. This of course is not to say that they exercise this
right.

OFFICIAL SECRECY AND ESPIONAGE

The first piece of American legislation to regulate the
release of government information was the Defence Secrets
Act of 1911. It is perhaps ironic that the USA and Britain
should both have introduced legislation on official secrecy
in 1911, although the fear of war was the immediate cause in
both cases. The 1911 Act made it an offence wilfully to
communicate defence information to an unauthorised person
and unlawfully to obtain defence information. The penalties
for such an offence were a fine of $1000, or one year in
prison, or both. If the offence involved a foreign government, the penalty increased to a maximum of ten years in
prison.[4] It is important to note that the Act is solely concerned with defence information, that mere receipt of information was not an offence, and that the prosecution would
have to prove that the communication was without lawful
authority.

This Act is the closest the USA has come to a comprehensive Official Secrets Act, but in fact it was repealed in
1917 and replaced by a new Espionage Statute. The reason for
the change was that the Justice Department considered the
1911 Act to be defective and difficult to operate, and
although the intention was not to replace the 1911 Act with
one which was more liberal, rather than more clear, this is
in fact what happened. The reason for this was the extensive
scrutiny which the proposed legislation received in Congress.[5] The proposed Espionage Statute was submitted to Con-

gress two days after the severance of diplomatic relations
with Germany, but the threat of war was not sufficient to
ensure a smooth and quick passage for the new Act. The major
congressional anxiety centred upon the powers which the Act
would give to the executive to control the flow of information, although this is not to deny that Congress was not
also concerned with the effect of such legislation upon the
public 'right to know'. Edgar and Schmidt pose the problem
as follows:

> In each instance, the legislative debates have focused
> on the problem of how to protect military secrets from
> spies without promulgating broad prohibitions that would
> jeopardise the legitimate efforts of citizens to seek
> information and express views concerning national
> security.[6]

Another problem is that in a pluralist society there are
always those who disagree with the policy of the executive
and who will see executive demands to control the flow of
information as an attempt to hide the true facts which, if
they were known, would show the inadequacies of present
policy. These dilemmas have led Congress to pass legislation
on the control of defence information which is distinguished
by its ambiguity rather than its breadth of scope or sev-
erity of penalty.

   The Espionage Act of 1917 makes the basic offence the wil-
ful communication of defence information such that: 'the
possessor has reason to believe [that the information] could
be used to the injury of the United States or to the advantage of a foreign power' (18 U.S. 793 (d)). The requirement
that the communication be to a person 'not entitled to
receive it' is retained from the earlier 1911 Act in the
1917 Espionage Act. However, nowhere in either Act is any
definition given of who is and who is not entitled to
receive defence information. None of the Acts make any
reference to the classification system or to the executive
rules on authorisation, and Schmidt concludes that: 'These
considerations suggest the odd conclusion that the key
phrase "entitled to receive" may be meaningless, leaving the
communication and retention offences a dead letter.'[7]

   The Espionage Act also requires that a certain intent be
established, that the offender had reason to believe that
the information was to be used to the injury of the United
States or to the advantage of a foreign power. The British
Official Secrets Act in Section 2 does not require intent,
and places the onus of proof that the communication was inno-
cent upon the defendant, the exact opposite of the United
States Act.

A further ambiguity of the Espionage Act concerns the section dealing with communication to the enemy in time of war. The Act makes it an offence to communicate defence information to the enemy, but only where the *intent* was to communicate with the enemy. This means that where information is released to the press, published and read by an enemy, no offence is committed unless it can be established that the intention was to communicate with the enemy.

The important point is that the ambiguities and uncertainties of the Espionage Statutes are a reflection of the congressional desire to square a circle; to protect defence information without this increasing the power of the executive to control the flow of information to the press and the public.

On the issue of protecting government information there is, and has been, a clear difference between the views of the executive and the legislature. In 1917 President Wilson asked Congress to pass legislation which would have made it an offence to publish defence information in defiance of presidential regulations and irrespective of intent. In 1957 a Commission on Government Security recommended that the publication of *classified* defence information be an offence. In 1975 a Subcommittee of the Senate Judiciary Committee, with the active support of the executive, proposed that the reform of the Criminal Justice Legislation include a provision which would have made the unauthorised release of classified information an offence.[8] Congress has steadfastly refused to acquiesce in what it sees as executive aggrandisement of its authority to withhold information.

A related issue is the legal status of the system in classifying defence information as 'secret'. The simple answer is that it has no statutory basis. There is no US Act which gives authority to the executive to classify information, and governs the principles of such classification and provides legal penalties for the unauthorised release of classified information. This is not to say, however, that consecutive Presidents have not claimed the authority to issue orders providing for the creation of a classification system. Presidents have claimed the authority to create a classification system by reference to the Constitution, which vests executive authority in the President and which makes the President Commander of the Armed Forces. Presidents have also appealed to various statutes such as the Espionage Statute, the Housekeeping Statute of 1789 amended in 1958, the Internal Security Act of 1950 and the National Security Act of 1947.

According to a study made by the House Committee on Government Operations in 1973, it was not until 1912 that

systematic orders were issued protecting certain kinds of
defence information, and not until 1917 that special mark-
ings of secret were established by the War Department. Only
in 1940 was the first Presidential Executive Order issued on
security classification.[9] The lack of a statutory basis to
the classification system exemplifies the American attitude
to official secrecy, which is that only specifically named
types of information should be given the protection of the
criminal law, in order to avoid providing the President with
a 'blank cheque' to protect whole classes of information.

LOYALTY

For the purposes of the present argument, the importance of
the American concern with loyalty is what it reveals about
the relationships between the federal bureaucracy, the President and Congress, and the climate of opinion which such
concern created. American concern with loyalty is not a
product of the cold war - indeed, it has its roots in the
War of Independence and the Civil War - but the legislation
which marks the beginning of the almost obsessional interest
in the issue is the Sedition Act of 1918. This Act made it
an offence to use disloyal, scurrilous or abusive language
about the American form of government. The leader of the
Socialist Party was sentenced to ten years' imprisonment for
expressing the view that the war was the 'curse of capitalism'. There were also lynchings of anti-war protestors and
pro-German supporters. The concern with loyalty was related
to the fact that the peak of immigration occurred in 1908-10
and that many of these immigrants were East Europeans who
did in fact make up the majority of the socialists opposed
to the war. The government did not try to place these fears
in perspective; rather they passed the Espionage and
Sedition Acts, legitimated vigilante groups, and instigated
an extensive campaign of domestic spying by the Military
Intelligence Division, the Secret Service and the FBI. The
situation has been described as follows: 'The United States
had fielded a corps of sleuths larger than any country had
done in all history. And they called it the American way.'[10]
The Justice Department issued some 200,000 badges to
'temporary agents' of the civilian American Protection
League and some three million investigations were undertaken,
but not one person was convicted of espionage.
    It is interesting to note that the specific concern with
the loyalty of civil servants arose at a time when Congress
felt that President Roosevelt was attempting to undermine
the career civil service by increasing the number of posts

which were held at his discretion. By 1936 only some 60 per
cent of civil service positions were covered by the competitive examination requirements (compared to 84 per cent
today), and Roosevelt had set up some sixty new agencies,
only five of which were placed under the Civil Service Commission.[11] This action by Roosevelt to create agencies which
were subject to his patronage reflected a desire to change
the ideological basis of the federal bureaucracy and to enable him to employ people who were in sympathy with the 'new
deal' style of politics. Roosevelt greatly increased the
number of college graduates and 'East Coast liberals' in the
federal bureaucracy: in my view, it is this more than anything which explains the subsequent congressional concern
with the loyalty of civil servants. The re-emergence of
patronage, the great expansion of the civil service with a
new ideology of 'liberalism', was a direct threat to congressional control and to Congress's image of itself as an
equal, if not superior, branch of government. Policy and
action were being carried out without waiting for Congress
to pass laws or to approve the new agencies. This was done
under the emergency powers which had been granted to Roosevelt to solve the economic crisis of the 1930s, but it
created a bureaucratic 'monster', staffed by people who did
not reflect the style or ideology of Congress. Congress re-
asserted itself through the attack on the loyalty of this
new breed of federal officers.

Loyalty is closely related to the question of political
neutrality, but it has some distinctive features such as the
investigations by Congress and the demands that civil servants be dismissed without arguing that their dismissal
improves the efficiency of the service. In fact, Congress
argued that even though such dismissals may actually harm
the service, they were necessary to preserve the security of
the nation. Whatever the intention of the loyalty orders, it
was undoubtedly the case that their consequence was to inhibit the expression of any but the most orthodox opinions
by civil servants.[12] Any expression of unorthodox views
could be, and was, used as a reason to investigate the
'loyalty' of the civil servant.

It is certainly true that those senators from the Mid-West,
who see civil servants as 'egg-heads' and remote from the
ordinary American, are right; an East Coast education does
not produce 'frontiersmen', lovers of open spaces, men of
moral virtue with the prowess to defeat the 'bad men', men
who despise 'learning' and who acknowledge the virtues of
practical experience, men of independence who make their own
way in the world, somewhat like the John Wayne hero. This is
quite different from the cultural attitudes of the Swede or

Briton towards the civil servant, who is admired for being a
gentleman and a scholar, with the virtues of controlled
emotions, impartiality and learning. The official in America
is of low status, his counterpart in Sweden and Britain of
high status.

Communism is seen as an ideology to which bureaucrats have
an affinity in that it is seen as implying the expansion of
bureaucracy, the control of the private sphere of life and
of the economy by the polity. The bureaucrats have to be
watched, otherwise they will extend their power without this
being a product of revolution, but simply by the insidious
and secret influence of those who are in positions of influence becoming Communists. This concern with internal subversion and Communism led to the famous or infamous activities of the Committee on Un-American Activities. This Committee is associated with the name of Senator McCarthy,
although the allegations that there were Communists in high
places began with the accusations of Congressman Dies.[13] He
argued that many civil servants were supporters of organisations which were subversive or were Communist front
organisations. This move from accusations of actual membership of the Communist Party to 'guilt by association' was
the most significant factor in the subsequent loyalty campaign. During this campaign it was sufficient to have spoken
in favourable terms to, or of, an organisation which the
Communists were known to favour or support, or were trying
to infiltrate, or was controlled by them. Not only organisations became tainted; the espousal of certain causes also
became the basis of accusations of being a Communist or
Communist sympathiser or supporter. Some of these ideas included racial equality, support for free speech, the constitutional rights of civil servants and blacks, advocacy of
nudism, technocracy, Republican Spain, world government, the
brotherhood of man and civil rights.[14] The original criticisms of the government, however, were not restricted to
civil servants, but included the President and the Cabinet.
The accusations of Congressman Dies were seen as an attack
upon the 'new deal' in that expansion of the role of government was seen by some members of Congress as being the start
of the slippery slope inevitably leading to totalitarianism
and Communism.

1940 saw the passing of the Smith Act, which made the
advocacy of the violent overthrow of the US government illegal, and this resulted in Congress increasing the Justice
Department appropriation for the purpose of investigating
subversives, those who advocated violent revolution. In 1941
Congress decided that every Appropriation Bill should have a
clause stating that no money should be used to pay anyone

who advocated violent revolution, thus declaring the intention of Congress to exclude Communists from government
employment and relief. As a result of the revelations of
Elizabeth Bentley, Whittaker Chambers, the Canadian Royal
Commission on Espionage and the case of the magazine
Amerasia, the federal government set up interdepartmental
committees to deal with the loyalty of federal employees. In
1945 Congress authorised an investigation by the Civil Service Committee of the House into loyalty among federal
employees. Hearings were undertaken and statements were
received from the Attorney General, the FBI and the Military
Intelligence Services concerning the danger from and extent
of subversion. The Attorney General argued that just one disloyal employee was dangerous, and the Military Intelligence
Services argued that subversion was the more dangerous as
the extent of federal government intervention increased, in
that the power to disrupt by subverting the federal service
became greater. The Committee recommended that a commission
be set up composed of members of the appropriate federal
agencies in order to carry out a more thorough study. Most
of the recommendations of the Commission were concerned with
criminal acts such as treason and sabotage, although they
also included connection with totalitarian and subversive
organisations and the disclosure of confidential information
as evidence of disloyalty. The Commission's investigations,
however, were considered to be ineffective and were replaced
by the Presidential Loyalty Order of 1947, which led to the
Loyalty Program and the Loyalty Review Board, whose job it
was to 'root out' subversives. This, however, required considerable personnel and funds, as some two million employees
would have to be investigated and some 500,000 new applicants
checked every year. The budget for this programme amounted
to some thirty million dollars, the money to be split between the Civil Service Commission and the FBI.

In 1953 the Executive Order on Loyalty, issued by Truman,
was superseded by a new Executive Order issued by Eisenhower.
The main difference between this new Order and the previous
one is that it makes specific reference to national security
and that the retention of any civil officer is 'clearly
consistent with the interests of national security' (E.O.
10450 Section 2).

The dismissal of a civilian employee by the Secretary of
Health, Education and Welfare was challenged in the Supreme
Court on the grounds that his dismissal could not be justified since his position was not 'affected with national
security'.[15] The decision to uphold Cole's appeal was a
majority one, the minority determining that it was entirely
a matter for the President as to what constituted national

security, and that no one else knew which positions were
sensitive and which not. The consequence of this ruling, however, was that the Justice Department issued a memorandum
stating that no further dismissal proceedings should be
undertaken against any employee not in a sensitive position.
This is the present position, although all civil servants
are still subject to the prohibition against the advocacy of
the violent overthrow of the Constitution.

The important point about the loyalty programme, for
present purposes, was the effect that it may be considered
to have had upon the level of government secrecy. The first
point to be made is that much of the effect must have been
related to a change in attitude on the part of civil servants
which will be difficult to document but is discussed by
Bontecou and Gelhorn.[16] The basis of this change in attitude
lies in the fact that what a civil servant did or said was
now a matter for investigation, and the definition of disloyalty was sufficiently vague and the procedures sufficiently different from those found in a court of law to
create a sense of uncertainty among civil servants as to
what was and what was not permitted. The consequence of this
was likely to be that civil servants would withdraw from any
active part in political life and would be extremely
cautious as to whom they talked and what they talked about.
It is impossible not to believe that it did not have a
chilling effect upon the civil service such that only the
most 'middle America' opinions became 'safe'. Also, by
making the disclosure of confidential information a breach
of duty and as part of the definition of *disloyalty*, this
again must have made civil servants more cautious about discussing federal information, especially to the press who may
use the information to criticise the government.

Congress, in recent years, has seen itself - and been seen
as - the champion of 'open government' and yet, by defining
the disclosure of information as disloyal, it has given to
the executive the basis for claiming that 'national security'
and secrecy were necessary in order to 'protect' the state,
and has been encouraged in this view by the loyalty campaign.
Congress considered that the level of state activity had
grown to the extent that its 'loyalty' was a matter of consequence, affecting the ability of the people to continue to
live the 'American way of life'. It was felt that the more
powerful government became, the more important was it that
the people exercising this power should be loyal, and loyal
not just to the government but to the way of life which had
become identified as 'American'. Neither Congress nor the
President was willing to admit that if the government acted
in ways which threatened this way of life, this was a matter

of policies for which they were responsible. The civil service was blamed because it was seen as the instrument by
which power was exercised.

ADMINISTRATIVE LAW

It was not by accident that the Administrative Procedure
Act[17] and the Loyalty Program occurred at the same time -
they were both symptoms of a fear of federal bureaucracy
which had its roots in the ambiguities of control which
characterise the American Constitution. These ambiguities
created anxieties over who controlled the federal bureaucracy. This led to fears that no one was in control and that
either the executive was out of control or that one branch
of the government was interfering to such an extent with the
activities of another, that it was no longer able to carry
out its duties. The first of these accusations is invariably
accompanied by claims that no one knows what is going on and
that an excessive level of secrecy exists, whilst the second
is accompanied by complaints that publicity is leading to
emasculation. In the case of the Administrative Procedure
Act and loyalty, the cause is the same; the fear that no one
is in charge and that to institute accountability requires
exposure, exposure to a new agency or an additional branch
of government. The Administrative Procedure Act and the
Loyalty Program exemplified the two different ways of ensuring that the policies which the bureaucracy is pursuing are
those that the electorate wishes; one is to ensure that a
certain type of personnel are in office, and the other is to
subject them to a system of scrutiny, in this case judicial
in nature.

Bernard Schwartz argues that the Administrative Procedure
Act was a product of anxiety concerning the increase and
authority of administrative agencies: 'Its enactment [the
Administrative Procedure Act 1946] gave clear evidence of a
congressional desire to call a halt to the process of administrative expansion.'[18] These anxieties centred upon the
powers of the regulatory agencies, and in particular upon
the publication and formulation of agency rules. The first
of the agencies created by Congress with wide powers of rule-
making, was the Inter-State Commerce Commission in 1887,
its duty being to safeguard the public interest in the
rapidly expanding railway industry. This agency was the
pattern for many other agencies, although the delegation by
Congress to these agencies of regulation of many parts of
the economy was not without resistance by the courts, who
argued that the Constitution provided that only Congress

could make laws and that limits to the rule-making powers of
the agencies must be clearly stated in law, otherwise the
law would be unconstitutional. The Supreme Court used this
reasoning to strike down the New Deal National Industrial
Recovery Act, although Schwartz states that this was almost
the last effort to inhibit congressional powers of delegation.[19] The Administrative Procedure Act however sought
to ensure that if these powers could not be denied then they
ought to be used according to certain procedures which Congress ought to lay down. This emphasis upon procedure has
been the dominant ethic of judicial review of administrative
action since then; there has been no attempt to restrict the
power of bureaucracy to regulate large areas of American
life, only to ensure that the power of bureaucracy be used
in accordance with due procedure. Provided a rule made by an
agency can be justified as being in the public interest,
then it is considered that the making of the said rule is
within its authority. The law has conceded that in these
fields of administration, the administrator is an expert in
his own right, with the authority to interpret the public
interest, without judicial interference.

The main element of procedure which was required by the
1946 Administrative Procedure Act was that decisions be made
upon the record and that those hearing the evidence should
be separate from those undertaking the investigation and
formulating the rules. There are other rules concerning due
notice, publication, review and the right of interested
parties to offer submissions to the agency. Another requirement was that the official record be made available to
persons concerned, except 'information held confidential for
good cause found'. This cause was left to the agency to
determine and was the object of investigations by Congress
from the mid-1950s as to what the agencies were using as
reasons to withhold information. This clause of the 1946 Act
placed the presumption that the information should be
released upon the claimant. He had to show that he was a
person properly and directly concerned and he had no power
to challenge a claim by the agency that they had good cause
to refuse him the information. The 1950s investigations
found that many of the agencies denied information to the
public on the grounds of administrative convenience, and not
because release of the information would cause specific
damage.[20] The consequence of giving discretion to the
agencies was that citizens did not ask for the information
in the hands of the agency since their right to know was
virtually without meaning; it was unenforceable.

The Administrative Procedure Act, then, is part of the
judicialisation of administration. This is legitimated by

the Constitution in the 'due process' clause; the Fifth and
Fourteenth Amendments require 'due process of law' before
federal and state governments can remove from the citizen
'life, liberty or property'. The main elements of due process, as compiled by Schwartz and Wade, are as follows:

> The right to notice, including an adequate formulation
> of the subjects and issues involved in the case;
> The right to present evidence (both testimonial and
> documentary) and argument;
> The right to refute adverse evidence, through cross-
> examination and other appropriate means;
> The right to appear with legal counsel;
> The right to have the decision based only upon evidence
> introduced into the record of the hearing;
> The right to have a written record which consists of a
> transcript of the testimony and arguments, together with
> the documentary evidence and all other papers filed in
> the proceedings.[21]

These have obvious implications for the right to information
and the corresponding illegality of 'secret' administrative
procedures.

As stated earlier, the Administrative Procedure Act requires that all 'adjudications', agency hearings leading to
formal rulings, be based upon a written record which is
available to the parties. This requirement for a written
record does not stem from a belief in 'open decisions, openly
arrived at'; rather it is a consequence of the fact that the
litigants cannot, without special circumstances, be denied
their right to judicial review. This right can only be
exercised if there is some way of discovering how the decision was arrived at, and this requires a written record.

It is the legalism which forced openness, not beliefs in
democracy. This will have important consequences when one
comes to analyse the reasons for the passing of the Freedom
of Information Act. The most important aspect of administrative procedure from the point of view of freedom of information is the requirement that a full record be made of the
proceedings; Section 7, para (d) of the Administrative
Procedure Act states:

> The transcript of testimony and exhibits, together with
> all papers and requests filed in the proceeding, shall
> constitute the exclusive record for decision in accordance
> with Section 8, and, upon payment of lawfully prescribed
> costs, shall be made available to the parties. Where any
> agency decision rests on official notice of material fact

not appearing in the evidence in the record, any party
shall on timely request be afforded an opportunity to show
the contrary.

The consequence of this formalisation of procedure is that
the process produces mountains of paper: it is very time-
consuming, and in the case of agency hearings, although not
welfare ones, it involves considerable expense.[22] It can be
argued that the insistence that all administrative decisions
should correspond to a 'trial' is time-consuming and unnecessary and that, especially in the case of agency hearings, the amount of time and effort means that the agencies
would rather not engage in such a process, but deal with the
'client' informally, leading to the well-known trap into
which agencies can fall of becoming partners of those whom
they are supposed to regulate. The judicial and open nature
of this process is, in my view, a form of compensation for
the fact that there are not clear lines of political responsibility to which these agencies are subject, such that
these techniques become a means of control. The fact that
they are not subject to clear lines of responsibility can be
seen from the fact that the heads of the agencies are
appointed by the President for a fixed period of time. It is
extremely difficult for the President to remove the head of
an agency who is carrying out a policy which he feels is in
conflict with his policies, and yet the agencies regulate
many of the most important areas of the economy.
  Openness in this area, as in so many others, is a replacement of clear lines of political responsibility by legal
means of control, which necessarily imply a higher degree of
'openness' due to the necessity for review.

FREEDOM OF INFORMATION

The discussion of the judicialisation of administration, the
fear of bureaucracy and the attempt to provide the citizen
with access to government information as a response to these
factors, brings one close to the Freedom of Information Act
(hereafter referred to as the FOIA).
  The immediate origins of the FOIA are basically four-fold:
as an extension of due process, as a response to the 'Cold
War', as part of the struggle between Congress and President,
and as a reaction to the increase in the size and complexity
of the federal bureaucracy.
  Openness had already become an important part of what the
courts considered to be fair and good administration. The
principle of due process, however, was concerned with open-

ness as an element of adjudication of the contest between
the individual and his government as to the legality of
government decisions and actions. Openness was part of what
the courts felt constituted a 'fair hearing', and persons
not involved in such a hearing had little right to any
government information. This meant that the basis of government policy and the information which led to that policy
were not accessible to public inspection, except in so far
as they were established by congressional investigation. One
area in particular was inaccessible, that of national security, involving foreign policy, defence and the intelligence
services.

It was in the area of national security that a great deal
of the public and congressional attention was focused when
examining the issue of official secrecy. This is not surprising since American society was, in the 1950s and 1960s,
gradually coming to terms with the implications of its new-
found role as a superpower. An early and oft quoted book on
the subject, *Freedom or Secrecy*, states the problem as
follows:

> [Secrecy] has come about, not by anyone's deliberate
> design or calculated conspiracy, but as a result of fell
> circumstances. It exists because a world in chaos, and in
> imminent threat of destruction, has imposed upon govern-
> ment and citizens disciplines to which they would other-
> wise never consent.[23]

It was only six months after the Senate had passed a motion
of censure against Senator McCarthy in connection with the
loyalty investigations that Congress set up a special subcommittee to investigate executive secrecy. The loyalty
programme had displayed the two contradictory desires of
Congress, to extract information from the executive by the
investigation of the civil service, and the desire to protect State secrets from the 'enemy', world Communism. On
balance, however, the loyalty issue had strengthened the
authority of the executive, as had the censuring of Senator
McCarthy by Congress, the National Security Act and the
Internal Security Act. It is, therefore, possible to see the
congressional decision to investigate executive power and
secrecy as reflecting a desire to readjust the balance which
Congress itself had upset by encouraging executive secrecy.
The absence of any authority within the American political
system which could take responsibility for determining the
balance between secrecy and disclosure must inevitably lead
to swings and fluctuations in attitude.

The Committee, which was created in 1955, was the Special

Government Information Subcommittee of the House Government
Operations Committee, headed by Representative John Moss.
The executive response to the investigations of the Com-
mittee into the Department of Defense was to appoint its own
Committee with the task of examining the executive classification system, under the chairmanship of a lawyer and former
Under-Secretary of Defense, Charles Coolidge. The Coolidge
Committee concluded that there were two main faults with the
classification system - overclassification and leaks. The
Committee argued that the two were interconnected in that
excessive overclassification encouraged an attitude of contempt and disregard for the system, even amongst those
involved in it, and that this was leading to the unauthorised release of classified information. The Committee
recommended that both problems ought to be dealt with: overclassification by restricting the number authorised to
classify, by creating an office of de-classification and by
restricting the secrecy stamp to matters of national security; and leaks, by appointing someone responsible to investigate them by calling newspapermen before grand juries in
order to force them to disclose the origin of the leak, and
by taking speedy and 'stern' disciplinary action against any
employee leaking information. The result of its report was
the creation of an office of de-classification in 1958, and
subsequent Presidents - Kennedy and Nixon - have sought to
reduce the number of those authorised to classify information and to make downgrading of information automatic
(with exceptions at the discretion of the executive) and to
make the criteria for each level of classification more
precise.

Paralleling the work of the Coolidge Committee was a Commission created by law which was sworn in 1956 and was composed of members appointed by the President, Speaker of the
House and President of the Senate (the Vice-President), and
chaired by Mr Lloyd Wright, a prominent lawyer. The main
conclusions of the Wright Commission on the classification
system were that the category 'confidential' should be
abolished and that criminal sanctions ought to be attached
to the unauthorised release of classified information. The
latter recommendation provoked considerable and violent
opposition in the press, which argued that such a law would
prevent the discovery of waste and corruption, and would
create executive censorship. In the event, neither of the
recommendations was implemented.

The Moss Committee is very important in that it created
the climate in Congress which led to the FOIA. The main
thrust of the Moss Committee was the investigation of the
Defense Department, because it considered that the new

American world position had created a serious threat to
democracy at home. The Committee argued that the consequences of defence and foreign policy were too grave to be
left to the executive - and in secret at that. The Committee
stated:

> Never before in our democratic form of government has
> the need for candour been so great. The nation can no
> longer afford the danger of withholding information
> merely because the facts fail to fit a predetermined
> policy.[24]

The Moss Committee's main criticisms were that the executive
misused the national security justification for secrecy as
an umbrella, with which to protect its policies and errors,
that the Housekeeping Statute was used to justify secrecy
when it was not intended to do any such thing, and that
executive statements on the virtues of disclosure were lacking in substance and were mere ritual incantations. The main
achievement of the Moss Committee, apart from changing
attitudes dealt with below, was to produce a change in the
Housekeeping Statute. The Housekeeping Statute of 1789 gave
the head of each federal department the authority to pre-
scribe regulations for the 'custody, use and preservation of
its records, papers, and property appertaining to'.[25] The
Moss Committee considered that this Statute had been used by
the executive to justify the withholding of information and
to create executive secrecy. The Moss Committee proposed a
Bill to the House, a similar Bill being sponsored in the
Senate by the Senate Committee on the Judiciary, which
stated that the Housekeeping Statute did not authorise the
withholding of information from the public. The Bill was
passed by Congress and approved by President Eisenhower in
1958. However, some members of Congress sought various
assurances that the Bill would not jeopardise 'legitimate'
executive secrecy, and there was in 1958 no general move in
Congress to insist on the elimination or severe reduction of
executive secrecy. The Moss Committee in a Report of 1960
admitted that the change in the housekeeping law had had
little effect on executive secrecy.

Another important agent in changing the climate of opinion
was the American press. The American Newspaper Publishers'
Association and Journalists' Association had committees on
freedom of information as early as 1948. According to a
report issued by the Moss Committee in 1960, approximately
one-third of the investigations into executive secrecy undertaken by the Committee were the result of cooperation between
the Committee and the press. Another form which that cooper-

ation took was the protection of the reputation of the press
by Representative Moss. The Wright Commission had sought
criminal penalties for the unauthorised release of classified documents, which were aimed at cutting off a source of
supply of information to newsmen. Moss asked Wright to
provide his Committee with the names of any journalists who
had 'purloined' any classified document, and Wright failed
to provide a single one. Of course the real issue was not
the names of journalists, but whether there had been newspaper stories based upon classified information. However the
challenge by Moss showed the importance which he placed upon
the reputation and freedom of the press. The media in the
United States have attached great importance to freedom of
information and have provided extensive publicity for the
issue, in editorials and books, and in their reporting of
Congress. This played a part in providing an incentive to
Congressmen to support freedom of information in that they
obtained favourable publicity for attacking executive
secrecy.

Senate and House Committees started hearings on an FOIA in
1963, which led to the presentation of a Bill to Congress in
1966 which was then enacted by both Chambers.[26] Most of the
factors which are important to an understanding of the FOIA
have already been mentioned and will not be repeated. However, two issues remain: one is that the executive departments were unanimous in their opposition to an FOIA, and the
second is that freedom of information has not been a partisan issue in Congress.

At the hearings which were held on the consequences of an
FOIA, various members of the executive were asked to testify,
and their objections to the Act can be classified under four
main headings: it was too inflexible; it shifted the balance
of power away from the executive to the judiciary; it placed
excessive burdens upon the executive because of the unlimited quantities of information which could be demanded;
and the exemptions were inadequate to cover all the information requiring protection.[27] The first objection made by
the executive summarises the whole dispute between the
executive and Congress over the issue of access to government information. The executive admitted that the Administrative Procedure Act gave each agency considerable discretion as to what type of information policy it adopted,
and the Moss Committee discovered a wide variation in information policy between the various executive agencies. This
was something which the executive thought desirable and
showed that each agency's policy reflected its particular
circumstances, whilst the Moss Committee saw this as evidence of abuse and that the executive was using its dis-

cretion to refuse to disclose. The executive saw discretion
as enabling it realistically to respond to particular circumstances, whilst the Moss Committee did not trust the executive to exercise its discretion, feeling that the executive
would always refuse access when in any doubt whatsoever.
There are, of course, those who feel that the present FOIA
still leaves too much discretion to the executive.

The FOI Bill was passed by acclamation in the Senate and
by a vote of 307 - 0 in the House. The sponsors of the Bill
made it clear that the FOIA was not a partisan matter and
was not directed against the incumbent President Johnson.
However, it was during his term of office that public concern with the Vietnam War became general, and the phrase
'the credibility gap' was coined. It is difficult to link
the FOIA too closely to the Vietnam War since the Bill had
been discussed in 1963 before public concern had become
acute. However, by 1965 the climate of opinion in the
country was one in which the executive had lost the trust of
the people over its conduct of the war and such a climate of
opinion must have had an effect on the unanimity of approval
with which the Act was received. In the House Debate on the
Bill not one single criticism was made of it.

The 1966 FOIA required the federal administration to adopt
the following procedures: to publish in the Federal Register
a description of its organisation, its functions and rules
of general applicability and to make available for inspection and copying final opinions and orders, statements of
policy and interpretation, and administrative staff manuals.
All other records which are required by the Act to be made
available or published must be indexed. The Act, however,
only required that a current index be kept, so that any
matter dealt with before July 1967 was not required to be
indexed. The Act also provided for the District Courts to
order the production of any agency records improperly withheld and placed the burden of proof that the records have
been properly withheld upon the agency. The Act required,
however, that a request for records be a request for
'identifiable records'. The records not exempt were to be
made 'promptly available'. The Act is limited to private
parties, excluding its use by one agency against another.
Moreover, the Act specifically states that the FOIA does not
provide any authority for the executive to withhold information from Congress.

The Act listed nine exemptions to which the provisions of
the Act would not apply. These were: national defence and
foreign policy; internal personnel rules and practices;
information required by other statutes to be kept secret;
trade secrets and commercial and financial information;

inter-agency or intra-agency memoranda and letters; personnel privacy; investigatory files; reports by any agency
responsible for the supervision of financial institutions;
geological information relating to wells. However, as a
result of the experience gained through application of the
Act, certain amendments were introduced to constrain the
agencies to comply with the spirit of the Act and to reduce
the scope of executive discretion. The main problem arising
as a result of the implementation of the Act was the use of
delaying tactics by the agencies.[28] These took the form of
delays in responding to a request under the Act and in dealing with appeals and with charging varied and excessive fees
in order to deny information to individual requestors. It
was also claimed that the agencies had used the fact that
one part of a document contained information exempt under
the Act to refuse access to any part of the document, and
that they had used the 'identifiable record' requirement as
an excuse to withhold public records. The specific exemptions were found to be inadequate as a guarantee of disclosure in that the courts had interpreted the first exemption, which stated that '[matter] specifically required by
Executive order to be kept secret in the interest of the
national defence or foreign policy', as prohibiting any
determination by the court that material was correctly withheld under this exemption. The courts argued that the word-
ing of the Statute precluded them from being able to determine whether the material ought to be so classified and that
a statement from the executive to this effect was final.[29]
The court ruling meant that for the first time a congressional statute was seen as legitimating executive
secrecy without any requirement relating to 'damage' or to
specific needs for secrecy, but solely to that which had
been seen by newsmen and others as *the* executive excuse,
national security.

The major amendments introduced in 1974 concerned the
following areas: indexing; the imposition of time limits;
uniform fees; disciplinary action; *in camera* inspections;
awarding of fees; revision of exemptions 1 and 7; breakdown
of records; and a requirement that an annual report be submitted to Congress.

One interesting revision concerns the imposition of strict
time limits in replacement of the requirement that records
be made 'promptly available'. These limits require that the
initial response to a request shall be answered within ten
working days and that an appeal shall be answered within
twenty working days. In unusual circumstances relating to a
particular request, the agency may write to the requestor
stating that an extension is necessary, the maximum exten-

sion being a further ten days. It is provided that if the
agency fails to meet these time limits, the requestor is
said to have exhausted the administrative remedies and is
permitted to apply to the court, which will then have jurisdiction in the matter. These time limits were considered to
be unworkable by the agencies themselves and were opposed by
them. The time limits were described by the Department of
State as 'not physically possible', by the Treasury as 'unrealistic', by Defense as 'totally impracticable'. The
Justice Department claimed that they would cause 'unnecessary
work' and the Atomic Energy Commission considered the limits
'unreasonable'; these views were shared by all the agencies
in some form or other.[30] This view was also held by President Ford, who entered office with a pledge to open government but who vetoed the proposed amendments to the FOIA, a
veto which was overthrown by a two-thirds majority of both
Houses. President Ford in his veto message stated that the
time limit requirements were 'simply unrealistic' and that
it was essential that additional latitude be provided. The
argument was that time limits may be appropriate for routine
inquiries or requests for a limited number of documents, but
where a large number of documents had to be checked and a
decision made as to whether all, none or some of the documents were exempt, this was simply unreasonable and would
lead agencies to make hasty decisions simply because of lack
of time to give due consideration to the request.

President Ford also objected to the fact that the courts
were given the statutory right in the amended Act to review
whether a particular classification of a document as secret
was in fact proper, and only in such a case was the document
exempt from disclosure. The President argued that the courts
should not have the authority to overturn an executive
classification which had a reasonable basis. The term
'proper' was considered to be too demanding, in that national
security could be jeopardised because a mistake had been
made in the procedures for classification of a document
which would, therefore, no longer be protected against disclosure. Agencies such as the Departments of State and
Defense argued that the judiciary had no constitutional
right to interfere in judgements of foreign policy or
national security, they had no responsibility for the consequences, nor expertise to make decisions. They claimed that
de novo review would place the courts in these positions and
that therefore the original Act should stand. President Ford
also argued that the requirement that investigative files
must be released unless specific harm can be shown and that
those parts which can be released must be separated from
those parts which cannot, simply could not be done with the

existing personnel, and could not be done within the time
limits allowed.

One interesting aspect of the FOIA is the fact that the
press are not major users of the Act. This was especially so
until the 1974 amendments, when the time limits under which
a request must be processed by an agency were made shorter.
However, the main benefit of the FOIA to the press has been
its existence rather than the need to use it. The press and
agencies know that a refusal to supply information may be
made the subject of court action, which would create damaging publicity for the agency, and that the Act is intended
to create a different climate of opinion within the bureaucracy and to encourage openness. There is every reason to be
helpful to the press, who may exchange one form of cooperation for another.

The effect of the FOIA has not been to alter the nature of
the political decision-making process, although it has
assisted individual citizens to discover the records of
administration. This is part of the process of appeal and
due process characteristic of the judicialisation of administration since the 1930s. It has also assisted special
interests to discover information not only concerning the
government but about each other, which can be seen as part
of the pluralist democracy which many Americans are concerned to preserve, in that it expands the degree of consultation and participation, although mainly at the level of
implementation.

OTHER LAWS RELATING TO GOVERNMENT INFORMATION

The FOIA is not the only Statute which Congress has enacted
relating to the rights of citizens to obtain access to
official information. The three most important are the
Federal Advisory Committee Act, the Privacy Act and the
Government in the Sunshine Act.

The Federal Advisory Committee Act of 1972 lays down
certain rules of procedure for the conduct of all advisory
committees to the federal government, whether established by
the State, the President or by federal agency. For present
purposes the most important feature of the Act is that it
brings advisory committees under the FOIA. The Act also
requires that the public be allowed to attend all meetings
and to request all papers, unless the subject matter of the
advisory committee is concerned with any of the exemptions
listed under the FOIA.

The Privacy Act was passed in 1974 and is not concerned
with protecting a civil right to privacy against other citi-

zens, but with the information held by government on private
citizens. The Privacy Act was seen as extending the protection offered to the citizen by the Fourth Amendment, which
is designed to protect the citizen from improper conduct by
law enforcement officers and, in particular, to ensure their
freedom from unreasonable searches and seizures of their
person, houses and papers. The Act provides that persons
shall have access to personal information contained in federal files and the right to correct or amend such information. It also provides that agencies should be prohibited
from passing information about individuals from one to the
other without the consent of the person, that federal
agencies must disclose the existence of all data banks and
files containing information on individuals. In addition, it
prohibits the keeping of information relating to the exercise of First Amendment rights, except where authorised by
Statute, approved by the individual, or in connection with
law enforcement. The Act also permits an individual to seek
an injunction to correct or amend such a file and to recover
damages where the agency has been negligent. Certain
agencies are exempted from these requirements, namely the
CIA, law enforcement agencies, the Secret Service (the
Presidential protection agency), as are references for federal employment, federal employment tests and historical
archives.

The background to the Act was an investigation by the
Senate Judiciary Committee, which found that the government
held at least one and a quarter billion records containing
personal information, and that some fifty-four agencies had
858 data banks between them.[31] The Committee also claimed
that there were undoubtedly more such data banks which they
had not been able to uncover. It also found that more than
half of the data banks had no explicit statutory basis and
that almost 100 had no statutory authority at all. It was
claimed that most individuals did not know that records were
kept on them, although the agencies knew of the records held
by other agencies and frequently exchanged information with
each other, including information collected under a pledge
of confidentiality, such as that obtained by the Internal
Revenue Service. This Act, then, does not seek to protect
government files from intrusion by non-government sources,
nor does it simply seek to limit the kind of information
which can be collected, except that concerned with politics,
religion and, in general, the exercise of free speech; what
it seeks to achieve is a right of inspection of those files
held by government which contain personal information. The
motivation behind the Act was again fear and suspicion of
the power of bureaucracy. The fear took the form of an appre-

hension that decisions would be made on the basis of inappropriate or false information and that the improved
efficiency offered by data banks should not be at the citizen's expense. Inappropriate information would be, for
example, that someone should be denied social security payments because they were a member of a Black Power movement,
and false information being that someone should not be
denied such payments on the grounds that they were cohabit-
ing without their having an opportunity to refute the record.

There is no conflict in principle between the FOIA and the
Privacy Act since the Privacy Act simply extends the principle of access to one's own records. However, there is a
conflict between openness and privacy in the sense that
others should not have access to records which contain personal information about oneself. The FOIA states that personal, medical and other similar files are exempt where
their disclosure would constitute a 'clearly unwarranted
invasion of personal privacy' (FOIA Subsection (b)(6)).
Personal information which is not held in such a file is not
exempt, even though its release would constitute a serious
invasion of privacy. It is also not sufficient that privacy
be simply affected; the FOIA requires a clearly unwarranted
invasion of such, and the court must balance the factors
involved. It was felt by Congress that to provide a blanket
protection for privacy would provide too broad an excuse for
the executive to withhold information and would therefore
lead to abuse. The courts have tended to demand a strict
interpretation of 'unwarranted invasion' before allowing
that a particular file is exempt from disclosure.

In 1975 Congress enacted a Bill which complements the FOIA,
namely the 'Government in the Sunshine Act'.[32] The essence
of the Act is that it requires independent federal agencies,
though not executive departments, to hold their meetings in
public, unless a majority vote is taken to the contrary. For
the purposes of the Act, an independent agency is one whose
members are appointed with the advice and consent of the
Senate and whose members are not subject to summary presidential dismissal, two famous examples being the Interstate
Commerce Commission and the Security and Exchange Commission.
The Act provides a list of topics which are considered to
provide grounds for a decision to hold an agency session in
private. They range from national security to personnel
rules and practices, law enforcement and commercial matters,
the reasons following very closely the exemptions contained
in the FOIA. The Act also requires that the public be informed of the place and time of meetings and that a record
be kept and those portions not exempt be disclosed. It also
provides for court supervision of the above provisions and,

like the FOIA, places the burden of proof upon the agency.
It also prohibits *ex parte* communications between the agency
and outsiders affected by agency business, requires the
registering of any contact with outsiders and states that
failure to meet these provisions shall be grounds for ruling
against the agency in the event of an appeal against its
decision. The purpose of the Act is to prevent the agencies
being partisan in the decisions they make and from becoming
clients of special interests rather than supervisors of
their activities. The Act is also sensible to provide adequate penalties in the event that the provisions are ignored.

The importance of this legislation is all too easy to
underrate in that it seems less general than the FOIA, but
in terms of the authority of the agencies it may be more
important, especially as it operates before decisions are
made.

CONCLUSION

In conclusion, the balance between secrecy and disclosure in
American government is a product of the growth of executive
authority, which increased fear of executive authority. The
structure of political authority in the United States is
such that the executive has not succeeded in becoming the
sole representative of the people and, therefore, it has not
had the authority to determine the balance between secrecy
and disclosure in accordance with its interests. The executive increase in size, influence and prestige led to a
series of moves by Congress, and others affected by this
rise, to institute new means of scrutinising the actions of
the executive. These were almost all of a legal nature, especially those which have become permanent, and include the
creation of a politically neutral civil service, the attempt
by the courts to control delegated legislation, the loyalty
programme, the Administrative Procedure Act and the Freedom
of Information Act. This is obviously an oversimplification,
however, because in times of crisis, mainly during a war or
threat of war, both the executive and Congress have expressed anxieties concerning the control of government information; but even in crises there has been a reluctance to
give authority to the executive to impose official secrecy,
since it was seen as giving the executive too much authority.
The Freedom of Information Act is just one stage in the
attempt by the American government to solve the problem of
controlling the federal bureaucracy and is part of the
judicialisation of the administration, which can only be

understood in terms of the absence of clear political responsibility for the actions of the bureaucracy. Whether the FOIA has succeeded is the subject of another dissertation, but it is worth noting that under the FOIA the Presidency is not an 'agency of Congress' and is not therefore subject to its provisions, and that given that much of the language used to justify the FOIA was the creation of a public right to know, it can hardly succeed in that objective, given that the Presidency, a powerful source of influence in government, is altogether excluded.

8. Swedish Government and Information

This chapter will deal with the political institutions of Sweden which are relevant to an understanding of the level of disclosure of government information. The first section deals with Swedish political culture, and the later sections with Parliament, the courts and the Ombudsman.

POLITICAL CULTURE

Sweden has been described as being a political system in which politics has become 'depoliticised'.[1] This is defined as being a type of politics in which there is a high degree of consensus within the society and as one in which the élites are coalescent. It is also used to describe a style of politics in which ideological differences are seen as less important compared to the consensus which exists concerning the goals which ought to be pursued: the only remaining debates concern the 'best' technical means for the implementation of the agreed goals. The depoliticisation is also expressed in the wide range of contacts which exist between the various organised interests and between the political parties themselves. The cooperation is reflected in the concentration within Swedish politics upon specific issues and by the isolation of these from one another. It is argued that only at elections, and only as a means of party identification, does ideology become a matter of public discussion. The structure of Swedish government and parliamentary life has encouraged the formation of contacts between the various parties and interests.

The advent of democratic government was achieved without violence, although not without the threat of violence. The spirit of compromise may have been affected by the fact that a class of fiercely independent members of the bourgeoisie has never really existed.[2] The relationship between capital and the state has not been based upon conflict with proud

and independent capitalists refusing to accept interference
in the running of business by any outsider. Although politics in Sweden is still influenced by the usual argument in
capitalist society concerning the use to which the State
should be put and, in particular, its power over private
property, there has not been a tradition in Sweden of resist-
ing an alliance with the State.

The Swedish Social Democratic Party was itself the object
of a battle over whether it should be a party of 'compromise'
or of all-out class war. This situation was in fact resolved
by the decision of the Social Democrats to place the introduction of universal suffrage as a precondition for the
attainment of socialism, but the actual date placed upon the
decision to become a 'reformist' rather than a revolutionary
party is the expulsion of left socialists who had threatened
to call a general strike in connection with the First World
War, in 1917.[3] After this the socialists did not seek the
nationalisation of industry.

Another famous compromise concerned the debate over what
policy should be adopted in response to the depression of
the 1920s. The socialists wished a high level of public
expenditure, whilst the non-socialist parties desired de-
flation with a low level of spending. The answer was a re-
alignment of the parties in that some members of the
agrarian and liberal parties were willing to support a high
level of spending, provided the expansionist policies were
also applied to agriculture. This was agreed.

During the war a National Coalition government was formed
and this was considered by some at the centre of the political spectrum to be so successful that a grand coalition
should become the basis of Swedish politics. However, this
was rejected by both the Social Democrats and the Conservatives. The politics of the post-war period has not, however,
been dominated by a choice between an ideology of 'leave
well alone' as opposed to interventionism. This has meant
that many aspects of the welfare state have been the result
of agreement upon certain basic values across all the main
parties.[4] Politics in Sweden, it is argued, encourages cooperation after a government has been formed and opposition
only at the time of elections. This situation is partly a
result of the organisation of the Riksdag and political
decision-making, and partly because of ideology. The voters
of Sweden see opposition as 'obstructionist' unless it is
opposition to a specific proposal based upon specific,
matter of fact and rational grounds.

THE DEVELOPMENT OF PARLIAMENTARY DEMOCRACY

Although Sweden has a parliamentary system of government, it
has had a far higher level of the separation of powers than
Britain. Although the Swedish cabinet is determined by the
support of the majority in the Riksdag it has been an important ideal that Parliament and the cabinet are separate
institutions with separate functions. The form that this
takes will be outlined during the following section, but
this situation arose because of the fact that those who
wrote the Swedish Constitution of 1809 saw the separation of
powers as part of the creation of a 'liberal' state.[5]

In 1772 King Gustav III carried out a coup against the
domination of the Four Estates and enacted a new constitution which gave more power to the monarch. The domination of
the King by Parliament, the Era of Liberty (1719-72), was
seen as having been an era of great instability and as a
period in which the direct intervention of Parliament in the
administration of the country had produced corrupt and ineffective government. This view was not only the King's view,
but also that of Parliament itself, and of the historians of
the period. It was this view which had important consequences
for the formulation of the Constitution of 1809.

The main principle which underlay the Constitution of 1809
was a balance between the powers of the crown and those of
Parliament. The main issue around which the powers were
divided was that of finance, with Parliament having the sole
authority to raise taxes, and the crown the authority to
determine how the taxes should be spent. A major motive for
the separation and balancing of powers was to create a
system of government in which both absolutism and parliamentary licence were to be avoided.

The next development was the abolition of the Four Estates,
which occurred in 1866 when the Four Estates were replaced
by a two-chamber Parliament. The first chamber was based
upon election by the local assemblies, and the second
chamber upon a limited popular franchise. It was hoped that
the new two-chamber Parliament would reduce the intensity of
the struggles between the office-holders and the wealthy,
and the peasant classes. In the event the two chambers, by
reason of the system of election, polarised precisely along
those lines. The first chamber was elected by indirect means
by the provincial and municipal assemblies, and though these
assemblies were elected by a larger proportion of the population than was the 'popularly elected' second chamber, the
fact that votes for the assemblies were allocated in proportion to taxable wealth ensured that control of the
assemblies went to the wealthiest 2 per cent of the popu-

lation.[6] The electorate of the second, or popular, chamber
was based upon owning land of a certain value, or having a
taxable income of a certain value, and this also restricted
those eligible to vote to the farming, office-holding,
merchant and professional classes. The most important consequence of the two-chamber system lay in the problem it
created for cabinet government.

   The main issue relating to cabinet, Parliament and
elections was whether the cabinet should be determined by
the popular chamber alone, or whether the first, the indirectly elected chamber, should also determine the cabinet.
There was also disagreement as to whether the franchise
should be extended in the case of the first chamber as well
as the second, thereby granting an equal legitimacy with the
second chamber. The Liberal and Socialist parties, which had
formed at the end of the nineteenth century, both took the
view that elections should be on the basis of the majority
principle and that the first chamber should remain oligarchic
but thereby weak. However, the Liberals were willing to
compromise with the Conservative demand that elections
should be based upon the principles of proportionality and
that extensions of the franchise should be undertaken only
if guarantees were provided. These guarantees amounted to an
attempt to maintain the power of the nobility and wealthy
whilst extending the franchise by proportionalism and by
maintaining bicameralism. The 1907 reform removed income and
property restrictions for the second chamber, introduced
proportional representation for both chambers, but retained
multiple voting, with a reduced number of maximum votes, in
elections for the first chamber. This was not finally abolished until 1919. After this change the problems of forming
a cabinet which was responsible to Parliament, to both
chambers, decreased in that there was a greater likelihood
that the party with a majority in the second chamber would
also have a majority in the first. The position remained
basically the same until the introduction of a one-chamber
Parliament in 1970.

   The most important problem created by a two-chamber House
is how decisions are to be made. In Sweden both chambers
voted on the same issue at the same time after a report had
been presented by a committee which contained equal numbers
of members of both chambers.

   However, the principle of simultaneous voting in both
chambers meant that an issue could not be passed by one and
then reviewed by the other; both chambers had to attempt to
resolve their differences in committee. This had the effect
of reducing the importance of debate on the floor of the
chamber and of encouraging a spirit of compromise within the

committees, as both chambers knew that a successful vote was possible only if the recommendation of the joint committee was followed.[7] Every legislative proposal goes to a committee for consideration and report, and it is seen as the constitutional function of these committees that they scrutinise proposals in an independent way. This is especially true of government proposals. Membership of these committees may be of long standing and may produce considerable expertise, which lends respect to their deliberations and leads to a situation in which ' ... seldom are decisions made which do not accord with the recommendations of a committee (or of a strong minority within it)'.[8] Membership of the committee is decided according to the proportion of seats held by each party. Membership is therefore determined by the parties and not, as was the case before 1909, by election by the chambers. This means that the role of the committees is not such an 'obstacle' to party government as would appear from the Constitution, in that the party in office will also have a majority of the members of the committees. There is one way, however, in which the 'independence' of these committees is maintained and which may be considered to be an obstacle to party government, namely the proscription upon Ministers attending or addressing these committees. It is considered that the committees are able to obtain the information they need concerning government thinking by means of the detailed proposals which are submitted by the government. This attitude is a reflection of the attempt by Parliament to be free of the King's influence in the days before party government. This 'independence' is further protected by the fact that the deliberations of the committee are closed, that no verbatim record of the proceedings is kept, and that the deliberations of the committee remain secret until the publication of their report. It is considered that these precautions ensure that the committees will be characterised by what the Swedes call *saklighet*, which approximates to 'objectivity', 'independent reasoning'.

From the reform of the first chamber in 1918 until the victory of the Social Democrats in 1936, the governments of Sweden were characterised by either minority or non-political civil service cabinets. In Sweden this did not take the form of actual coalition governments, but rather the formation of understandings concerning the legislation which would be supported by one of the other parties.

One factor which may have affected the viability of these loose coalitions is that under the Swedish Constitution, the power of the Prime Minister to dissolve Parliament is limited. This is mainly a consequence of the fact that the length of time for which each Parliament runs is set by the

Constitution - at present it is three years. Should the
government order new elections during the three years, any
assembly elected at those elections will sit only for the
remainder of the three-year period. This means that a member
elected at an extra election called by the government in its
second year of office will sit for only one year before
having to contest the seat yet again. The government is also
constrained in its use of the dissolution power by a clause
in the Constitution which states that no extra election can
be called for a period of three months after any previous
election. The consequence of this system is that the government is effectively deprived of a political or tactical
weapon and is evidence of the Swedish tendency to reduce
such weapons to a minimum.

PARLIAMENT AND DISCLOSURE

Parliament has important rights of access to official information. This, however, is achieved not through the parliamentary question but rather through the work of standing committees, which are composed of members of all the major
parties.
    There existed in the 1809 Constitution a clause prohibit-
ing the consideration or investigation by the Riksdag of the
decisions of officials, the judgement of executive and
judicial authorities, the private affairs of citizens, or
the execution of any law. This was a serious prohibition
upon the powers of the Riksdag to ask questions or investigate the executive when the separation of powers was a
reality and the government was appointed by the King, and
was not based on parliamentary support. However, the more
Sweden has moved to a majority party system of government,
the less of a prohibition has the clause been. The relatively late rise of parliamentary questions can be seen from
the fact that a specific time was not set aside for the
answering of such questions until 1964. There are, by tradition, two main types of question which may be asked -
interpolations which relate to matters of policy and the
more 'political' issues, and ordinary questions which are
meant to elicit matters of fact. The old rules were as
follows. In the case of an interpolation, the House was free
to debate the matter once the answer had been given, but in
the case of ordinary questions a vote of the House had to be
taken before the question could be debated. They have since
been revised such that in the case of an interpolation any
member may ask supplementary questions, whilst in the case
of an ordinary question only the member who put the question

and the Minister who replied may question and reply. A
Minister may refuse to answer a question, although he must
make a statement giving his reasons for so doing after a
period of four weeks. One may argue that the main reason why
questions have never assumed importance is due to the absence of ministerial responsibility for administration, in
the sense that most of the administration is not under his
direct control, but more important than this in my view is
the fact that questions are not related to votes of no
confidence. Questions have never been used to embarrass a
Minister or to show that he is lacking in wisdom or political finesse, since the consequences of this could not have
been the downfall of a Minister or the embarrassment and
downfall of a government.

Question time has not been used to show that the government is full of weak and vacillating men unaware of what is
happening in their ministries or the country, that is for
the purposes, not of eliciting information but of exposing
the government as politically unfit to govern, and this is
because of the absence of the motion of no confidence. This
was not allowed by the Constitution until recently. The 1809
Constitution prohibited the Riksdag from expressing mere
opinions on a vote which did not lead to some other form of
action, such as the passing of a law. Under the revised
Constitution of 1974 it is now possible to declare that a
particular Minister, including the Prime Minister, does not
have the confidence of the House and in those circumstances
the Minister must be removed. However, it is only in the
event of the Prime Minister being discharged that the government falls, and in other cases a Minister may be discharged
without this affecting the life of the government as a whole.
The object of this clause is to replace the archaic procedure of impeachment and is not intended to be used for
political ends, but to get rid of an incompetent or dis-
honest Minister. The object is not to make the bringing down
of the government the main task of the opposition.

The right of impeachment was related to the right of the
Standing Committee of the Constitution to examine the minutes of the King's Council.[9] The King's Ministers were
responsible on an individual basis for the advice which they
gave to the King and the Parliamentary Committee on the
Constitution could initiate a criminal prosecution against
a Minister, the prosecution being undertaken by the
Ombudsman. The minutes of the King's Council not only
contained a record of its decisions, but also of the advice
which was offered by the Ministers. It was also a requirement of the Constitution that any dissent be minuted; otherwise, each was held responsible for the advice as if he had

proposed it. The possibility of criminal sanctions was only
resorted to for a brief period: it was last used in 1854 and
was unsuccessful on this as on all four previous occasions.
The Committee could also ask the King to remove one of his
Ministers if the advice which had been given was not, in the
eyes of the Committee, impartial and in the true interest of
the State. These rules are no longer in force (1974 revised
Constitution) and in terms of the reality of parliamentary
government they have long been archaic.

What they do indicate is the tradition that Parliament is
expected to be impartial in its scrutiny of the activities
of government, and although this has obviously declined with
the advent of majority party governments it is still part of
the culture of the House that the committees ought not to be
mere 'hacks'. This conviction is part of the basis of self-
respect which sustains Members of Parliament. It also highlights the importance of individual responsibility to the
law as an integral part of the development of 'popular control' of government and the extent to which the Swedes, at
least on paper, have sought to retain that continuity. The
access of the Committee to the State Papers of the King's
Council is particularly important in the light of the fact
that the members of the cabinet, its papers and its decisions, are not subject to review by either the courts or
the Ombudsman. This can be illustrated by an example based
upon the cabinet's right to classify certain papers as
secret on the grounds of national security which, given the
immunity from review which decisions of the cabinet possess,
would not be subject to any scrutiny were it not for the
right of the Committee on the Constitution to have access to
the minutes of the King's Council and to call for all papers
relevant to the matter under investigation. Certain matters,
however, used to be kept on separate minutes - for example,
foreign policy and matters of military command - and these
could be refused to the Committee. Since 1974 all such
minutes are available. The scrutiny of the decisions of the
Council (cabinet) by a Committee composed of representatives
of the various parliamentary parties has political overtones
The majority, or government party, is unlikely to accept
criticisms of its own Ministers and there have been several
cases in which the Committee has been very closely divided
along party lines over whether to criticise a Minister. However, it has been argued that these Committees have a role
which is based upon the scrutiny of the activities of
Ministers as administrators, rather than as political advisers to the crown, i.e. the government.

As stated earlier, these Committees meet in secret, so
there is no right of the public to have access to the docu-

ments which are at the disposal of the Committee; however, information is produced in the form of the report of the Committee, and the Committee does have the right to release those documents in its possession, especially if a criticism of a Minister is made. The Committees are assisted by members of the State administration being seconded to them. The purpose of these experts is to provide the Committee with the background to any proposal which it may be considering, and this also provides the Committee with access to the thinking and experience of civil servants.

The Swedish Parliament has some of the characteristics of the British Parliament and some of the United States Congress. However, the similarity with the US Congress is the more important to an understanding of the Swedish Parliament's attitude to government information. The absence of a system of ministerial responsibility, of which more in the subsequent chapter, the importance of Committees and the remnants of a system of separation of powers all produce a situation in which Parliament would view government as being only partly a matter of politics. The Riksdag, unlike Congress, does not see itself as acting as an opposition to the executive, but neither does it see itself as a divided legislature in which the primary duty is either to oppose or support the Ministers in office. The Swedish Parliament views itself as often being engaged in debates which are concerned with matters which do not affect the rise and fall of the government, and thus views much information as being politically neutral. Information defined as politically neutral does not need the protection of secrecy.

THE POSITION OF THE COURTS

In Sweden the ordinary courts of law have little to do with the State since the review of administrative acts has long been seen as being part of the system of administration, rather than a duty of the ordinary courts. The tradition in Sweden has been that the rule of law in the sphere of State action is best preserved by means of a system of judicial or quasi-judicial appellate bodies within the administrative hierarchy itself. From a very early date Swedes have enjoyed the right to 'go to the King' when they wish to contest any administrative action.

In the nineteenth century two developments took place which led, in 1909, to the creation of a new institution, the Supreme Administrative Court, which took over many of the appellate activities of the King in Council. The two were, the politicisation of the cabinet (the King in Council),

and the sheer number of cases with which the cabinet had to
deal.[10] The Supreme Administrative Court is the final court
of administrative appeal concerning the actions of the
administration, especially in so far as the appeals are concerned with the legality of administration actions. The
government itself still hears appeals against the decisions
of the cabinet or Ministers, especially in so far as such
appeals are concerned with the exercise of discretion.[11] However, one consequence of this division is that no body,
other than the government itself, has the right to review
the actions of Ministers, since the ordinary courts and the
administrative courts are excluded from this role.

As well as the Supreme Administrative Court, there also
exists the right to appeal against a decision of an administrative body to the next rung in the administrative hierarchy, except where statute requires that an appeal must be
made to an administrative court.

A general rule governing all appeals, either to administrative courts or to a superior authority, is that the
appellate body has the same powers as the body appealed
against. That is, the appellate body cannot only assess the
legality of the action but also the quality of the decision
and may not only overturn the decision but may also replace
it with one of its own.[12] This stems from the fact that the
system of appeal is part of, and has the same powers as, the
administrative authorities. One advantage of the Swedish
system of appeals is that the appellate bodies do not seek
to emulate the procedures of ordinary courts of law. This
means that the administrative courts will normally base
their decisions upon written submissions, and the appellant
is not obliged, and very often does not, use legal counsel.
The court has a duty actively to seek out the appellant's
case and to frame it in legal terms, if this has not already
been done.

The ordinary courts of law, as stated above, have little
importance in understanding the legal control of administration. It is a general principle of Swedish administrative
law that the ordinary courts are prohibited from reviewing
administrative decisions, and it is only if administration
happens to be the arena for some private or criminal case
that the ordinary courts may become involved with administration.[13] Such cases are those concerning contracts,
salaries, those where an indictment is being sought for
failure to obey an administrative order, suits for damages
against officials, or, traditionally of the greatest importance, prosecutions of officials for neglect of duty. The
reason for the qualification 'traditionally' is that in 1976
the number of actions for which a civil servant was crimi-

nally liable was reduced. This further reduces the number of
occasions on which ordinary courts will deal with cases
relating to administration.

The importance of the above analysis for the argument is
not that the courts force the government to reveal more
information than they would wish (although more of this in
the next chapter), but rather that it shows the Swedish
attitude towards administration. The Swedes do not consider
that administration is a part of the political system, but
rather part of the legal one. Government administration is
treated as requiring the qualities of impartiality and
independence similar to that of the judiciary. The division
between politics, administration and the law is different in
Sweden from either Britain or the United States. In Sweden
administration is seen as quasi-judicial in nature and not
quasi-political. In Sweden there is considerable judicialisation of administration, but this has not been imposed by
courts - rather, it has evolved with the notion of a constitutional state. The judicialisation of administration was,
and is, seen as being a safeguard of the citizen's rights
and liberty, and this has led to the creation of a system of
administration in which the principles of legal responsibility and legal accountability are enshrined within the
administration itself. It is in this context that disclosure
of government information must be understood.

THE ROLE OF THE OMBUDSMAN

Another institution which is part of the judicialisation of
administration is the *Justitieobudsman*, the Ombudsman. The
office of Ombudsman was created in the Constitution of 1809
as the agent of Parliament with the duty of supervising
civil and judicial administration. The office of Ombudsman
is based upon one of the principles of Swedish constitutional
government, the responsibility of public officials to the
law. One of the main tasks of the Ombudsman is to investigate complaints against the work of the Central Administrative Boards. In the past this meant enforcing the law
against individual state employees. This reflected the individual responsibility of each state employee for the
decisions which he made. It also reflected the fact that
each state employee had security of tenure in that dismissal
required court action.

However, it was accepted by Parliament in the middle of
the nineteenth century that prosecution in the courts was a
very heavy-handed way of dealing with minor infractions of
good practice by state employees, and that a public repri-

mand may be sufficient; this was made part of the Parliamentary Directives governing the conduct of the office of the
Ombudsman in 1915.[14] The Constitution of Sweden, however,
did not expressly include criticism as part of the duties of
the Ombudsman, his duty being defined in terms of prosecution, and the change led to a debate over the position of the Ombudsman. In 1915 and in the 1950s, Members of
Parliament argued, unsuccessfully, that public criticism
without prosecution failed to give the admonished official
the right to test the case before a judge and that therefore
the Ombudsman would be acting as both prosecutor and judge
in the same case.[15] At present the Ombudsman is required to
present the complaint to the official concerned and to give
the official a chance to reply, but in terms of the canons
of natural justice or due process, and especially if this
leads to an official being denied promotion or some other
such loss, one can understand the objection. In a way this
situation arises because the Ombudsman is an institution
which arose under a set of circumstances which no longer
exist and from the attempt to adapt an old institution to
new circumstances.

It is recognised by the Ombudsman that his role is increasingly concerned with good administrative practice, as well
as with individual responsibility to the law, and such
practice may not be the responsibility of any one individual.
In order to maintain the usefulness of the office and make
it responsive to the demands of citizens, it has been
necessary to allow criticism to be made without a prosecution being instituted. The authority of the Ombudsman is,
however, limited to issuing admonishments, advice or prosecution; he is not able to instruct an official to alter his
decision, although he can suggest that an individual be
compensated or that redress be made. This aspect of the
Ombudsman's work led to adverse comment, particularly in the
1950s. It was claimed that the Ombudsman was attempting to
instruct officials to compensate persons he felt had been
aggrieved by suggesting that his decision not to prosecute
was dependent upon compensation being forthcoming. One case
applied to judges of a Court of Appeal and in another an
Ombudsman wrongly requested that compensation be made: the
Ombudsman had no recourse other than to refund the money
which had been paid out in compensation upon his request.[16]

The nature of the institution of the Ombudsman has changed
over time in that election to the office was more of a
political affair than it has now become, due to the fact
that in the nineteenth century, before the advent of parliamentary government, the Ombudsman acted as the prosecutor in
cases of impeachment brought by the Constitutional Committee

of Parliament against the highest members of the judiciary
and against the members of the Council of State. However,
the Ombudsman has not been asked to bring such a case since
1853. The Ombudsman has also become more restrained about
making suggestions for changes in the law, which he is entitled to make, since the advent of parliamentary government,
and the present Ombudsmen seek to make their office as
apolitical as possible.

THE OMBUDSMAN AND DISCLOSURE

In principle the Ombudsman could be a considerable producer
of information, in that he has a statutory right to have
access to every document held by all public authorities;
this includes the army and the courts, as well as the administrative bodies and the municipalities. The only documents from which the Ombudsman is excluded are those relating to the work of cabinet Ministers, members of the Riksdag
and municipal councils, that is those elected representatives
holding public office. The Ombudsman has the right to
investigate at his discretion, he does not need to wait for
a complaint to be made, and his investigation need not be
restricted to the initial complaint but can be extended to
cover the activities of a particular office or agency, and
to cover all decisions of a certain type. The Ombudsman used
to have a duty to carry out inspections of certain public
authorities, but in 1975 this duty was modified in order to
limit the amount of work handled by the Ombudsman; now the
Ombudsman need only inspect those authorities which he
believes are unsatisfactory. The idea for an investigation
or inspection may come about through press reports, receiving a number of complaints concerning the same authority,
or simply because of a lapse of time since the last inspection. The Ombudsman has the right to receive complaints from
anyone; this includes public officials, elected representatives and non-nationals. The complainant need not have any
special standing in order to make the complaint, nor is
there a time limit upon the period by which a complaint must
be made, although if it is later than two years then the
Ombudsman can refuse, if he believes the issue is not one of
wider public interest. It is also not necessary that all
other remedies be exhausted before a complaint is made. As
well as access to all documents, the Ombudsman must be given
whatever lawful assistance he demands when investigating a
case; therefore he has the right to investigate on the spot
and to interview those personnel concerned. These powers
could give the Ombudsman the potential to 'reveal' almost

all state secrets; however he is not obliged to produce the
evidence that he used in making his decision; he does not
act as a court of law, he either acts as a special prosecutor or as a superior disciplinary officer. He acts to re-
assure the public, not by establishing the thoroughness and
justice of his case in public, but by the impartiality and
prestige of the office.[17] When the Ombudsman acts as a
special prosecutor, his case is brought into open court and
is dealt with by the courts as is any other criminal prosecution, in public. This was an important mechanism in the
establishment of the prestige of the office, as was the fact
that the Ombudsman was often a judge from a high court and
was always a respected legalist.

The Ombudsman does, however, produce information which
would not otherwise be available, and this takes the form of
summaries of his investigations. For instance, the Ombudsman
investigated allegations that the Swedish intelligence service had collaborated with foreign services, had engaged in
unlawful surveillance, and had infiltrated informers into
political and other organisations. Although the Ombudsman
did not give any details of what the documents contained, or
the results of his interviews, he did state that certain
operations were performed involving foreign citizens within
the realm and that domestic intelligence activities were a
cause for concern. The danger in relying upon the Ombudsman
and the integrity of his office is that such matters will
not be disposed of to the satisfaction of those who see such
matters as being of a political nature, involving the integrity and nature of government. In other words, the nearer
the Ombudsman approaches a politically sensitive area -
entirely excluding the activities of the cabinet, of course -
the more he places his integrity in jeopardy. The closer he
stays to everyday matters, the more he acts as an ordinary
superior would act in any hierarchical organisation. It is
argued that because he is independent, his criticism carries
greater weight and that he is necessary because Swedish
civil servants have such a high level of individual responsibility that they are not subject to hierarchical control. It
is true that in a normal system of hierarchical control,
those superiors who are criticising their subordinates are
not independent and may, because they are also partly responsible for the decisions, be less likely to criticise the
actions of their subordinates than someone outside, but it
must be remembered that the Ombudsman is, so to speak, an
occasional or emergency superior, not a regular and routine
part of a system of supervision. The latter is considered to
be more desirable in most administrations because of the
need for ensuring regularity and equality and conformity of

decisions. Of course, to have an Ombudsman as well as this
may be desirable, but in Sweden, at least in theory, it is
because this system of supervision is lacking that the
Ombudsman exists. This is compounded, as will be seen in the
following chapter, by the absence of subordination to an
'outside authority' such as a Minister or other elected
representative who has the power to intervene and modify
decisions that he considers to be wrong. This possibility is
far more limited in Sweden than in Britain or the United
States. However, in terms of 'hard fact' the Ombudsman does
not extend citizen access to information to any great extent.

CONCLUSION

This chapter has sought to establish that Parliament, the
courts and the Ombudsman all operate on the principle that
there are large areas of apolitical government activity
which do not threaten the government's authority or prestige.
The other principle upon which all three operate is that
there are many areas of government which are judicial or
quasi-judicial in nature and that the law is the most appropriate method of controlling such areas. The courts and the
Ombudsman are excluded from interfering in the workings of
administration, except in so far as they act as appeal
bodies. However, when they do have the authority to intervene, they are not restricted by any need to determine 'fact
and law'; they have the right to comment upon the advisability of the decision as well as its legality. It is also
the case that the political culture of Sweden is based upon
the view that many activities of government are not ideological, not political, and that objectivity, reason, consultation and compromise are the most appropriate values to
apply. One other fact which has been established is that
none of these institutions is a significant producer of
government information. None of them has, as a main duty, to
struggle with the government to extract from it information
which otherwise it would choose not to reveal. It is not
through competition and political struggle that Sweden is an
open society. The description and explanation of why Sweden
has the level of disclosure of government information it
does is the subject of the following chapter.

9. Secrecy, the Law and the Civil Service in Sweden

Sweden is of particular interest because it was the first State to establish a right of citizen access to government documents. There are, however, two points which must be made.

  There is no hierarchy of authority from the lowest civil servant to the most senior Minister, and this raises the question of to whom, and how, civil servants are made responsible. The second point is that Swedish civil servants were, until recently, individually legally responsible for their administrative acts. Given these two elements, disclosure of government documents becomes not only comprehensible but also, one could claim, necessary. One other important fact is that the legislation establishing the right of access to government documents was introduced before the advent of popular government. It was part of the parliamentary attempt to create a 'liberal' rather than a democratic polity. Disclosure of government documents was something that democracy inherited rather than created. The motive for the creation of such a right was suspicion of the crown by Parliament during a period of parliamentary ascendancy. These facts raise doubts about the connection between legislation granting citizens access to government documents and democracy, just as much as the lack of such access does in some contemporary democratic societies.

THE ORIGIN OF THE PUBLICITY PRINCIPLE

The period during which the publicity principle was established is known as the Era of Liberty (1719-72) and is a period in which the Swedish Riksdag or Parliament was dominant over the monarchy.

  The politics of this era were determined by a struggle between two political 'parties', the Hats and the Caps. The names derived from the fact that one group, who considered themselves to be adventurous, labelled their more cautious

rivals the 'nightcaps'. The Caps may be compared to Whigs
and the Hats to Tories. The Hats supported a mercantilist
economic policy, sought to restrict recruitment to the civil
bureaucracy to the nobility, disapproved of attacks upon
aristocratic privileges, and sought a restrictive political
and ecclesiastical censorship. The Caps tended to be of the
lesser nobility and the newly ennobled bourgeoisie, and
although they were also mercantilist they tended to be more
radical, supporting greater economic freedom, equality within
the bureaucracy, freedom of assembly, and of the press.[1]
    Despite the fact that the Riksdag was by no means represen-
tative, it did incorporate important elements of a parliamentary constitutional government and may, therefore, be seen
as a liberal polity. Among the elements introduced were the
insistence that the King should only rule in accordance with
the advice of the Council of the Realm, that the policies of
the Council should not be contrary to those of the Estates,
that the representatives of the Estates should be subject to
election by the provincial assemblies, and that there should
be a constitutional guarantee of the freedom of the press,
except on theological matters. The Freedom of the Press Act
of 1766 was introduced by the Caps after the election of
1764 and was a response to the use of censorship by the Hats
during the previous twenty years when they had been in power.
The Freedom of the Press Act, however, not only gave the
press the right to publish without government control, but
also included a clause providing for free access to government archives and for the taking of copies of the documents
contained in them. This right to inspect documents was not
as comprehensive as the present one, although it does share
the most important characteristic with the modern Act, which
is that this right is given to every citizen. It is not
possible, according to Nils Herlitz, to extract from the
existing sources an exact explanation of the reasons for
extending this right to all citizens, as opposed to Parliament alone. However, the ideology of the Caps and their
suspicion of bureaucracy and of monarchy provide the background to the Act.
    The Caps' suspicion of bureaucracy stemmed from the fact
that higher positions were the monopoly of the nobility and
by the fact that the Hats had barred commoners from advanc-
ing to the highest positions within the bureaucracy by
prohibiting the creation of new peers. The Caps also resented the number of officials with seats in the Riksdag who
were there by virtue of the monopoly of the nobility upon
such positions. There had also been an attempted royal coup
in 1756. The object of the coup was a return to absolutism
and the reimposition of royal control of the Council of the

Realm. The coup failed, however, and only provided grounds
for suspicion of royal motives within the Riksdag. Freedom
of the press and access to documents were part of a desire
to reduce the power of the monarch and the high nobility and
to prevent a re-emergence of this power without public aware-
ness. The fundamental motive, then, was suspicion.

THE STRUCTURE OF THE CIVIL SERVICE

The most striking difference between Britain and Sweden is
the absence of a concept of ministerial responsibility. The
concept of ministerial responsibility is best understood as
a dual hierarchy, one internal to the government administration and ending in the Minister, the other consisting in
the responsibility of the Minister to Parliament, for all
those who are responsible to him.

In Sweden, a Cabinet Minister is not held responsible for
administration, for he is not the head of a hierarchy whose
duty is the administration of government policy. Before the
advent of 'popular' government, administration was a matter
for the King, who appointed his own Ministers and adminis-
tered in accordance with the law. It is the latter concept
of responsibility to the law which has been the central
pillar of Swedish theory concerning the responsibility of
both Ministers and state employees. The development of
parliamentary government in Sweden did not lead to a subordination of administration to Parliament. The 1809 Constitution recognised the separation of powers, and although
this effectively ended with the completion of parliamentary
democracy in 1918, the institutional framework and the
culture derived from an earlier period persisted.

With the advent of universal suffrage, some of these
institutions were adapted, some ignored, but the principle
that administration should not be subordinate to a political
master has always been accepted in Sweden. Any move to
change this is rejected as an attempt to 'politicise' what
ought to be non-political acts. Swedes argue that the security of the citizen is best protected by ensuring the
'independence' of administration. It is felt that this has
been the best safeguard against an attempt by a monarch to
misuse his power, and that it was also a protection against
the misuse of political power by a democratically elected
government in attempting to interfere directly in the
decisions made by those whose duty it was to carry out the
law. This 'independence' of administration is instituted in
the fact that the ministries are small, with some 2000
persons in total, whilst the Central State Boards, who carry

out government administration, are staffed by many hundreds of thousands of employees. The independence of these Boards was first recognised in the Instrument of Government Act of 1634 and has only been subject to question at the beginning of this century when popular government was introduced and when the Socialists felt that the independent Boards were too conservative and would therefore have to be brought under direct control.[2] However, they had neither the political authority nor the support of the political culture for such a change. Before discussing the relationship between these Boards, Parliament and the government, I will describe the relationship between these Boards and the Law.

THE CIVIL SERVICE AND THE LAW

One of the mainstays of the legal control of administration was the individual legal liability of each state employee for his own decisions. The Swedish Penal Code, until 1976, made neglect of duty a criminal offence. This, it is argued, means that an employee not only has to consider how his actions look in the eyes of his superiors, but also how they may look to a judge. This in turn produces a 'judicial' frame of mind within state employees.[3] Indeed, before the days of the 'interventionist' state there was little difference between judicial and administrative decisions, and law was considered the natural training for a career in administration. Another parallel between the judiciary and administration was that both, from an early date, had security of tenure: employees could only be dismissed by court action for having committed a criminal act. The judiciary and administrators also shared a similar class background in that both tended to be from the nobility; indeed, the higher positions in the State administration were reserved for members of the nobility. It was an important fact of Swedish political life, especially until the advent of full democracy, that the nobility who constituted one of the Four Estates of Parliament, and supplied many of the State administrators, played an active part in political life. This was also true of judges. It is also the case that neither judges nor state employees are restricted in any way from exercising the normal rights of citizenship, such as participation in politics, expression of political views, membership of any political party, or membership of Parliament. The above facts are important when considering the consequences of the 'publicity' rule which 'exposes' the opinions of the State administrators and therefore brings them into the political arena. They have never been excluded

from that arena. In Britain, I have argued, the exclusion of
civil servants from that arena was seen as a necessary consequence of the move to full democratic government.

Tenure is no longer a matter of the Constitution, but part
of budget legislation; however, security still exists for
most employees except the highest officials. It is also the
case that since 1 January 1976, the element of criminal
liability of civil servants has been reduced. This simply
took the law into line with practice, in that superiors were
reluctant to discipline their subordinates by use of the
courts, and had for years relied upon internal discipline
procedures. Criminal sanctions were retained in three areas,
however: breaches of the duty of silence; bribery; and
severe breaches of duty such as illegal seizure of property
or illegal arrest. The responsibility of individual civil
servants to the law, allied to security of tenure, was seen
as ensuring the legality of administration and the independence and impartiality of administration. Given this
separation of administration from politics, it was not seen
as necessary to restrict administrators from taking an active
part in political life. The problem of a civil servant
having to be responsible to masters of differing political
views did not arise, since he was not responsible to them in
the first instance. In Sweden, the law and public accountability are seen as the mechanisms for ensuring that administration is responsible to the people.[4]

POLITICAL CONTROL OF THE ADMINISTRATION

The independence of Swedish administration creates an
apparent problem in that the government appears to be incapable of ensuring that its policies are executed. Apart
from legal responsibility and security of tenure, the main
form which independence takes is that Ministers are unable
to issue instructions to the Boards as to the decisions they
make in particular cases. The Boards have autonomy of interpretation in most routine applications of the law, except
where the government is given a right to intervene by
statute. The government's principal means of instructing the
Boards is in its attempt to ensure that its legislative
programme will be passed by Parliament and that the laws
which the Boards carry out express its desires. The government can also lay down certain duties upon these Boards in
terms of their structure and finance, which provide additional means of control. The Boards do not raise finance
and their budget is determined by the government. The
government may also require that the Boards adopt 'good

administrative practice' and can inspect them to ensure this
is carried out. The government also appoints the Heads of
the Boards in whose name decisions are made. The Heads of
the Boards are always appointed under the auspices of the
appropriate Minister and, although the appointments are not
normally rewards for party service, they are almost always
given to people who share the government's political
persuasion. This makes informal consultation between Boards
and the ministries somewhat easier, and this is normally
sufficient to circumvent the rather cumbersome process of
issuing government decrees, even where they are provided for.

It is obvious that in practice there may be little difference between the disinterest of a British Minister in the
routine decisions made by his department, and the formal
disinterest required of his Swedish counterpart. However,
the lack of a system of ministerial responsibility does have
important consequences for the publicity principle, in that
openness is seen as a necessary safeguard, given the absence
of a hierarchy of control leading to elected representatives.
It leads to a different principle of accountability of
officials, although it is difficult to judge whether one
system is more or less democratic than another.

THE PUBLICITY PRINCIPLE

Many of those who have compared the Swedish laws on access
to official documents with those of their own country have
been impressed and astonished at the apparent openness with
which government business is conducted. This has led them to
the conclusion that the high level of secrecy which they see
in their own country is unnecessary. They see the lack of
secrecy in Sweden as conclusive evidence that democratic
government does not require a high level of secrecy and that
all the arguments which suggest that this is the case are
false. However, what this fails to recognise is that the low
level of secrecy, granting that this is the case for the
moment, may be dependent upon the specific way in which
democracy is expressed, and that the adoption of Sweden's
laws concerning the availability of government documents may
also require the adoption of other Swedish institutions
which provide the context within which these laws operate.
It is my belief that the openness of Swedish government
reflects particular arrangements of political authority and
responsibility.

The publicity rule is part of a Constitutional Act which
is known as the Freedom of the Press Act. The status of the
Act means that it cannot be altered, except by the decision

of two Parliaments, separated by an election and voting upon
an identical motion.

The law on availability of documents is, in principle,
very simple.[5] All 'official' documents are available for
inspection and/or copying. The term 'official' applies to
any document which may be held by a public authority, including Parliament, the government and its ministries, the
courts, State and Municipal Authorities, and all Authorities
'which constitute integral parts of the State administration'.[6] The rules even apply to the General Assembly of
the State Church. They do not apply, however, to public
corporations, which are defined as commercial enterprises.
The word 'document' is also interpreted in a very wide sense
and includes recorded information, which may be read only by
means of technical aids, as well as maps, pictures, drawings
and normal State papers. There are, however, problems as to
when a particular document becomes 'held' by an authority,
and thereby becomes 'official'. The main problem is that the
Act does not specify whether all pieces of paper, or other
means of recording information, must be retained and not
destroyed; rather it states that the public only has access
to those that are retained and have been 'taken care of for
the purpose of being filed'.[7] This licence to destroy,
which may be removed by other statutes or decrees, refers to
internal memoranda and these are not considered to be
official documents until the case or matter has been finally
settled and the papers 'taken in charge'; that is, when
minutes have been signed or decrees are ready for use. The
Supreme Administrative Court of Sweden ruled, in 1971, that
where an internal working document contained facts which
formed a part of the case or matter, then the document
should not be destroyed. This was added as a requirement
under the amendments to the Freedom of the Press Act in 1976.
This duty is one, however, which is obviously difficult to
enforce and is potentially open to abuse.

There is, however, a rule concerning the despatch and
receipt of documents by an authority which serves as a way
of ensuring that some internal working documents come to
light before a case or matter is finally settled. It is that
documents received by an authority become 'official' documents, as do those which have been despatched by an authority. This means that those memoranda which pass from one
authority to another have the status of official documents
and, therefore, become subject to the rules of publicity.

However, it is also the case that what many people in
other countries would consider a private letter, that is,
any letter written by them about a personal matter, is considered to be an official document. It becomes an official

document when it is received by an authority under the rule
stated above.

It is important, however, to realise that although belonging to the category of official document is a necessary step
if the publicity rules are to apply, it is by no means the
case that all documents which are official are in fact available for public inspection. There are exceptions to the
general principle such that certain documents are 'officially
secret'.

OFFICIAL SECRECY

The basic exceptions to the requirement of public access to
official documents are laid down in the Freedom of the Press
Act and these principles of secrecy form the criteria according to which more detailed laws of secrecy are formulated.
There are four main areas which are considered to need the
protection of secrecy: national security and foreign affairs;
suppression of crime and illegality; protection of legitimate economic interest; and personal privacy. However, the
interpretation of these general categories is not left to
the courts or to the administrator: they are simply taken as
the basis according to which Parliament then specifies in
greater detail the type of documents which are to have the
protection of the law. The detailing of the type of documents to be protected used to be done in the Constitution
itself, but this is no longer the case. It was felt that the
listing of protected documents was too cumbersome to be part
of a constitutional Act and that it prevented easy amendment
of the list of protected documents. The detailing of exceptions has been done in the Secrecy Act since 1937 and only
the general principles, derived from the existing exceptions,
are stated in the Freedom of the Press Act.

The Secrecy Act

The Secrecy Act contains some forty sections and not only
specifies the type of document to be kept secret, but also
the length of time for which it is protected. This can vary
from two years to seventy years, or indefinitely.

The nature of the Secrecy Act can be seen from the section
dealing with national security where the government is
allowed to protect documents dealing with mobilisation, concentration or activities of the armed forces in war or threat
of war, supplies and equipment, fortifications and installations, naval stations, military airports, military positions and mine defences, other technical materials destined

for wartime construction and use, military communications,
experiments and inventions, planning for civil or psycho-
logical defence. The government is also given latitude to
decree that certain documents relating to production, trade,
transport, etc. may be protected in time of war or danger of
war. However, it is important to recognise that defence or
national security information can only be protected if it
can be shown to come within the specified categories.

Some of the documents which are granted protection seem
excessively trivial to be specified in a Secrecy Act - for
instance, the logbooks of state- or municipally-owned vessels
engaged in collisions - but the Secrecy Act is not an attempt
to establish a limited set of principles governing disclosure. It is rather a list of specific exceptions which
have been determined by time and experience. No country
introducing such an Act could hope to emulate the Swedish
detail as to which documents deserve protection and which do
not; it could only hope to introduce certain principles and
to leave the detailed application of these to the courts.
After several years a set of more detailed exceptions would
emerge and could possibly be incorporated into a revised Act.

The provisions which derive from the protection of personal
privacy are of great importance in that Sweden has an extensive State welfare service which demands that individuals
produce large amounts of information in order to gain the
benefits offered. The majority of documents dealing with
public health, sickness, probation and social work are protected. Information derived from the census or State ethno-
graphic studies is also protected in so far as the reports
contain information concerning an individual's personal
circumstances, although that information may be released to
bona fide scholars. This protection is not, however, accorded to the decisions of an authority, even though such
decisions may contain personal information. Exceptions to
this general rule apply to decisions relating to child care,
temperance, sex determination, venereal diseases, abortion,
sterilisation or castration. Where personal information contained within a decision is not protected, it is felt that
in most cases, except the most sensitive, the need to ensure
public scrutiny of decisions outweighs the need for personal
privacy. In practically all of the above cases, however, the
information, which must legally be kept secret by the authority concerned, may be released to the person whose privacy
is being protected. The individual whose privacy is being
protected has greater rights of access than the public, as
he cannot be damaged by receiving information about himself,
except in very special circumstances. These circumstances
are allowed for in the Act. In the case of someone whose

health or mental state may be affected by the receipt of his
own hospital or other medical reports, the documents may be
withheld. The principle governing release, however, remains
the same: damage to the individual.

Enforcement of Secrecy

Obviously the law requiring that public authorities keep
certain documents secret can only be enforced if the employees who actually hold these documents obey the law. In
Sweden this is of particular importance in that the decision
to release or to withhold a document is made by the official
who is responsible for the particular document requested. In
Swedish law it is his responsibility if he releases a document which ought to have been withheld, or refuses to
release a document which ought to have been released. In
either case the official is liable to a reprimand, fine, dismissal or even imprisonment. As a result, the official concerned seeks advice from the legal counsel of the authority
or from the Ombudsman. However, the decision cannot be
delegated or 'shared'; it remains a matter of individual
responsibility.

There are three ways in which a civil servant may commit
an offence by disclosing information. The first of these,
and the least important, concerns communication which constitutes espionage, treason or sedition by those in public or
military service. It is least important in that there have
been very few prosecutions under this clause of the Freedom
of the Press Act. The second concerns a duty of silence
which is placed upon certain civil servants either by decree
or statute. Certain categories of public officials have a
specific duty laid upon them not to reveal information protected by the Secrecy Act. For example, social workers have
a statutory duty of silence placed upon them. The object of
such a duty is to make it an offence to release information
verbally, since the Secrecy Act refers only to documents.
The duty of silence also prohibits a civil servant volunteer-
ing information without its having been requested. The
situation is complicated in that certain officials are subject to decrees requiring them to be silent, whilst others
have a statutory obligation on them to be so. As will be
discussed later, this has important repercussions in connection with the press. The duty of silence does not inhibit a
civil servant from verbally releasing information which is
not protected by the Secrecy Act. The third provision is
part of the Secrecy Act and states that it is a breach of
duty to release any document protected by the Act. The normal
penalty is a fine, although certain sections of the Act are

protected by the possibility of prison sentences, these
being foreign affairs, defence matters, certain economic
information acquired by compulsion and records of cases
heard by a court in camera.

THE OPERATION OF THE PUBLICITY PRINCIPLE

The Freedom of the Press Act does not require the identification of a specific document; there is a duty upon all
public servants to assist the public, and this includes
assisting them to discover the documents in which they are
interested. It is also the case that a citizen or the press
can ask for all the papers relating to a certain issue, or
dealt with by a certain individual, or arriving on a certain
day. There are no limits on the number of documents which
may be requested and no prohibition upon 'fishing' ex-
peditions amongst the archives. There is no requirement in
the Act to make indexes and registers of documents; this is
not necessary as the indexes and registers of the Authorities themselves must be made available, even though they
list documents which are classified as secret. The Freedom
of the Press Act does not create a classification system of
'classified', 'secret' and 'top secret' and there is no
other statute which does this. Documents are either identified in law as public or secret, although the period for
which a document remains secret varies. Certain documents
may be stamped 'secret', although this in itself does not
protect the document from disclosure unless the civil servant who has authority to deal with such documents considers
it to be a protected document, and further that in the event
of an appeal the authority or the court decides that the
particular document is covered by· statute. It is also
required that any such stamp must be accompanied by the
appropriate provision of law by which it is claimed it is
protected, the date on which it was stamped, and the person
or authority who caused the stamp to be made. It is also the
case that in the area of national security the government is
given the right to specify that only an authority named by
it has the right to release certain documents. In this case
the appeal is to the Minister concerned and there is no
appeal against his decision, not even to the courts. As
stated in the preceding chapter, this is because of the fact
that government decisions are immune from judicial review.
    There is one aspect of the law which causes particular
problems to administrators and it involves the amount of
time taken in complying with the Act and the difficulty of
being certain that one is not breaking the law. It lies in

the requirement that an authority determine whether all, or
only a part of a document, is protected by legislation. An
authority is not allowed to deny access to an entire document or set of documents and files if only a part of the
document may be considered secret under law. The authority
must make available the part of the document which is not
secret, excluding the protected matter. This provision can
involve very elaborate and time-consuming reading and
searching of documents. For example, in the case of a medical or mental patient who applies for access to his own file,
there is a legal obligation to hand over that file to the
person, unless ' ... there is sufficient reason to assume
that by release of the document the purpose of the care or
treatment would be impeded or someone's personal safety
would be jeopardised, then release may be refused even if
release should take place according to the regulations in
the first paragraph'.[8]

The determination of whether or not release may harm the
patient or endanger others, or whether only part of it may
be so found, may only be answerable by a medical doctor who
may therefore be required to spend time making the decision
concerning release of the document. Apart from the time,
there is also the difficulty of making such a decision and
of not only protecting the patient's best interests, but
protecting the doctor from possible legal action for breach
of silence. Another problem for administrators, caused by
the right of an individual to have access to his own documents, is that the individual has the right to reveal whatever proportion of the document released to him he wishes
and to whomsoever he wishes. However, this does not release
the authority from its duty of silence concerning any other
documents they may have relating to the case or any part of
the document which the party himself has not released. This
has meant that it is possible for an individual to release
some part of a document containing statements by an authority or by some person in the authority which may not be in
the best or highest traditions of the civil service, or
which are simply wrong, without the authority or any member
of it being able to release those parts of the document
which the party possesses but has not released, in order to
protect itself from accusations of incompetence. This
becomes particularly acute, in the eyes of administrators at
least, if the party to whom the documents have been partially
released has been the press. Administrators are not so keen
on the freedom of the press as others, not only because of
their Weberian penchant for secrecy, but also because they
feel so vulnerable to the press releasing documents or
filing stories based upon only part of the information,

either an early statement or plan, or only on the citizen's
story or on what some party has partially released. This
problem is compounded by the fact that complaints which
enter the office of the Ombudsman are available to the press
before the Ombudsman has investigated the case, so that the
press are able to report upon accusations. Administrators
also say that the press are much more keen to report the
accusation than the Ombudsman's final report, especially if
this should prove to be a vindication of the actions of the
accused civil servant.

Some of the above problems relate to the expense of oper-
ating the publicity principle and the time taken to determine what part, if any, can be released. This would certainly
be a major factor in any country with a large population,
especially given the lack of restrictions upon access to
documents, characteristic of Sweden. The rule is that any
document which has been requested must ' ... be made available, immediately or as soon as possible ... '.[9] This
requirement can be met either by allowing the person to read
the document or to copy it. This can be done either where
the document is kept or, if this raises 'considerable difficulties', at some other place. Documents which require
mechanical recording must be made available in a readable
form or in some form that can be listened to. In the case of
secret documents where only some part may be revealed, there
is no obligation to allow the person to see the document; a
copy may be provided with the secret part removed.

There is also an obligation under the Decree on the Public
Service issued by the government to give information in whatever form it is requested, unless this interferes with the
primary tasks of the authority; for example, to give information orally or by telephone. This provision does not
remove any legal obligation but is an additional requirement
to offer assistance.

A decision by a civil servant that a particular document
is secret under the Secrecy Act can be appealed. In the
first instance the appeal will be made to the authority itself, but in the event of an appeal being disallowed by the
authority there is the right of appeal to the Administrative
Courts. The system of appeal is, however, very simple in
that the court hearing takes the form of the examination of
written statements. It does not include the examination of
witnesses under oath nor does it involve an adversary type
of procedure. Very often the citizen will have written his
own statement and a lawyer will not be involved. The court
itself has a duty to comprehend the statement of the citizen
in legal terms.

It is understandable that civil servants in Sweden will

refuse access to certain categories of documents, those
protected by the criminal law, when in doubt as to whether a
citizen is entitled to access to such documents. This is so
for two reasons: one is that there are no criminal penalties
for refusing access when a citizen is legally entitled to
access, although an admonishment may be issued; and the
other is that because of the ease and cheapness of appeal,
refusal is not a serious obstacle to the citizen finally
obtaining the access to which he is legally entitled.

THE ANONYMITY PRINCIPLE

There is a further principle of the Swedish Constitution
which is important in affecting the amount of government
information which is disclosed - the 'anonymity rule'.
   The anonymity rule was first introduced in 1949 as part of
a revision of the Freedom of the Press Act. The rule stated
that anyone had the right to write for, or give information
to, the press, anonymously. The anonymity rule meant that
public officials could give information to the press, which
would otherwise have been illegal if given to an ordinary
member of the public, with virtual impunity. The Freedom of
the Press Act stated that no investigation or prosecution
could be undertaken of the source of information given to
the press. This rule was reinforced by two other rules, one
being the designated editor rule, and the other being the
requirement that all criminal cases arising under the Freedom of the Press Act be heard by a jury and not by judges.
The designated editor rule states that one person must be
named to the authorities as the responsible editor such that
he alone is responsible for the content of the newspaper.
   These provisions were felt to give complete security to
the press in Sweden, the Freedom of the Press Act clearly
stating what classes of documents should not be published
and could be subject to prosecution, who could be prosecuted,
and how the case would be tried, but this interpretation was
proved to be false. In 1973 a case occurred which involved
two journalists who were tried and convicted for espionage,
not under the Freedom of the Press Act, which includes the
offence of espionage as part of its prohibitions, but under
the Espionage Act. This meant that none of the normal rules
protecting journalists applied. This provoked many complaints
concerning the case and led to the amendment of the Freedom
of the Press Act in 1976. The revised Freedom of the Press
Act which came into force in 1978 gave greater protection to
informants, made all prosecution of the press a matter for
the Attorney General alone, and made such cases subject to

trial by jury. The situation remains complicated, however,
because the exact nature of the regulations controlling the
verbal release of information is unclear. This has been the
subject of a government Commission, and a set of proposals
has been produced but a decision has not yet been taken.[10]

   The effect of the anonymity rule is to make it possible
for civil servants to ignore the Secrecy Act and other
statutes which place obligations of secrecy upon them,
except for certain types of crimes specified in the Freedom
of the Press Act, such as espionage and treason.

THE PRESS AND FREEDOM OF THE PRESS

The press, then, has great potential as a provider of information which would not be available to the public according
to the publicity rule. This is mainly due to the anonymity
rule rather than to a tradition of investigative journalism.[11] Such a tradition is inhibited by the party allegiance
of the press and by the fact that few newspapers are of
national standing, able to afford the time and number and
quality of journalists needed to sustain such a tradition.

   In the case of political journalism, that is, access to
political information related to the political parties
(which are not considered public authorities and, therefore,
not subject to the publicity rules), the same 'traps' of
acquiring information by becoming a trusted confidant and
yet becoming bound to preserve this relationship by being
circumspect as to what is published, still apply in Sweden.
Such information tends to be as secretive in Sweden as any-
where else. A recent interesting development in government-
press relations is the accusation by the non-socialist
coalition that certain members of the public service are
'leaking' information protected under the rule concerning
'preparatory' documents and that this is happening with
greater frequency than under the socialist government. Members of the press admitted that this was the case, but
argued, first, that it was a consequence of an attempt by
the then government to restrict access to the press and to
restrict access to themselves, secondly, that a coalition
was more interesting as a political situation than a majority
government and, thirdly, that members of the coalition were
themselves leaking information which other members of the
coalition would rather remained secret. This aspect of the
relationship between press and government can be illustrated
by the fact that the Prime Minister's Press Secretary issued
a confidential memorandum asking that the Ministries and the
Central Boards should remember to utilise the Press Officers

and not to give personal interviews to the press - the next
day this 'confidential' memorandum was published in one of
the newspapers. Practising journalists are much more sceptical of the value of the publicity rules than are lawyers and
politicians. The journalists are willing to admit that there
is still a role for investigative journalism and, indeed,
that the Freedom of the Press Act may have led them to be
less inquisitive than they ought to have been.

Political journalists must maintain contacts with the
government, bureaucrats, trade unions, etc. if they are to
obtain 'inside knowledge' of the meetings, plans, intrigues
and negotiations, many of which are not subject to the
publicity rules. For example, in 1976 the Prime Minister was
elected on an anti-nuclear platform and yet this was not
supported by the other parties in the coalition, nor by the
Central Energy Board. A change of policy on the Prime
Minister's part would have been front page news, and would
have had important political implications for the next
elections, but such a policy change would have been totally
hidden from view until the decision had been made, unless
reporters investigated, talked to opposition Members of
Parliament, members of the Boards and of the government.
Before judging the value of the publicity principle, however,
it is necessary to take into account another very important
mechanism for producing public information: the remiss
system and government commissions.

GOVERNMENT COMMISSIONS AND THE SYSTEM OF REMISS

The important point about the remiss system and government
commissions is that they solicit public opinion and the
opinion of the public authorities *before* action has been
taken. On the other hand, the publicity principle as described up to this point is largely operative *after* a
decision has been made. This is because the publicity principle operates as a part of the system of administrative
control and to enable the principle of individual responsibility of civil servants to be enforced.

It is not necessary that the decisions of the administrators be subject to scrutiny before a decision has been
made in order that criminal liability for those decisions
be meaningful. This was rejected because it was considered
that to insist that the civil servant always be open would
disrupt administration: citizens would take action to
prevent what they expected would be illegal or bad decisions
and this would bring smooth and effective administration to
a halt. The remedies against illegal action by adminis-

trators, then, comes after the decision has been made.

In the case of political decisions, however, the Swedes have a strong tradition of discussion and consultation before a decision is taken. It was a requirement of the 1809 Constitution that the opinions of the relevant administrative offices be obtained before the submissions of any matter to the King in Council, and since 1918 the duly elected government has consulted the opinion of the administrators before proposing legislation to Parliament. This has since been widened to include the opinion of the relevant organised interests. The Constitution of 1974 requires that administrators be consulted: 'To the extent necessary associations and private subjects shall be given an opportunity to express their views'.[12]

This system of the circulation of draft proposals is known as 'remiss' and it plays an important role in the formation of public support, if not always public policy. Another means of producing information relevant to legislative proposals is the setting up of a commission of inquiry. These commissions are appointed by the government and vary in composition from inquiries headed by one man, usually a civil servant and assisted by various experts, to inquiries headed by government Ministers and containing civil servants, Members of Parliament, members of the opposition, representatives of various interests and experts. The terms of reference of the commission are defined by the government and may be widely or narrowly drawn.[13]

It is an important consequence of the publicity rule, as specified in the Freedom of the Press Act, that documents sent from one authority to another, unless protected by the Secrecy Act, are open to the public. This means that the opinions of civil servants are available to the public, and the position taken by the civil servants is expected to be an 'independent' one reflecting their experience and expertise and independent position. This means that the views of civil servants, whether supporting or opposing government proposals, are known; here apparently there are no statesmen in disguise!

This is particularly true of the system of 'remiss'. In the case of the commissions, however, they work in secret until the publication of their report; this, it is felt by many, is where the real bargaining of Swedish political life takes place. Because these commissions are so 'representative' in composition, it is felt that their conclusions have particular weight and are not to be altered by Parliament without very good reason. Of course, given the fact that members of the government, the majority parliamentary party, the minority parliamentary party and members of the

main interests concerned are commission members, any rejection of the commission consensus by Parliament is highly
unlikely.

Very often the report itself will then be circulated,
rather as a draft Bill would be, under the remiss principle,
thus ensuring even greater opportunity for the expression of
views and consultation. The main decisions, however, are
taken by the cabinet in secret, the cabinet and outside
bodies in secret, the commissions in secret, or by parliamentary committees in secret. It is certainly true that when
these reports are published, the public are provided with
access to a wide range of fact and opinion and this can lead
to extensive discussion in the media concerning the proposals. However, one must also admit that the main point at
which influence is exercised by those outside the government
upon the government is by means of organised interests, and
these operate not by applying 'pressure' or the articulation
of interests, but as part of the decision-making élite of
Swedish political life. This takes the form of participation
in commissions of inquiry, through membership by Members of
Parliament of these organisations, and by direct negotiation
between them without the interference of the government, by
membership of the Boards of the Central Administrative
Bodies, by membership of the Labour Court and the ownership
of newspapers. This is not a simple case of pressure groups
transmitting information and articulating demands, but of
such groups actually participating in the formulation of
policy and application of that policy through representation
upon quasi-judicial and administrative bodies. The influence
of such groups is also reflected in the fact that they are
often given the right to nominate who shall represent them
upon a commission of inquiry. This is not to say that the
government is not the main centre of decision-making power;
it decides whether to have a commission in the first place
and also determines its size and basic composition. But the
fact that these outside interests and opposition and 'back-
bench Members of Parliament' sit on these commissions, etc.
also means that they have access to a wide range of information, a wider range than that which is finally published
and available to the public.

The other main consequence is that the opinions of the
civil servants do not remain hidden, but are matters of
public knowledge. This is part of the traditional role of
civil servants in that for most of the nineteenth century
governments contained many civil servants as Ministers, they
were a major part of Parliament, and are still eligible to
be elected as Members of Parliament. It is considered a
necessary part of public life that the views of the 'expert',

the professional, often legally trained, always well edu-
cated, and independent civil servant should be available so
that the public can judge the wisdom of the actions of the
government.[14]

LOYALTY AND NEUTRALITY

This availability of civil service views is reflected in the
fact that civil servants are not subject to any restrictions
upon their political activities and that until recently
Sweden did not scrutinise the 'loyalty' of public employees
in any way. There is still no law relating to the loyalty of
public employees, although in 1963 a government regulation,
entitled Personnel Control, was introduced which gives a
public authority the right to check police files as to
whether there is anything known, in the sense of whether or
not someone is actually suspected of breaking the law. The
authorities are prohibited from investigating the opinions
of an employee or prospective employee, and the process of
checking applies only to a limited number of positions,
which are determined by the government. This government regulation was introduced after a spying case in 1963 involved
an RAF Colonel who was found guilty of passing information
to the Soviet Union and was sentenced to eight years' imprisonment. A committee was set up to investigate the case
and the new regulations were the consequence. Such cases,
however, come as something of a surprise to Swedes, who take
each other's basic loyalty to the State very much for
granted.
    This situation may, however, appear to create a paradox,
namely that a civil service which is required to be 'independent', 'neutral' and 'objective' should also be part of
political life, both through active engagement in Parliament
and participation in party politics, and through public
statements taking 'sides' on what in other countries would
be seen as political matters. How is it possible for the
Director General of the Board of Energy to argue for the
necessity of nuclear energy and for the Prime Minister to be
publicly opposed to the use of nuclear energy, and for these
two to see each other as 'neutral', 'objective' or 'independent'? The answer lies partly in the sense which Swedes give
to the word 'political'; to many Swedes political means ideological as opposed to rational. The civil service therefore
remains neutral as long as it remains non-ideological, but
this does not require non-participation in 'rational' arguments about issues which are a matter of discussion between
the political parties. The main test of neutrality is that

each issue be treated in isolation, and Swedish political
life encourages this treatment of issues in isolation.
Indeed, one can argue that this is the basis of the Swedish
political style. This fragmentation of issues means that it
is possible for the various elements of the Swedish political élite to arrive at a consensus without this ever becoming
a matter of the fall of the government, a matter of principle. It is very rarely that such matters cannot be handed
over to a commission in order that a 'rational' debate can
take place and so avoid the polarising of the issue between
government and opposition.

CONCLUSION

The main area of *political* life is hidden in Sweden, as else-
where. No publicity rule can give access to the political
basis behind a decision, the political thinking and calcu-
lations, the inter-party and intra-party disputes; in other
words what the Swedes would see as politics. Once the political decision as to the direction which is to be taken has
been made, then the details of how best to implement this
decision are much more open to view, especially the factual
basis used by the government to justify its decisions. The
irony, however, is that because of the nature of Swedish
politics, the availability of information does not lead to a
lively political debate and to the rise and fall of governments. The opposition parties do not seem to benefit from
this freedom of information. It is a perennial complaint in
Swedish politics that the opposition parties are relatively
impotent: the issues which have led to a real political
battle since the Second World War are very few in number.
However, the issue of nuclear power and the two defeats of
the Social Democratic Party at the elections in 1976 and
1979 suggest that this situation may be changing. Notwith-
standing this there has been a generally accepted view that
the style of Swedish politics is 'depoliticised', 'compromised', 'pluralistic', 'bureaucratic' and 'organisational'.
All of these terms do not imply that 'open government' leads
to an active political system, but rather the opposite, at
least in theory, of the oppositional style of politics
characteristic of Britain.

10. Conclusion

Government secrecy is mainly a product of the control of civil service or government bureaucracy and not ideology, inefficiency, corruption, national security, good or bad politicians, right- or left-wing government, pressure groups or paternalism. This is not to say that these factors are irrelevant to an explanation, but there is little to be gained from a mere compilation of 'influences'.

It is within the area of civil service/government relations that the level of secrecy or openness is determined. In the countries that I have examined, the level of secrecy is affected by two factors: the degree to which the civil service or administration is the direct responsibility of elected representatives, and the extent to which that responsibility is undivided and hierarchical. The relation of the above to secrecy is that where administration is clearly subordinate to elected representatives, then information becomes an important element in the political struggle for office and therefore something which governments will seek to control. This desire for control is also affected by the existence of other groups who are also elected representatives, but whose political base is not dependent upon the success or otherwise of those who are directly responsible for administration, and yet who are constitutive of government. In such a situation the desire for control will be contested by those seeking to establish their own reputations either by thwarting that desire, or by seeking to establish a level of control of their own.

DEMOCRACY AND FREEDOM OF INFORMATION LEGISLATION

It is of vital importance that one recognises what kinds of information one would ever be able to obtain from any democratic government, and especially by means of a statutory right. One can never envisage a situation in which politicians would be forced to divulge what was in their minds by virtue of any piece of legislation. One cannot force politicians to state what they think they may do, what is possible or impossible. In one sense it is impossible to prohibit secrecy.

This raises the question of whether this vitiates any attempt to legislate for more open government. The answer is that it does not, and the reason for this is simple. All governments in the course of making decisions will communicate in writing, either within the government or between the government and outside bodies, and this is a necessity if the government is to function at all. It is access to the documents which do exist which is the basis of open government, and it is on the basis of this record that judgements on government will be made. The important thing is that the existing record to which one does have access should justify the decisions taken, and once the principle of access is established then the government will feel an obligation, simply to protect itself, to ensure that the record is sufficiently complete so as to justify the decisions taken. The fact that there may be other considerations which are not part of the record is irrelevant, since their exclusion from the record means that the government cannot defend its decisions by using these arguments. If the government has omitted arguments which others feel are important, then this is a form of criticism which undermines the validity of government arguments and one which they will seek to avoid. Openness then does not guarantee that the government will provide access to all of its thinking and information, but it does provide an incentive to the government to ensure that what the public does have access to is complete enough to protect itself. Without legislation providing for public access to government documents, the incentive for the government not to provide half truths and lies is much less. What open government legislation does is to raise the cost to government of attempting to 'fool' the public. It does not eliminate that possibility, but this is not to deny the benefit of increasing the difficulties of governments attempting to do so.

On the basis of the above arguments, one can conclude that it is in the area of routine government decisions that access will be of most benefit. The reason for this is that the more routine the decision, the more likely it is that standard forms and procedures will exist, and those higher in the government hierarchy will see it as part of their method of controlling subordinates that procedures are closely adhered to and that the record is complete. The hierarchical nature of bureaucracy is one of the main safe-

guards against secret government when legislation on access
exists.

Most routine decisions, by their very nature, will only be
concerned with a particular individual or firm; for example,
granting social security payments or awarding import/export
licences. These types of decisions, however, make up the
vast majority of administrative acts and public scrutiny of
these has as its object to ensure that they are lawful, are
based on accurate facts, and are consistent. The public has
an interest in these decisions on the basis of self-interest,
to ensure that they are receiving their legal rights, and
access to the record is important in so far as it enables a
person to appeal against a particular decision. However, the
possibility of appeal depends upon the existence of an
appellate body and access to the record is only of value in
so far as an adequate system of appeal exists. By adequate,
I mean a system of appeal which is inexpensive, quick and
has a measure of independence.

The important factor affecting this is whether the appeals
system involves lawyers and a judicial type of procedure.
The more information available the more likely it is that
lawyers will have to spend a greater amount of time on the
case, and this will increase the expense to the client. Only
if the appeals procedure dispenses with the assistance of
lawyers will the balance of improvement in justice gained by
more information not be lost by a reluctance by members of
the public to appeal because of the expense. One can argue
that many members of the public would consider that a more
important alteration in administrative law would be to enable appeal bodies to award damages for administrative error,
even when made in good faith, rather than to have increased
access to documents. Most remedies in administrative law do
not involve damages, but merely the setting aside of the
decision. The possibility of obtaining some form of recompense may be a greater incentive to appeal against decisions than access to the record.

POLITICS AND SECRECY

As I have repeatedly stated, no Freedom of Information Act
gives, or will ever give, access to politics. By this I mean
that no Freedom of Information Act will give access to the
inner workings of political life. Politics is not simply a
matter of making 'rational' decisions, but of making judgements of popularity and ideology, and these judgements will
inevitably be opposed by some group, especially in a democratic society. This means that politics and politicians in

a representative democracy are subject to two potentially
conflicting demands; on the one hand to be accountable to
the electorate, and on the other to have sufficient authority
to take decisions. These tensions would become intolerable,
leading either to 'popularism' or autocracy, were it not for
the role which secrecy plays in maintaining the boundaries.
The boundaries between strong, effective and decisive government and popular government are maintained by secrecy.
Governments know that they will not satisfy every member of
the electorate, but that this must not prevent them from
taking decisions.

This is not to say that all governments have the same
degree of secrecy; indeed, the point at which secrecy operates tells one what balance between these two possibilities
a particular society has adopted. However, I wish to empha-
sise that 'strong' government does not necessarily mean
undemocratic government; as I stated in the second chapter,
democracy is defined in terms of the power of removal and
the right to organise and express opposition and to form
political parties for this purpose. However, within this
definition, democracies vary as to the values which are
given predominance and, in particular, the ones mentioned
above; namely, 'strong' government, or 'popular' government.
I find it difficult to produce a term which accurately describes the second type in that the opposite of strong is
weak, but this is certainly not what is meant, nor does
consensus apply in that this type of government is no more
or less likely to produce a consensus than strong government.
I use the term 'popular' in the hope that it signifies a
style of government in which there is an obligation to search
for agreement, one which encourages consultation and in
which government is seen as simply one party to the law-
making process, but not the sole or dominant one. The United
States and Sweden are examples of 'popular' governments, and
Britain of 'strong'. Only in Britain is there no legal
obligation to consult interested parties, little attempt by
the courts to interfere with administration, no powerful
legislative committees and no fixed terms of election.

The idea that secrecy is a boundary indicator is best
summed up in the idea that it acts as the dividing point at
which politics is said to cease and 'reason' begin. Secrecy
will cease at the point at which politics ends and reason
begins. This opposition between politics and reason is somewhat formal, but politics is distinct from reason in that
politics is the art of making judgements of popularity and
of values, and reason the process of solving problems, the
problem being defined in factual terms. Politics is the art
of defining what the problems are, and reason the art of

solving them. Politics is that part of political life in
which politicians have the duty to determine what the
aspirations and goals of the society are, in the sense that
they have to judge the nature of popular aspirations and
also to give them substance. All political systems recognise
that, however far participation and consultation may go,
some political body has to carry out this task, will have
responsibility for supplying direction and coherence to
government. Depending how narrowly or widely this body extends its net depends upon how far secrecy spreads.

POLITICS IN THE THREE COUNTRIES

This argument links with the earlier discussion on responsibility. Where political responsibility spreads into many
areas of political life, then secrecy will be widespread;
where political responsibility is narrowly drawn, then
secrecy will be limited. It is the penetration of the 'responsible body' into many areas - administration, the courts
and law-making - that gives rise to secrecy and the contain-
ment of this body which enables openness. Strong governments,
namely those in which politicians have their responsibility
clearly defined and widely drawn, will be secretive. Governments in which responsibility is narrowly drawn and not
clearly defined will be characterised by openness.

In Britain, at least until recently, the government has
had almost sole responsibility for making political decisions, and the responsibility has been widely defined in
that there are few areas of political life for which it has
not been responsible. All kinds of decisions were seen as
having implications for the competence of politicians and
their ability to make political judgements. Politicians have
had little competition from other groups or bodies in defining the goals of the society and in defining the general or
public interest. This is reflected in ministerial responsibility, the penetration of administration by politics, and
in a sense its contamination, such that few administrative
decisions have been seen as having little or no reflection
upon the competence of politicians and upon their authority.

The situation in Sweden and the United States is different.
In Sweden, politics has traditionally been seen as something
which arises at election time, whereas the art of government
involves very little of it and mainly involves reason or
'sensibleness'. In Sweden, politics is seen as being 'ideological', as something to be kept to a minimum, whilst
problem-solving and consultation are seen to be sensible and
as values which should be maximised. This belief is expressed

in the separation of administration from direct ministerial
control and in the judicialisation of administration, the
replacement of politics by law. It is also found in the
remiss system, the requirement that consultation takes place
before legislation is passed and by the important role
played by commissions of inquiry and parliamentary committees
in the definition of problems, their solution, and in the
formulation of legislation. Sweden is also a multi-party
system and one which has had a considerable number of coalition governments. Sweden is a society which in religious,
language and cultural terms has a remarkable degree of
homogeneity. It is also a society which views its history as
being one in which success has been associated with neutrality, cooperation and consensus, and its failures by times
of war and dominance either by Parliament or the monarchy.
The attitude of compromise is found in the area of industrial relations in which trade unions and management have
been formed into central negotiating bodies and in which the
law and arbitration are identified with economic success.[1]
Economic success is seen as being a product of State intervention, or perhaps more accurately, State participation.
The Swedish 'bourgeoisie' have not seen the State as an
object of fear, but as an institution which has been a source
of finance and the provider of a framework within which all
interests can cooperate. There has been remarkably little
argument concerning the goals of Swedish society, 'caring'
and economic success being dominant, and this has meant that
politics has been seen as limited, and somewhat remote from
'solving problems'.

The United States has certain similarities with Sweden,
but also some differences. The United States is similar to
Sweden in that certain important administrative agencies are
autonomous, for example, the Interstate Commerce Commission,
although the US has not adopted this as a principle of good
and lawful administration. The US also has a system of powerful legislative committees, which hold extensive and detailed
hearings involving evidence from many outside bodies and
interests. These hearings are empowered to question civil
servants and to receive from them written submissions; there
is little anonymity of administrators. The US courts 'compete' with both administrators and legislators in that the
courts have sought to lay down certain procedures which
administrators must follow if their decisions are to be
counted as fair. The courts also have the right to test the
constitutionality of legislation, and there has been far
less reluctance on the part of US courts to state what they
consider the public interest to be and to deny to the executive the sole right of definition of that interest.

The United States system is however different from both
Britain and Sweden in that it is a presidential system and
separates the executive from the legislature. This means
that no single body has the authority to make political
judgements. This competition for sovereignty necessarily
involves a search for compromise: the more 'extreme'
measures are liable to be vetoed by one side or the other
and this tends to produce a limitation upon the potency of
politics. However, the tendency identified by many political
commentators for one party, namely the Presidency, to become
dominant or 'imperial', has been seen as a cause of a higher
level of secrecy than was to be found before the Second
World War. This, however, has provoked a reaction by Congress and has led to the passing of the Freedom of Information Act and other Acts to combat the fear of an imperial
presidency which they saw vindicated by the Vietnam War,
Watergate and the activities of the CIA. It has been an
intuitive belief of many Americans that the centralisation
of political authority in one body would lead to an increase
in the degree of secrecy and this is true, except that it
can never go as far as Britain. Congress can, however, never
become dominant in that it does not control administration,
nor does its structure lead to the production of a united
consensus on what the goals of American society can be, so
the congressional role is to prevent secrecy rather than to
achieve dominance, which would produce its own desire for
secrecy. The American system of government could never
produce a situation in which one body obtained sole political authority which would enable it to impose secrecy,
except in an emergency situation.

GOVERNMENT INFORMATION IN THE THREE COUNTRIES

I have discussed the difference between these countries in
general terms, but not the differences in the information
which is available. This second task involves asking whether
some information is produced in one country but not in the
others. This depends upon what exactly one means by information. For example, the British system produces clearer
information concerning the goals and aspirations of the
various parties competing for power than either the US or
Sweden. It also produces information concerning who is
responsible for what more clearly than any other system,
although this could be more accurately characterised as a
past, rather than present, virtue. The British parliamentary
question can also be said to produce information concerning
the character and competence of a Minister with more fire

and precision than any hearing or access to documents. This is especially so in the case of political competence, the ability to feel the mood of the House and of the nation. The British system encourages the Member of Parliament's political talents, his ability to make judgements and not simply to administer, although the parliamentary question is under attack as a mechanism for controlling administration. However, it is clear that if one means by information the production of documents or government facts, then the British system is the least adequate. This must not lead to the view that the British system therefore produces no infor- mation; as I have stated above, it can be argued that it is the best system for producing certain kinds of information and especially that which I would describe as political.

The Swedish and American political systems both produce a substantial amount of information concerning the basis of policy, both the reasoning behind it and its factual basis. However, neither system produces what political consider- ations have been made by the cabinet, Prime Minister or President, what advice they have received from their im- mediate aids or senior civil servants, what meetings the senior political figures have had or what was discussed at them. The main type of information produced in both countries is the record of administrative acts and the factual and legal basis of them. This means that the major beneficiaries of such an Act are those who have dealings with adminis- trative agencies either as private citizens or as private corporations. The main benefit accruing to these groups is the increased ability which information provides in appeal procedures either in the courts or within the administrative hierarchy. The major use, and major justification, of a Freedom of Information Act is in relation to the judicial- isation of administration, to an increase in the ability of those subject to administrative acts to ensure that the decisions are impartial and follow the requirements of due process or natural justice. However, the American use of the Freedom of Information Act is different from the Swedish one in that there has been considerable use of documents to check on the abuse of individual civil rights undertaken by administrative agencies, mainly law enforcement or intelli- gence ones. The American Act has also increased the number of consumer and other 'citizen protection' private interest groups. This is very important in that it has helped to compensate for the fact that the United States has no federal Ombudsman and therefore no 'cheap' or, indeed, free way of using information to formulate criticism of agency procedures in general.

However, the United States Freedom of Information Act and

the Swedish Freedom of the Press Act both exclude internal
minutes and memoranda which act to preclude access to information whilst decisions are at the formative stage, before
decisions have been made. This would reduce the value of
such Acts almost entirely to aids in the appeal process,
having little or no effect upon the political process. However, both countries have important additional mechanisms
for producing information of the above type.

In the case of Sweden there is the rule concerning the
sending of documents such that they are no longer internal
and no longer protected, except by subject matter, and also
by the requirement that the government consult interested
parties and affected agencies before presenting legislation.
In the United States the congressional committees and their
hearings perform a similar function in that interested
parties and the administrative agencies will submit written
statements and may also be questioned by the committee. It
is important therefore to recognise that legislation on its
own is not sufficient to produce what one may call 'open
government'. The political system must be structured in such
a way that consultation takes place, in public, if 'openness'
is to be achieved. It is difficult, if not impossible, to
legislate for this in a Freedom of Information Act; it
requires change in the constitutional arrangements by which
authority is exercised. This statement has important implications for those attempting to reform the 'British tradition of secrecy'; an Information Act will not suffice if
their stated aims are to be achieved.

THE COST OF SECRECY

So far I have been concerned with the causes of secrecy without assessing its costs. One very real cost is a financial
one. It can be argued that freedom of information is extremely expensive, in that a great deal of administrative
labour is required to operate such legislation, but it is
also true that secrecy is expensive. For example, in 1971
the US General Accounting Office estimated that the cost of
security classification in four major agencies with classification authority, the Departments of State and Defense, the
Atomic Energy Commission and the National Aeronautics and
Space Administration, was $60.2 million in one financial
year.[2] This however did not include the cost of the security
system to defence contractors, all of whom are obliged to
maintain secrecy under their contracts and all of whose
employees with access to secret information are obliged to
submit to security investigations. In 1974 some 11,000

industrial firms and research centres had research defence
contracts worth some $9,000,000,000 and the additional cost
to the State of security requirements was estimated to be
$63 million.[3] However, no reliable estimates of the total
cost exist and the above estimates are thought to be conservative. Also the above figures take no account of the
intelligence budget; they are simply the cost of administering the security requirements within particular agencies and
firms. No estimate exists of the cost to the British taxpayer of having to protect its government secrets, although
one would suspect that given the potency of the Official
Secrets Act perhaps less effort has to be taken to protect
classified documents as such; however, in so far as these
require special handling and procedures, then the costs
would be comparable. A Freedom of Information Act which made
documents available to the public and therefore no longer
requiring special protection would reduce the security costs
and these would have to be subtracted from the cost of such
an Act if a true estimate of its cost was to be made.

A hidden cost of secrecy is that much research and development is not available to other firms or to other scientists,
which may impede the very development which governments are
seeking. This is extremely difficult to assess but there can
be no doubt of the existence of such an effect. Science is
an activity which requires the free interchange of ideas and
any restriction upon this will impede, in some measure, its
progress. This becomes particularly important when one considers the proportion of research which is sponsored by
governments. In the United States it is estimated to be more
than half of all research and development,[4] and the potential
effect of secrecy is quite horrifying, especially since no
Freedom of Information Act applies to the work performed by
these private firms. Relating to this is the fact that much
of modern science raises questions of morality and safety,
both for the public at large and for employees, and it is
difficult to see how these fears and problems can be adequately discussed if research is being conducted in conditions of secrecy.

Secrecy also has a financial cost in that it may make the
scrutiny of the efficiency of administration and the cost-
effectiveness of government policies more difficult. There
are two elements to this proposition: one is that incompetence will not be detected by outside groups and that it
is not in the interests of the government or bureaucracy
that it should be detected, and the other is that it dis-
courages those within the bureaucracy who may wish to remove
inefficiency from making their findings public. Bureaucracy
may not have an interest in exposing inefficiency, but

particular individuals may, especially if they are able to establish a reputation as efficient managers and thereby win public esteem. Secrecy then may stifle initiative by allowing the corporate interest in 'quietude' to dominate by not encouraging individual initiative and speaking out. This is especially likely to happen when politics becomes involved with administration when such 'speaking out' becomes seen as a political move tantamount to 'opposition' to government policy and, therefore, an act which may be seen as implying support for an alternative political party.[5] There is also the problem of 'team loyalty'. In so far as the law or the government supports a high level of secrecy, then this will provide a reinforcement of the natural loyalties which officials feel towards each other. However, I do not then wish to support the use of the 'leak', the unauthorised release of information, as an acceptable solution to this problem of the reluctance to disclose embarrassing information. Rather the only acceptable solution is to create a situation in which it is made clear that officials are authorised to release certain information and that the public has a right to obtain it.

Another area in which secrecy has a cost to the public is the withholding of government investigations of public health, factory safety, drug safety and the reliability of consumer products. Only in Britain are such reports withheld and in recent years several ironic situations have occurred in which such information not available in Britain has been accessible in the United States under the Freedom of Information Act.[6] In some circumstances the cost to the public could be high, for example, where a factory was endangering life by inadequate safety precautions.

There is another argument against secrecy which is that the taxpayer has paid for certain investigations to be carried out and is, therefore, entitled to the results. The more the government intervenes and the more information it demands from the public, the more it seems logical that the public should be entitled to receive information from the government. It can also be argued that the more active the government becomes, the more the public is in danger from government mistakes and, therefore, the greater the need for public access to government information. It is also the case that intervention makes less plausible the argument that the government requires a high level of secrecy because it is dealing with politics and not 'rational solutions to particular problems'. It seems that governments are making decisions which are more and more based upon expertise, science and technique, and that there is less justification for arguing that government is concerned with issues of national policy

and not 'ordinary' decisions concerning efficiency, pro-
ductivity and profitability which are based upon public or
accepted principles. As government becomes more active, so
the number of 'ordinary' decisions increases and the argument for secrecy is further weakened.

DEMOCRACY, SECRECY AND RESPONSIBILITY

I now wish to return to some of the issues raised in Chapter
2. One may well ask why notions of democracy are important
in relationship to secrecy, and the answer is that secrecy
is an indicator of the boundaries which exist between one
aspect of the political system and another. It marks off the
sphere within which authority and responsibility are clearly
delineated such that those with authority have autonomy. One
of the main problems which all democratic systems had to
solve was the extent to which the 'public' were expected to
intervene within the political process, the extent to which
civil servants, the courts and the legislature were expected
to intervene with the operations of the executive. For
instance, within the British parliamentary system the
Opposition has no responsibility for the actions of Her
Majesty's Government. The Opposition therefore has a limited
basis for arguing that they have a right to know in so far
as that right is predicated upon the sharing of responsibility, upon a desire to participate. The problems of the
right to know, participation and responsibility can be understood in terms of debates concerning the separation of
powers. A situation in which each branch of government has a
distinct and separate existence implies that each branch is
autonomous and that no other branch of government has any
right to interfere with the actions of any other. In terms
of the ideal type of the separation of powers as defined by
Vile,[7] the personnel of each branch are also distinct, in
that no person can serve in both branches simultaneously and,
therefore, the only information which each branch will have
about the workings of any other is no more and no less than
that which is available as a result of observation or of the
voluntary release of information by one branch to the public
at large. It is not a situation, however, in which any
branch can claim a right of access to the information
possessed by any other branch based upon some special
relationship or special duty *vis-à-vis* any other branch -
the extreme separation of powers precludes this by definition.
  The idea that this 'extreme' system will produce harmony
is unrealistic; however, if the desire is to prevent any

positive act being made by the State, or if one wishes to produce impotent government, then one may see disunity as desirable.

Nineteenth-century government differs from twentieth-century government in this respect. In the latter, the demand that the State plays an active role in guaranteeing the conditions necessary for the security and safety of each citizen is incompatible with an extreme separation of powers. The tendency in all Western industrial states is for the unity of the State and this can only be achieved by the balanced or pluralistic state. However, there are various ways in which this can be achieved. It can be achieved by one part of the government gaining dominance, it can be achieved through the partial integration of the branches, or it can be achieved by all the branches becoming part of a wide system of power-sharing in which consensus becomes the norm - not only consensus within the three branches of government, but within the society as a whole. In the latter case the State becomes simply the institution within which the consensus is arrived at, but not the centre at which power lies; power becomes diffused.

Each of these systems has its own particular problems, especially when it comes to allocating responsibility for the actions which result from the government and the relationship between the allocation of responsibility and elections. If then it is a basic part of any democratic polity that there be elections which are based upon the principle that the decision by the voter will be and ought to be a consequence of the actions undertaken by those who have power and who are therefore responsible for the actions of the State, then the less clearly are the lines of responsibility drawn and the more difficult it is to exercise one's vote in a rational or meaningful way. However, the clarity of lines of responsibility is a conflicting requirement of the demand that power be decentralised in order to prevent its abuse.

Clear lines of responsibility also conflict with 'participation' unless those who participate are actually part of the decision-making process, otherwise participation becomes consultation. The alternative is that participation becomes the exercise of influence without this influence being clearly acknowledged so that it can be challenged or accredited by the electorate.

GOVERNMENT SECRETS AND THE SECRETS OF GOVERNMENT

There is the question of whether 'secret' influence is the

opposite of good government - this goes to the heart of the question concerning the kind of considerations which it is legitimate for a politician to take into account when making his decisions. One of the most important of these questions concerns re-election - is it legitimate that a politician undertakes a particular course of action in order to be re-elected? The answer depends upon the balance between particular interests and the 'general interest'.

The fact that the government must constantly debate whether or not to undertake a particular action, and whether this will win or lose votes, is a legitimate consideration. However, what if this were the only consideration? Take, for instance, the case of a 'hand-out' pre-election budget: the government knows, or has reason to believe, or has been advised by the civil service, the press and other groups, that the budget will be bad, but it nevertheless goes ahead with this plan; is this legitimate?

There are two relevant considerations here. The first is that accusations against the government that it has done such things, if they are considered to be illegitimate, may have the effect of damaging the government's popularity with everyone who has not been a party to these particular ben-efits. The government may be seen as too sectarian and there-fore will lose support at elections, so that such issues are part of political realities in so far as these accusations play a part in winning and losing electoral support. The second is that if one does think that such actions are il-legitimate, then it seems to me to be relevant to ask whether the rules of political life encourage or inhibit these kinds of political decisions. To say that such things happen is not to conclude that they cannot be affected by further actions which can be undertaken; to do otherwise is to imply a kind of crypto-conservatism and to abdicate responsibility both on the part of politicians and of aca-demics. It is obviously a part of every democracy that the government must keep in mind that at some point it must face the electorate and this necessity must play a part in the decisions which it makes.

This discussion is concerned with the kinds of consider-ations which a government will wish to keep secret. One mean-ing of secret does not apply to governments, namely the meaning which implies that government has secret objective knowledge, knowledge of mysteries which are denied to the public. Of course they do know some things which the public do not, but the question is what kind of things? By objec-tive knowledge I mean that they know what consequences will follow from the building of nuclear reactors, or whether British Leyland can be made profitable, or whether the Middle

East problem is capable of solution and what the solution is, or how to help Russian dissidents. It does not know any of these things to a greater or lesser degree than other experts. Government secrecy, then, does not involve concealing objective knowledge to which only the government has access and to which the rest of us are denied.

The implication of this is that there is very little factual government information which it is essential to protect, perhaps only the range and speed of missiles, but even to have defence plans made public would not necessarily mean that a war would be lost. What then is the reason for government secrecy? In my view it is based upon the desire on the part of governments and politicians to preserve an area of autonomy, to protect the point at which politics comes to rest from the infinite demands to which it is subject, and to protect the political process from arbitrariness and collapse. This is based on a particular view of the political process, one which sees the making of decisions as involving considerations which are not purely 'rational' but, for instance, relate to popularity and ideology. The argument for open government is often based upon the view that 'political' considerations ought to be eliminated, that all decisions should be the product of 'science' and that this can only occur where there is the maximum freedom of information. The difficulty with this view is that it is wrong. 'Science' does not produce the obvious or sole answer as to what is the best policy and, therefore, those who make decisions must be protected from the constant accusation that a particular decision is not the correct or 'rational' one. It is a curious irony that those who see politics as a bargaining process between various interests, as a pluralist democracy, should argue for open government when the fact that bargains have to be made means that the exposure of these leads to the denial of one of the fundamental principles of democracy, namely the obligation to act in the general interest; this obligation can only be sustained if the bargaining process can always claim to produce a consensus or a decision which reflects the majority view. The difficulty is that the consensus arrived at may be at the expense of all those who have not participated in the bargaining process. The more groups involved in this bargaining process, the more difficult it becomes to arrive at a consensus and the more likely it is that some interest will feel itself to have been neglected and to regard the political process as unjust. These conflicts between 'participation', bargaining and the general interest are related to the question of responsibility and the clarity with which such responsibility can be assigned, and also with the prob-

lem of equality versus hierarchy. Effective action seems to
imply the centralisation of decision-making, but centralisation implies hierarchy and clear lines of responsibility.
There is also the problem that once the government intervenes in a greater number of areas, the more it impinges
upon 'private life', then the more it requires the cooperation of other non-government agencies, who are not part
of the hierarchy. These requirements however are contradictory in that intervention and effective action require
centralisation and such action also requires the cooperation
and participation of persons who are not part of the hierarchy.

DEMOCRACY AND THE RIGHT TO KNOW

This discussion raises the question of what democracy is
and whether it necessarily implies a 'public right to know'.
This phrase is very rarely defined, especially as to what
the public have a right to know about, but it is seen as
being important for the vitality of democracy and the mean-
ingfulness of elections. These claims are extremely broad
and would seem to imply that a country that does not allow
for the public right to know barely, if at all, constitutes
a democracy. At the very least, any country without such a
right would lose points in the ranking of how democratic
that country was, compared to the ideal. I do not consider
this to be justified. This way of thinking is false in that
it implies that democracy is a bundle of characteristics,
albeit that some may be more important than others, and that
judgement of whether a political system deserves the accol-
ade of democracy depends upon how many of these characteristics it possesses. The difficulty with this viewpoint is
that the decision as to what to include or exclude from
one's 'bundle' seems very arbitrary and becomes so large as
to include all desirable political qualities. Democracy
then becomes the equivalent of the 'good society'. One may
approve of good societies, but it is careless to pretend
that one is talking of democracy. A political system is democratic in so far as the government is removable as a result
of periodic election, and in which the public is entitled to
express political views and to organise to that end.
    The definition that I have offered implies that the import-
ant factor in a democracy is the ability of the public to
express its opinions. It does not imply that the public have
a right to the opinions of any others, whether the government or otherwise. Given this right to express views and
organise accordingly, there will necessarily be competition

for office and this will force the government, or any other
contender for office, to state what it intends to do and to
defend its past performance. It then becomes a matter how
the competition for office is organised and how office-
holding is organised as to how much information will be
released. An irony of fierce political competition is that
it forces political parties to be articulate on the one hand,
but also makes them aware that any information which they
make available will be 'taken down and may be used in evidence against them'. However, in the countries studied, the
number of parties competing for office does not seem to be
an important factor in explaining openness. It is certainly
true that Sweden is a multi-party system, but openness
existed long before any thought of political parties or
democracy, let alone terms like multi-party. Also, neither
Britain nor the United States are multi-party systems and
yet they have wide contrasts as to the amount of information
to which the public have access. The conclusion to be drawn
from this is that elections and competition for office do
not require that governments release documentary information,
since the electorate have never made it a price of office-
holding that they do so. The electorate, as many studies
have shown, are remarkably ill-informed about the information to which they do have access, and those countries
characterised by openness do not seem able to improve the
standard of public performance in this area. Perhaps the
public are more concerned with what they think the government will do, rather than in reading the reasons for its
past failures, especially when they have actually experi-
enced these at first hand. One of the few essential features
if democracy is to survive is that the public are not
completely malleable, that they do reflect upon what has
happened and state whether they approve or disapprove of
what has happened, and whether they wish those happenings to
continue. It is perhaps more difficult to do this as governments become more complicated, and assume responsibility for
events which are difficult for governments to understand,
let alone control. Indeed, I see this as being why so many
countries are now considering Freedom of Information Acts.
It is a response to this complexity, but I doubt whether
such Acts can make it easier for the public to form political judgements about which party to vote for. It may rather
be the case that Freedom of Information Acts are a symptom
of the increasing impossibility of having a democracy, that
they are a sign of the end of democracy rather than a
further flowering, that they are a vain attempt to make
government responsible and responsive. I see open government
as evidence of a new stage in political development, but a

new stage which is characterised by increasing technocracy, complexity and bureaucracy in which democracy becomes increasingly difficult to sustain. Freedom of Information Acts are a consequence of the recognition that this is happening.

CONCLUSION

My answer to the above problems is that it is only in democracy, as I have defined it, that these problems are capable of solution. The problems exist and cannot be wished away or solved by the adoption of any simple political formula. Only where there is the potential for views to be expressed and for those who hold these views to be organised in political movements and to compete for office can the adoption of simple solutions be prevented. In my view the problem is not particular policies, but rather that government has become so complicated that elections have ceased to be an important mechanism by which the public can influence what the government does. Open government is a product of the recognition of this situation, although not in my view a solution to it.

Notes and References

CHAPTER 2: DEMOCRACY AND SECRECY

1. The classic exposition of this view is by Madison: 'Knowledge will forever govern ignorance. And a people who mean to be their own governors must arm themselves with the power knowledge gives. A popular government without popular information, or the means of acquiring it, is but a prologue to a farce or tragedy, or perhaps both.' Letter to W.T. Barry in S. Padover (ed.), *The Complete Madison* (New York: Harper, 1953).
2. 'Any lessening in available information results in lessened participation.' Senator Ervin, Government Operations and Judiciary Committee Hearings, *Secrecy in Government*, 1973, 93rd Congress, 1st Session, US Government.
3. This is the dominant view. See E. Shils, *The Torment of Secrecy* (London: Heinemann, 1956); F. Rourke, *Secrecy and Publicity* (Baltimore: Johns Hopkins Press, 1966); C.J. Friedrich, *The Pathology of Politics* (New York: Harper and Row, 1972); I. Galnoor (ed.), *Government Secrecy in Democracies* (New York: Harper and Row, 1977).
4. For an account of this view, see V. Himmelstrand, 'A Theoretical and Empirical Approach to Depoliticization and Political Involvement', *Acta Sociologica* (6) 1962.
5. 'Liberalism', *Dictionary of the History of Ideas* (New York: Scribner, 1973).
6. This is reflected in the almost obsessive interest Americans have in the doings of spies, the best being: H. Ransom, *The Intelligence Establishment* (Cambridge, Mass.: Harvard University Press, 1970); R.H. Blum (ed.), *Surveillance and Espionage in a Free Society* (New York: Irvington, 1973); D. Wise, *The Politics of Lying* (New York: Vintage Books, 1973); M. Halperin *et al.*, *The Lawless State* (New York: Penguin, 1976).

7. Sir Isaiah Berlin, *Two Concepts of Liberty* (Oxford: Clarendon, 1958).

8. C.J. Friedrich and Z.K. Brzezenski, *Totalitarian Dictatorship and Democracy* (Cambridge, Mass.: Harvard University Press, 1965); C.J. Friedrich, 'Secrecy versus Publicity', *Nomos* (12) 1970; C.J. Friedrich, *The Pathology of Politics*, 1972; *Constitutional Government and Democracy* (Waltham, Mass.: Blaisdell, 1968).

9. H. Gerth and C. Wright Mills (eds.), *From Max Weber* (London: Routledge & Kegan Paul, 1967).

10. See David Beetham, *Max Weber and the Theory of Modern Politics* (London: Allen and Unwin, 1974) Chaps. 4 and 8.

11. H. Gerth and C. Wright Mills (eds.), *From Max Weber*, 1967, p. 233.

12. Ibid., p. 233.

CHAPTER 3: BRITISH GOVERNMENT AND SECRECY

1. For a useful summary of this view see Potter in R. Dahl (ed.), *Political Oppositions in Western Democracies* (New Haven: Yale University Press, 1966).

2. For a traditional exposition see S. de Smith, *Constitutional and Administrative Law* (Harmondsworth: Penguin, 1974) pp. 188ff. For a more critical view see R. Wraith, *Open Government* (London: Royal Institute for Public Administration, 1977) pp. 33ff. For a journalistic view see David Leigh, *The Frontiers of Secrecy* (London: Junction Books, 1980).

3. As expressed by the Home Secretary in the debate on the famous Crichel Down Affair. 530 H.C. Debate, pp. 1289ff.

4. For example: A. Hanson and H. Wiseman, *Parliament at Work* (London: Stevens, 1962); A. Hill and A. Wichelow, *What's Wrong with Parliament* (Harmondsworth: Penguin, 1964); N. Johnson, *Parliament and Administration* (London: Allen and Unwin, 1966); B. Crick, *The Reform of Parliament* (London: Weidenfeld, 1968).

5. 'Consensus politics resulting from an objective search for truth would be dull politics and let Ministers off too lightly. Over concern with a search for facts could deliver Members of Parliament into the hands of experts and make them remote from the people they represent.' Ryle in S. Walkland and M. Ryle (eds.), *The Commons in the Seventies* (Glasgow: Fontana/Collins, 1977) p. 20.

6. Ibid., p. 255.

7. Ibid., Chap. 12.

8. de Smith, *Constitutional and Administrative Law*, pp. 618ff; J. Jacob, 'Discovery and the Public Interest', *Public Law*, Summer 1976.

9. *Duncan* v. *Cammell, Laird* [1942] A.C. 624.
10. [1942] A.C. 624, 632.
11. [1942] A.C. 624, 636.
12. *Conway* v. *Rimmer* [1968] A.C. 910.
13. House of Lords, 6 June, Hansard 197, pp. 741-8.
14. [1968] A.C. 910, 924.
15. For a discussion of the two cases see de Smith, *Constitutional and Administrative Law*, pp. 517ff and 581.
16. S. de Smith, *Judicial Review of Administrative Acts* (London: Stevens, 1973) pp. 142-55.
17. de Smith, ibid.
18. B. Schwartz and H.W.R. Wade, *Legal Control of Government* (Oxford: Clarendon Press, 1972) p. 238.
19. *Coleen Properties* v. *Minister of Housing and Local Government* [1971] 1 WLR 433.
20. *Secretary of State for Education and Science* v. *Tameside Metropolitan Borough Council* [1975] 3 WLR 641.
21. *Sunday Times*, 8 August 1976. For his general comment on this problem see H. Griffiths, *The Politics of the Judiciary* (Glasgow: Fontana, 1977).
22. R.H.S. Crossman, *Diaries of a Cabinet Minister*, vol.1 (London: Hamish Hamilton, 1975). The following report of the case is based upon *The Times* Law Reports of 26 June, 27 June, 22 July, 28 July, 29 July, 1 October and 10 October 1975. The political editor of the *Sunday Times*, Hugo Young, also published a book on the case, *The Crossman Affair* (London: Cape, 1976).
23. Law Report, *The Times*, October 1975.
24. Report of the Privy Counsellors on Ministerial Memoirs 1976, Chairman Lord Radcliffe, Cmnd. 1681 (London: HMSO, 1976).
25. Ibid., paras. 1-13.
26. Ibid., p. 7.
27. The PCA Act 1967, sec. 11, para. 3.
28. Ibid., sec. 7, para. 2.
29. In the years between 1967-72, some 310 out of some 1875 cases which were wholly or partially investigated, were found justified. Compiled from R. Gregory and P. Hutchesson, *The Parliamentary Ombudsman* (London: Allen and Unwin, 1975) pp. 179 and 404.
30. de Smith, *Constitutional and Administrative Law*, p. 558.
31. de Smith, *Judicial Review*, pp. 184-5.
32. Ibid., pp. 178ff.
33. Ibid., p. 129.

CHAPTER 4: THE DEVELOPMENT OF OFFICIAL SECRECY IN BRITAIN

1. F. Wilson, 'Ministries and Boards', *Public Adminis-tration*, 33, 1955; G.K. Clark, 'Statesmen in Disguise', *Historical Journal* (2)1, 1959; H. Parris, *Constitutional Bureaucracy* (London: Allen and Unwin, 1969).
2. Parris, *Constitutional Bureaucracy*, pp. 64-6.
3. Wilson, 'Ministries and Boards', pp. 48ff.
4. Parris, *Constitutional Bureaucracy*, p. 82.
5. Wilson, 'Ministries and Boards', p. 47.
6. Parris, *Constitutional Bureaucracy*, p. 138.
7. L. Brown, *The Board of Trade and the Free Trade Movement* (London: Oxford University Press, 1958) p. 215.
8. Ibid., p. 22.
9. Ibid., p. 226.
10. Parris, *Constitutional Bureaucracy*, p. 94.
11. J. Leese, *Personalities and Power in English Education* (Leeds: E.G. Arnold, 1950) Chap. 2.
12. Ibid., p. 43.
13. H.C. Debate, 18 April 1864.
14. Space prohibits a full listing of Public Record Office files but the most useful are: WO/32/6347; T1/8308B/16646; HO45/10501/120695; ADM1/8030; HO45/9813/B7315A; ADM1/8533/216. Unless otherwise indicated statements are based upon research undertaken in the Public Record Office.
15. *The Times*, 6 December 1858.
16. D. Williams, *Not in the Public Interest* (London: Hutchinson, 1965) pp. 17-19.
17. Parris, *Constitutional Bureaucracy*, pp. 102-4.
18. Hansard, vol.217, pp. 1223-4.
19. W. Bagehot, *The English Constitution* (London: Watts, 1964) pp. 190-1.
20. A. Beattie, *English Party Politics*, vol.1 (London: Weidenfeld and Nicolson, 1970) pp. 136-55.
21. Parris, *Constitutional Bureaucracy*, Chap. vi; G. Fry, *Statesmen in Disguise* (London: Macmillan, 1969) Chap. 1.
22. Larceny Act 1861 24/25 Victoria c 96. S30.
23. The Official Secrets Act 1889.
24. Hansard, 20 June 1889.
25. *Echo*, 20 March 1893.
26. Statement made by the Lord Chancellor to the House of Lords, May 1908.
27. Williams, *Not in the Public Interest*, pp. 59-60.
28. Letter from Sir Robert Chalmers of the Treasury to the Committee, 18 December 1912.
29. E.C.S. Wade and G. Philips, *Constitutional Law* (London: Longman, 1970) p. 222.

30. Public Records Act 1958/67; Report of the Committee on Departmental Records, Cmnd. 9163 (London: HMSO, 1953-4).
31. As reported and the text reprinted in *The Times*, 7 March 1978.
32. Foreign Office Minute, 1910.
33. Treasury Minute, 19 November 1891.
34. Committee Report, p. 3.
35. Ibid., p. 5.

CHAPTER 5: OFFICIAL SECRECY IN BRITAIN

1. Departmental Committee on Section 2 of the Official Secrets Act, Chairman Lord Franks, Cmnd. 5104 (London: HMSO, 1972). See evidence from Home Office Vol.2, part 1 and that of the Director of Public Prosecutions and Attorney General in Vol.3.
2. D. Williams, *Not in the Public Interest*, p. 28.
3. Ibid., p. 34.
4. Memorandum by the Secretary of State for War to the Cabinet, 25 September 1918.
5. T. Bunyan, *Political Police* (London: Julian Friedmann, 1976) p. 10.
6. Section 6 of the draft National Security Bill.
7. Cabinet Committee on Official Secrets Act, 1938, p. 9.
8. Bunyan, *Political Police*, p. 12.
9. Franks Report, Vol.1, pp. 116-18.
10. Biafra Case, see below. The ABC Case refers to the initials of the surnames of the three defendants, Aubrey, Berry and Campbell.
11. For an account by a defendant see J. Aitken, *Officially Secret* (London: Weidenfeld and Nicolson, 1971).
12. Aitken, ibid., p. 198.
13. Account based upon reports in *Guardian Weekly*, 26 November, *Daily Telegraph*, 18 November and *Sunday Times*, 19 November 1978. Crispin Aubrey, *Who's Watching You* (Harmondsworth: Penguin, 1981) arrived too late to be included.
14. *Sunday Times*, ibid.
15. Mr Justice Mars-Jones, as reported in the *Daily Telegraph*, 18 November 1978.
16. *Daily Telegraph*, ibid.
17. Radcliffe Report on Security Procedures in the Public Service, Cmnd. 1681 (London: HMSO, 1962) Chap. 9.
18. Radcliffe Report, para. 131.
19. Ibid., para. 139.
20. D. Jackson, 'Individual Rights and National Security', *Modern Law Review* (20) 1957.

21. Bridges–Day, Joint Committee to consider the Political Activities of Civil Servants, Cmd. 8783 (London: HMSO, 1953).
22. The Canadian Royal Commission on Espionage, 1946.
23. Report of the Conference of Privy Counsellors on Security, Cmnd. 9715 (London: HMSO, 1956).
24. Radcliffe Report, Chap. 1.
25. Bunyan, *Political Police*, p. 165, and P. Seale and M. McConville, *Philby* (London: Hamish Hamilton, 1973).
26. Report of the Committee on the Political Activities of Civil Servants, the Masterman Report, Cmd. 7718 (London: HMSO, 1949).
27. Bridges–Day Committee.
28. Ibid.
29. As a representative sample: 'Some of the complaints against the departments are well founded, yet with all its faults, the British Civil Service is unsurpassed.' G. Campbell, *The Civil Service in Britain* (Harmondsworth: Penguin, 1955) p. 365.
30. Report of the Committee on Minister's Powers, The Donoughmore Report, Cmd. 4060 (London: HMSO, 1932).
31. de Smith, *Constitutional and Administrative Law*, p. 332.
32. Some of the more famous critics are: A. Shonfield, *Modern Capitalism* (London: Oxford University Press, 1965); E. Nicholson, *The System* (London: Hodder and Stoughton, 1967); and H. Thomas (ed.), *Crises in the Civil Service* (London: Anthony Blond, 1968).
33. Report of the Fulton Committee on the Civil Service, Vol.5, Cmnd. 3638 (London: HMSO, 1968) p. 1098.
34. Ibid., Vol.1, Chap. 1.
35. Ibid., p. 91.
36. Departmental Committee on Section 2 of the OSA, Chairman Lord Franks.
37. Examples of the academic literature expressing this view are: Williams, *Not in the Public Interest*; D. Rowat, 'The Problem of Administrative Secrecy', *International Review of Administrative Science*, 1966; J. Jacob, 'Some Reflections on Government Secrecy', *Public Law* 1974; J. Christoph, 'A Comparative View: Administrative Secrecy in Britain', *Public Administration Review* 1975; R. Wraith, *Open Government* (London: Royal Institute of Public Administration, 1977). Some of the bodies advocating reform are: All Party Committee for Freedom of Information, Freedom of Information Campaign, NEC of the Labour Party, NCCL, Outer Circle Policy Unit, Justice, and individual MPs who have introduced Bills, the most celebrated being that of Clement Freud, MP, in 1979.
38. Justice, *Freedom of Information*, Chairman Anthony Lincoln QC (London, 1978) p. 15.

39. Outer Circle Policy Unit, Official Information Bill (London, 1978) p. 5.
40. See *The Times*, *Daily Telegraph* and the *Guardian*, for 20 July 1978.
41. Green Paper on Open Government, Cmnd. 7520 (London: HMSO, 1979); Disclosure of Official Information: A Report on Overseas Practice (London: HMSO, 1979).
42. Green Paper on Open Government, p. 3.
43. Green Paper, ibid., paras. 44 and 45; Report on Overseas Practice, paras. 11.11, 11.20 and 11.26.

CHAPTER 6: AMERICAN GOVERNMENT AND SECRECY

1. E. Corwin, *The President* (Princeton, New Jersey: Princeton University Press, 1957) pp. 15-16.
2. E. Goffman, *The Presentation of Self in Everyday Life* (Garden City, New York: Anchor Books, 1959); *Stigma* (Englewood Cliffs, New Jersey: Prentice-Hall, 1963).
3. Malcolm Shaw, *Anglo-American Democracy* (London: Routledge & Kegan Paul, 1963) pp. 32-3.
4. Except, of course, where there is a legal basis for the claim.
5. On the history and meaning of impeachment, see R. Berger, *Impeachment* (Cambridge, Mass.: Harvard University Press, 1973). Berger is the leading commentator on these issues but for a recent critical review see L. Fisher, 'Raoul Berger on Public Law', *Political Science Review* (8) 1978.
6. Berger, *Impeachment*, p. 79.
7. R. Berger, *Executive Privilege* (Cambridge, Mass.: Harvard University Press, 1974) pp. 35-6 and 262-3.
8. Commentators aware of this are: R. Rourke, *Secrecy and Publicity* (Baltimore: Johns Hopkins Press, 1966), Chap. 3; and Gore in N. Dorsen and S. Gillers (eds.), *None of Your Business* (New York: Penguin, 1975).
9. US Senate Hearings on Executive Privilege, 93rd Congress, 1st Session, 1973, p. 20 (US Government).
10. For a discussion of these cases see J. Hamilton, *The Power to Probe* (New York: Random House, 1976) pp. 37-45.
11. Berger, *Executive Privilege*, p. 1.
12. US Senate Hearings on Executive Privilege, 1973, vol.11, p. 56.
13. I. Younger, 'Congressional Investigations and Executive Secrecy', *University of Pittsburgh Law Review* (20) 1959.
14. S. Scher, 'Congressional Committee Members as Agency Overseers', *American Political Science Review* 1960, p. 912. See also, Scher, 'Conditions for Legislative Control', *Journal of Politics* 1963.

15. Hamilton, *Power to Probe*, Chap. 2. For the texts of the various cases see A. Boyan, *Constitutional Aspects of Watergate* (Dobbs Ferry: Oceana, 1976).
16. Younger, 'Congressional Investigations', pp. 768-9; Berger, *Executive Privilege*, pp. 234-5.
17. Relyea, in US Senate Hearings on Executive Privilege, 1973, vol. III, p. 227.
18. *Congressional Quarterly Almanac (CQA)* 1971, p. 123.
19. *CQA* 1975, pp. 26ff.
20. *CQA* 1975, p. 402.
21. Hearings before the Joint Committee on Congressional Operations, Constitutional Immunity of Members, 93rd Congress 1st Session (US Government, 1973).
22. 395 US, 486, 502 (1969).
23. *Gravel* v. *US*, 408 US, 606, 616 (1972).
24. B. Schwartz, *A Commentary on the Constitution of the US* (New York: Macmillan, 1963) vol.I, p. 110.
25. As quoted in *Executive Privilege: A Brief Overview* (Library of Congress, 1974) p. 265.
26. 272 US, 602 (1926).
27. Somers in W. Sayre (ed.), *The Federal Government Service* (Englewood Cliffs, New Jersey: Prentice-Hall, 1965); J. Harris, *Congressional Control of Administration* (Washington: Brookings Institution, 1964) p. 42.
28. D. Wise, *The Politics of Lying*.
29. R. Fenno, *The Power of the Purse* (Boston: Little, Brown, 1966) pp. 101-2.
30. B. Schwartz and H. Wade, *Legal Control of Government* (Oxford: Clarendon Press, 1972) p. 6.
31. C. Pritchett, *Congress Versus the Supreme Court* (Minneapolis: University of Minnesota, 1961) pp. 15ff.
32. 345 US, 1, 8 (1953).
33. Wise, *The Politics of Lying*, p. 25.
34. *CQA* 1975, p. 544; *CQA* 1976, p. 240.

CHAPTER 7: SECRECY, THE LAW AND THE CIVIL SERVICE IN AMERICA

1. For a description of the spoils system see D. Rosenbloom, *Federal Service and the Constitution* (Ithaca, New York: Cornell University Press, 1971) Chap. 2.
2. Rosenbloom, ibid., pp. 114ff.
3. *United Public Workers* v. *Mitchell* 330 US 75, 67 (1947).
4. *Congressional Digest* 1975, p. 258.
5. Schmidt in T. Franck and E. Weisband (eds.), *Secrecy and Foreign Policy* (New York: Oxford University Press, 1974).
6. H. Edgar and B. Schmidt, 'The Espionage Statute', *Columbia Law Review* 1973, p. 939.

7. Schmidt, in Franck and Weisband, *Secrecy and Foreign Policy*, p. 199.
8. All three are referred to in the *Congressional Digest*, 1975, pp. 258–67.
9. House Committee on Government Operations, Availability of Information to Congress, 93rd Congress, 1st Session, 1973.
10. Elliff in R. Blum (ed.), *Surveillance and Espionage in a Free Society* (New York: Irvington, 1973).
11. These figures taken from Kaufman in W. Sayre (ed.), *The Federal Government Service* 1965, p. 42.
12. Rosenbloom, *Federal Service*, pp. 166 and 217 and E. Bontecou, *The Federal Loyalty–Security Program* (Ithaca, New York: Cornell University Press, 1963) pp. 150–1.
13. Bontecou, ibid., pp. 8ff.
14. Bontecou, ibid., Chap. 4 and E. Shils, *The Torment of Secrecy* (London: Heinemann, 1956) Part 3.
15. *Cole* v. *Young* 351 US, 536 (1956).
16. Bontecou, *The Federal Loyalty–Security Program*, pp. 150–6 and W. Gelhorn, *Security Loyalty and Science* (Ithaca, New York: Cornell University Press, 1950) Chap. 2.
17. The Administrative Procedure Act was passed in 1946.
18. B. Schwartz, *Administrative Law* (Boston: Little, Brown, 1976) p. 21.
19. Ibid., pp. 19–20.
20. The House Committee on Government Operations, Subcommittee on Government Information, Chairman Representative John E. Moss. The Committee held hearings between 1956 and 1958.
21. Schwartz and Wade, *Legal Control of Government*, pp. 107–8.
22. Ibid., pp. 108 and 317.
23. J.R. Wiggins, *Freedom or Secrecy* (New York: Oxford University Press, 1956) p. 93.
24. Report of the Subcommittee on Government Information, 1958, p. 152.
25. 5 USCA Section 22 (1789).
26. A useful publication is the *Freedom of Information Act and Amendments of 1974: A Source Book* (US Government, 1975).
27. Summarised in the *CQA* 1966, pp. 557–8.
28. 21st Report of the House Committee on Government Operations, *Administration of the FOIA*, 92nd Congress, 1st Session (US Government, 1972).
29. A ruling made in the case of the *Environmental Protection Agency* v. *Mink* by the Supreme Court 410 US (1973).
30. House Government Operations Committee, Hearings 1973. Reports from Departments and Agencies.

31. *CQA* 1974, p. 292.
32. For the background see *CQA* 1975, pp. 725ff and *CQA* 1976, pp. 473ff.

CHAPTER 8: SWEDISH GOVERNMENT AND INFORMATION

 1. Lijphart, *Politics in Europe* (Englewood Cliffs, New Jersey: Prentice-Hall, 1969); B. Peters *et al.*, 'Types of Democratic Systems and Types of Public Policy', *Comparative Politics*, April 1977; Stjernquist in R. Dahl, *Political Opposition in Western Democracies* (New Haven: Yale University Press, 1966).
 2. T. Tilton, 'The Social Origins of Liberal Democracy: The Swedish Case', *American Political Science Review* (68) 1974.
 3. D.A. Rustow, *The Politics of Compromise* (Princeton, New Jersey: Princeton University Press, 1955).
 4. O. Ruin, 'Patterns of Government Opposition in Multi-Party Systems: Sweden', *Scandinavian Political Studies* (4) 1969; B. Molin, 'Swedish Party Politics', *Scandinavian Political Studies* (1) 1966.
 5. Stjernquist in S. Koblik (ed.), *Sweden's Development from Poverty to Affluence 1750–1970* (Minneapolis: University of Minnesota Press, 1975).
 6. Rustow, *Politics of Compromise*, p. 21.
 7. N. Elder, 'The Parliamentary Role of Joint Standing Committees in Sweden', *American Political Science Review* (45) 1951.
 8. N. Herlitz, *Elements of Nordic Public Law* (Stockholm: Norstedt, 1969) p. 73.
 9. N. Elder, *Government in Sweden* (Oxford: Pergamon Press, 1970) p. 158.
10. K. Holmgren, 'The New Swedish Legislation on Administrative Jurisdiction', *Scandinavian Studies in Law* (18) 1974, pp. 73–7.
11. N. Herlitz, *Elements of Nordic Public Law*, pp. 233–5.
12. Holmgren, 'New Swedish Legislation', p. 76; N. Herlitz, 'Legal Remedies in Nordic Administrative Law', *American Journal of Comparative Law* (15) 1967; H. Ragnemalm, 'Administrative Appeal and Extraordinary Remedies in Sweden', *Scandinavian Studies in Law* (20) 1976.
13. O. Westerberg, 'Judicial Review of Administrative Decisions', *Scandinavian Studies in Law* (16) 1972. 'It may be said that the Swedish public administration is almost entirely removed from judicial review', p. 323.
14. D. Anderman, 'The Swedish Jutitieombudsman', *American Journal of Comparative Law* (11) 1962; S. Jägerskiöld,

'The Swedish Ombudsman', *University of Pennsylvania Law Review* (109) 1961.

15. Anderman, 'Jutitieombudsman', p. 231.
16. Jägerskiöld, 'Swedish Ombudsman', pp. 1089 and 1091-2.
17. Herlitz, *Elements of Nordic Public Law*, p. 191, shares this view.

CHAPTER 9: SECRECY, THE LAW AND THE CIVIL SERVICE IN SWEDEN

1. Carlsson in S. Koblik (ed.), *Sweden's Development*.
2. Elder, *Government in Sweden*, pp. 65ff.
3. Herlitz, *Elements of Nordic Public Law*, p. 146.
4. The following literature stresses the importance of the legal control of administration: Herlitz, ibid.; F. Schmidt and S. Strömholm, *Legal Values in Modern Sweden* (Stockholm: Svenska Bokförlaget, 1964); R. Ginsburg and A. Bruzelius, *Civil Procedure in Sweden* (The Hague: Martinus Nijhoff, 1965); V. Merioski, 'Legality in Administrative Law', *Scandinavian Studies in Law* (4) 1960; N. Elder, 'Regionalism and the Publicity Principle in Sweden', Commission on the Constitution (Research Papers No.3) (London: HMSO, 1973).
5. For accounts see: N. Herlitz, 'Publicity of Official Documents in Sweden', *Public Law* Spring 1958; S. Anderson 'Public Access to Government Files in Sweden', *American Journal of Comparative Law* 21(3) 1973; S. Anderson, 'Some Essential Characteristics of an Effective Public Records Law', *Administrative Law Review* 25(3) 1973; D. Campbell, 'Free Press in Sweden and America', *South Western University Law Review* 8(1) 1976; B. Wennergren, 'Civic Information - Administrative Publicity', *International Review of Administrative Science* 36(3) 1970; Holstad in D. Rowat (ed.), *Administrative Secrecy in Developed Countries* (London: Macmillan, 1979).
6. Freedom of the Press Act, Chap. 2, Article 5.
7. Ibid., Chap. 2, Article 9.
8. Secrecy Act, Section 14, para. 2.
9. Freedom of the Press Act, Chap. 2, Article 12.
10. Holstad, in *Administrative Secrecy*.
11. K. Gustaffsson and S. Hadenius, *Swedish Press Policy* (Swedish Institute, 1976). 'Only infrequently have Swedish newspapers independently scrutinized political and other decisions affecting the general public' (p. 56) This view was repeated by Professor Hadenius in conversation and was also accepted by Ulla Persson of the Swedish Union of Journalists. And this despite the anonymity and publicity rules.

12. Instrument of Government Act, Chap. 7, Article 2.
13. The recent trend has been for the government to exercise greater control over the commissions. Elder, 'Regionalism and the Publicity Principle', para. 102; H. Meijer, 'Bureaucracy and Policy Formation in Sweden', *Scandinavian Studies in Law* (4) 1969; N. Elvander, 'Interest Groups in Sweden', *American Academy of Political and Social Sciences*, May 1974.
14. Herlitz has argued that there is a tendency for their views to be weighted too heavily; Herlitz, 'Publicity of Official Documents', p. 56.

CHAPTER 10: CONCLUSION

1. T. Anton, 'Policy Making and Political Culture in Sweden', *Scandinavian Political Studies* (4) 1969.
2. House Committee on Government Operations, 3rd Report (US Government, 1973).
3. A. Cox, *The Myths of National Security* (Boston: Beacon Press, 1975) pp. 79 and 192.
4. Cox, ibid., p. 79.
5. For a comparison of the willingness of British and American politicians and administrators to speak out, see E. Weisband and T. Franck, *Resignation in Protest* (New York: Penguin, 1976).
6. For example, see the articles by James Michael in the *Sunday Times* for 13 January 1977 and 27 August 1978.
7. For the various meanings of the term: M. Vile, *Constitutionalism and the Separation of Powers* (Oxford: Clarendon Press, 1967) Chap. 1.

Index